Praise for *Being an Early Childhood Educator*

'This book is gold! It features useful practical components as well as a strong focus on teacher qualities and reflection. It perfectly supports the new professionalism we aspire to for today's early childhood teachers.'
Joanne Orlando, PhD, Centre for Educational Research, University of Western Sydney

'This excellent text has the potential to support pre-service teachers as they explore and traverse the territory of their initial teacher education course and the early childhood education profession. It will also be a valuable companion text as they cross the uncertain boundaries between pre-service teacher and beginning teacher. It is a practical and well-theorised text for all early childhood pre-service teachers.'
Louise Thomas, PhD, Director—Accreditation, Faculty of Education and Arts, Australian Catholic University

FELICITY MCARDLE teaches undergraduate and postgraduate education students at Queensland University of Technology and Charles Sturt University. She publishes nationally and internationally, and is co-author of *The Trouble with Play*. Felicity taught in primary schools and preschool settings in Queensland for over fourteen years before coming to QUT. She has also led the design and implementation of programs of study for pre-service teachers, and regularly conducts professional learning programs for in-service teachers.

MEGAN GIBSON is a lecturer in the School of Early Childhood, QUT. Her key areas of interest for research and teaching include teacher professionalism, leadership and management, and policy and sustainability. Megan has worked across a range of diverse early childhood contexts, most notably in child care. Her doctoral research examined early childhood teachers' professional identities. She currently works with pre-service teachers and leads professional learning programs with practicing educators in the early childhood field.

LYN ZOLLO is a lecturer in early childhood education at QUT. She has extensive experience teaching in a diverse range of early childhood settings both in Australia and internationally including long day care, kindergarten, preschool and primary school. She has worked in the roles of teacher, director, a validator for the National Childcare Accreditation Council, a consultant and as a TESOL teacher of children and adults, and is an active member of a diverse range of related advisory committees and professional organisations. Lyn's particular interest with pre-service teachers is preparing them to create and enable quality learning and teaching in the early years.

BEING AN EARLY CHILDHOOD EDUCATOR

Bringing theory and practice together

Felicity McArdle | **Megan Gibson** | **Lyn Zollo**

Routledge
Taylor & Francis Group

LONDON AND NEW YORK

First published 2015 by Allen & Unwin

Published 2020 by Routledge
2 Park Square, Milton Park, Abingdon, Oxon OX14 4RN
605 Third Avenue, New York, NY 10017

Routledge is an imprint of the Taylor & Francis Group, an informa business

Cataloguing-in-Publication details are available
from the National Library of Australia
www.trove.nla.gov.au

Index by Puddingburn Publishing Services
Set in 11.5/13 pt Adobe Garamond Pro by Midland Typesetters, Australia

ISBN-13: 9781760111182 (pbk)

Contents

List of figures and tables

Figures

Tables

Introduction:
How to use this book

So you have decided to study the art and the craft of teaching? Whatever your reasons for making this decision, in this book we are committed to providing you with the best support we can, to help you become an excellent teacher. This is because we believe that teaching is a noble profession—indeed, one of the oldest and most important occupations—because it has played such a significant role in shaping the world. Congratulations on your choice of career!

We also believe it is very important to be inducted into the profession. While just about everybody, at some point in their lives, has experienced both the act of teaching and the act of learning, this is not the same as becoming a member of the community of teachers—the profession of teaching. Teaching is complex, sometimes difficult, sometimes thankless, sometimes easy, sometimes pleasurable and sometimes frustrating. It is certainly not for the faint-hearted. When asked 'Who taught you how to make art?', the responses from very young children in Hong Kong and Australia included, 'Nobody—I just knew' and 'Nobody *doesn't* know how to make art' (McArdle & Wong, 2010). Good teachers make it look easy—and this means that the best teaching can sometimes go unnoticed.

Good teaching and learning can also take many forms. We begin this book by acknowledging the traditional owners and custodians of the land

?

Did you know?

Defining terms
is important, as
language shapes
thinking. Many of
the key terms differ
across contexts
and between
jurisdictions: states,
territories and
countries. We use
the term 'teacher'
to refer to all
educators of young
children. We use
'prac' as a short-
hand term for field
experience, work
placement and
work-integrated
learning.

on which we live. Indigenous Australian peoples have played and continue to play an important part in the care of our land and the development of our culture. Children and families have always been of the utmost importance to almost every aspect of the lives, cultures and histories of Australian Aboriginal and Torres Strait Islander peoples. We pay our respects to their elders, and acknowledge the long history of teaching and learning in this land. We are committed to teaching and learning in partnership with Aboriginal and Torres Strait Islander peoples, and acknowledging Indigenous ways of knowing, seeing and being. Throughout this book, you will find reminders of Indigenous perspectives and knowledge. These are important to all teachers in Australia, not only those who will be teaching Aboriginal and Torres Strait Islander children.

Think about it

Consider your current perspective:
- non-Indigenous teacher teaching Indigenous children
- non-Indigenous teacher teaching non-Indigenous children
- Indigenous teacher teaching non-Indigenous children
- Indigenous teacher teaching Indigenous children.

What will be different in each situation? What will be the same?
For more on this, see Phillips (2011).

If you are using this book in another country, the perspectives of the Indigenous people in that country are equally important to acknowledge. This is an essential part of every teacher's worldview. There are some parts of this book that are uniquely Australian because this is our immediate context; however, they are likely to be equally relevant to other places and systems. There are some things about teaching and learning that are universal.

Think about it

Make a note in your professional reflection journal on some 'universals' about teaching and learning.

Other factors are unique to specific cultural contexts, social situations, geographical locations, individual people and particular groups. Differences can occur at a national, state, regional or local level, and apply to a town or even to an individual centre/school.

Think about it

In your reflection journal, make a list of issues that are local to your particular prac setting. This will help you to develop insights into the unique aspects of this setting.

In writing this book, we are determined to encourage you to avoid the trap of thinking that education comes in a kit, packaged and portable, which is transportable to any educational setting to be assembled according to the 'model'. Instead, we begin with a firm commitment to recognising and celebrating differences and diversity. Every prac you do will be different. Every year you teach will be different. And the children with whom you will work will be different. It will be part of your work to acknowledge differences, and include them in all your plans and thinking. Australia is a multicultural country, but even 'multiculturalism' is enacted differently in different countries, and through different policies and practices.

The overall guiding principles for working with differences are fairness and equity. A good teacher will aim for the success of *all* children. There are many other places in your course where you will give more thought to the ideas of difference, diversity and equity, but prac often provides the most immediate opportunities to try out your principles in practice.

Master and apprentice

Historically, teachers learned their profession through an apprenticeship model, and student teachers worked alongside the 'master' until they were deemed capable of being independent teachers themselves. In some countries, this is still the way teacher preparation is carried out. More recently, the apprenticeship model has been augmented with other forms of teacher preparation, and in many countries now involves increased requirements for various formal studies and qualifications, examinations and accreditations. Nevertheless, the master–apprentice model has not disappeared entirely.

Taking it further

Throughout your studies, there are a number of terms that you are likely to hear frequently. Eventually they will become very familiar to you. When preparing for each prac, it is useful to have a quick reference guide to some of the terms that are part of the professional language. At this stage, they might not be part of your everyday vocabulary.

It is important that you add to this list, and build your own glossary of terms. Like the rest of your toolkit, this is likely to be a lifelong exercise.

?

Did you know?

A *practicum or prac* is a field experience placement where a pre-service teacher/student spends time in an educational context and implements key university requirements while being supervised by a classroom teacher, and supported by the other staff within the context (e.g. director, deputy principal).

During the practicum (prac) component of your program of study, you will be assigned to a more experienced and qualified teacher, who will serve as a model for you to observe, and from whom you will learn. You will have opportunities to watch and learn, and to try out your own developing skills, theories and understandings about children, teaching and learning. Initially, you will do this under the watchful eye of a mentor—sometimes more than one. The relationships you form will be crucial to your successful prac and transition to teaching, and in this book you will find support for your management of the various prac relationships and those you will encounter when you begin work as a teacher. Later, it will be important for you to manage the relationships as an experienced teacher who, in turn, contributes to the profession by inducting new teachers.

One of the trickiest spaces to negotiate is your transition. For all of your previous experience with learning and teaching, you have been positioned as the student—a learner. On prac, and as you begin to work in the profession, you are becoming a teacher.

Ideas that shape this book

We begin by asking you to consider why you wanted to become a teacher, and what kind of a teacher you want to be (see Chapter 1). It is important to reflect on these questions before your first prac. We suggest you form the habit of keeping a journal, if you do not already do this. A professional journal is different from other journaling you might do. When you think about the kind of teacher you want to be, write your ideas down, and constantly revisit them—before each prac, after each prac, and sometimes during your prac. You should also continue to ask them throughout your teaching career, particularly over the first few years. And also remember to ask them, when later, you are mentoring new teachers. Your answers to these questions will quite possibly change as you progress through your studies and begin to teach. We hope your goals and objectives become clearer and closer with each step in the process.

Chapter 2 looks in more detail at the nature of pracs, explains broadly how prac works, draws your attention to the key people and emphasises the important relationships you will need to build.

Chapters 3, 4 and 5 form the core of this book, and we expect that you will revisit them with each new prac experience, and once you begin teaching. We draw from the literature and growing body of research into education, early education, higher education, teaching and learning, teacher education and professional identities. Alongside the practicalities

of achieving success in your prac and future work as professional educators, we share the theories and ideas of a range of researchers and students of teaching and learning, from John Dewey, who wrote about active learning in the United States in the early twentieth century, to Jean Phillips, who writes about Indigenous knowledges and the needs of those who are becoming teachers in Australia in the twenty-first century. You will learn more about theories in your coursework as you progress through your program. Here we combine theories with practice, as you will on prac, and later when you begin teaching.

When you have completed your studies and hold your graduation papers in your hand, then you are ready for your next transition—to employment. But working to improve your employability has to start long before that point. In this book, you will find strategies for enhancing your employability as you go (see Chapter 6). This will enable you to show yourself in the best light when it comes to finding a job—and remember, there are many possibilities. The skills, attributes and capacities that are indicated by your qualification are not limiting you to the obvious. You might be employed as a teacher in a long day care setting, in a kindergarten, in a nursery or in a school. Equally, you will be highly employable further afield. We know graduates who have found employment in galleries, museums, recreation agencies, training institutions, travel companies, creative endeavours and professional organisations. Employers in all of these contexts require people with a package of skills that include teamwork, people skills, organisational skills, initiative and self-direction. Good teachers have all of these attributes, and more!

One of the unique aspects of the field of early childhood education and care is the diversity of the workforce, due partly to the wide range of different settings in which we work. In other teaching contexts (primary, secondary), the pracs are staged and sequenced. With each return to a similar setting, you gradually build your skills and capacities, and finally you are given more responsibilities. This is not the case in the early childhood field. Each setting for your prac will be different—a primary school (lower grades), a kindergarten, a preschool, a prep class, a child care centre. Each of these contexts can be very different—subject to different regulations, policies and organisational structures. In this book, we provide the means by which you will become 'readers' of the various settings, curricula, hierarchies and cultures you encounter (see Chapter 7).

Finally, we finish this book with a 'toolkit' (see Chapter 8). With all the complexities and differences that we keep emphasising, it is understandable that some students interpret this as meaning that 'every place is different', so it is pointless and impossible to be prepared before the

Did you know?

A *pre-service teacher* or *student teacher* is a student who engages in a field experience placement, attending to prac requirements and taking opportunities and initiative for professional growth and learning!

specific context is known. This logic is flawed. A good teacher builds a whole range of strategies and a repertoire of skills and knowledge, and is able to call on the most appropriate of these in response to their growing ability to 'read' an opportunity for teaching and learning. In Chapter 8, we have collected numerous 'tried-and-true' tips, strategies and pedagogical aids that will help you to succeed in your prac and your early years in the profession. Some of them are particularly useful for the prac situation in which you are working with a group of children who are relatively unknown to you, and who do not know you in the same way that they know their regular teacher. This sometimes calls for strategies that are not so necessary when you are a qualified teacher, and have the opportunity to build and develop sustained relationships with the children and their families. 'Behaviour management', for instance, is sometimes difficult for pre-service teachers on prac. You will find some useful tips in this chapter to assist with this.

Making this book work for you

The design of this book is based on the rhizome—a complex kind of rootstock in which the roots branch out in many different directions. You can read this book from front to back, and follow along as we try to capture the importance of becoming a *good* teacher (and we want you to be a *good* teacher). Alternatively, consider the rhizome. Dip in and out of the book according to where you are in your studies—whether you are preparing for prac, in the middle of your prac, or reflecting after the completion of your prac, or once you have begun teaching.

Like the rhizome in Figure 0.1, there are threads of ideas that weave throughout the book, sometimes colliding with other concepts, sometimes meeting and collecting around nodal points, and sometimes heading off in directions that only you will understand. If this sounds complex and uncertain, that is good! If you can begin to feel comfortable with complexities and uncertainties, then this is an excellent starting point for a successful prac and your future career as a teacher.

The book has many nodes and sections. There are places where you will find information, and places where you are provoked to think your own way through numerous possibilities. We invite you to revisit sections in this book each year, and to return to topics and ideas throughout your studies and into your early years as a qualified teacher. You might skip things in this book that you already know, and you might shoot off in other directions, adding to this information with ideas and knowledge of your own.

Figure 0.1: A rhizome, with multiple, non-hierarchical entry and exit points

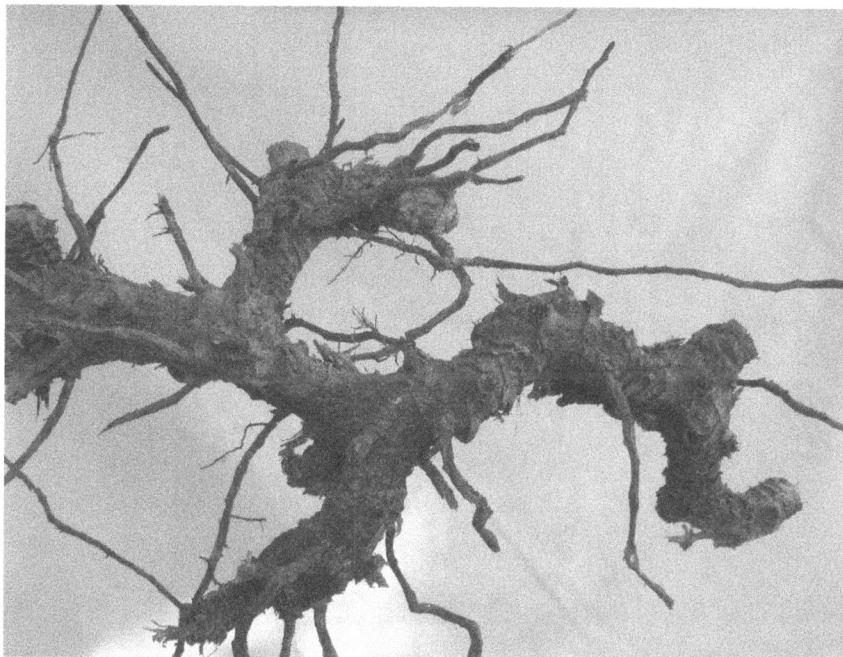

There are parts of this book that examine individual matters, like identities. *What kind of a teacher do you want to become?* And there are parts that invite you to work in partnership, and in relationships, with your peers, with your mentor teacher, with children and with community members.

There are three key ideas threading through the chapters of this book, and they are represented in the photograph of Luca and his Nonna (Figure 0.2), whose intertwined hands form a rhizome of their own. These ideas are:

- *Images of children.* The teacher can make a difference to children, and children can make a difference to teachers. The ways in which teachers come to see and understand children can profoundly affect and shape the children in their care.
- *Relationships.* The things children learn do not automatically result from what is taught. All learning occurs in strong relational and cultural contexts. Relationships play an important part in what makes a good teacher.

❝ ❞

The ideas that run through this book provide a way of planning and mapping your prac experiences—and supporting your thinking, doing and reflecting.

Figure 0.2: Luca and Nonna—images of children, relationships, pedagogies

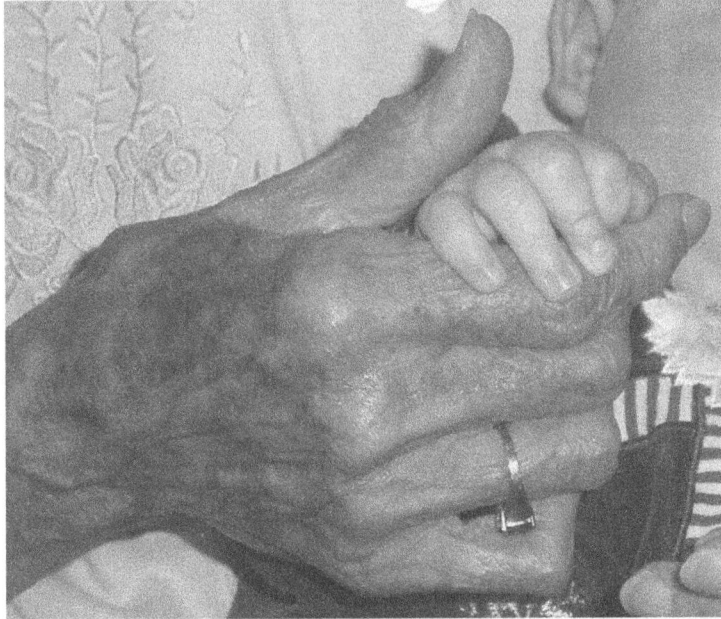

- *Pedagogies*. When it comes to teaching and learning, it is tempting to pay most attention to what the teacher says and does. Pedagogy is a term that captures everything that happens between teacher and learner, including careful listening, thoughtful reflection and considered responses.

Your success in prac and in your early years of teaching will largely be shaped by *you*:

- how you see/think about children
- the relationships you build and maintain with children, your mentor teacher, other professionals with whom you will be connected, families and the community
- how and what you learn about pedagogies, and the connections you make between your prac experiences with particular children and contexts, and the bigger picture of teaching and learning. This will be enriched by thinking, broader reading and reflection.

Elsewhere in your course, you will learn more about these three focal points: images of children, relationships and pedagogies. When it comes to your prac experience and all of your later experiences as a teacher, they are key. This is why there are reminders throughout each chapter of this book. You are prompted to continually ask yourself:

- How am I seeing this child/these children? What do I believe about children?
- Where are the important relationships here, and how am I connecting and contributing?
- What makes a good teacher in this situation? What pedagogies are most appropriate here?

66 99

Remember: Every one of your prac experiences will be different.

In conversation

I think my child care prac was amazingly rewarding and exciting, and I learned heaps! (Della, third-year undergraduate, 2011)

My kindergarten prac was a nightmare. The teacher did not like me, and I reckon it was one of the most difficult times I have ever had. Still, I made it through, and it required more of me than I ever thought possible. (Daniel, fourth-year undergraduate, 2012)

I never really felt part of the team when I was on prac. I think the first time I felt like a 'real teacher' was when I had my own group of children, in my first year as a graduate teacher. (Suellen, graduate teacher with three years' experience, 2012)

I learned more on prac than I did throughout my entire university degree. (Cara, graduate teacher with two years' experience, 2011)

The things I learned at uni made sense when I went out on prac and vice versa. The more pracs I did, the more I understood what the theories were about. (Joanne, practising teacher, eight years' experience, 2012)

Key features of this book

Throughout the book you will find some special features designed to enrich your experience and guide you on your prac.

On track on prac

Talking and making sense of what you see and do are integral to growing, learning and evolving as an early childhood teacher. During your prac, make it a priority to find time to have regular chats with your host teacher—this may be at the conclusion of every week, at the end of the day or some other time that suits you both. At the end of this book, as part of your 'toolkit', we have included discussion points that might help you get started for these sessions. The discussion starters are called 'On track on prac'. They can be useful as check-ins, to ensure everyone (you and your host teacher) is 'on track'.

Together, you might arrange to have a cup of tea together in the staffroom or a local café one afternoon after work. You might decide to go for a walk together—find a time/space/place that suits you and your host teacher. The important thing for 'On track on prac' is that you and your supervising teacher have time to talk—about the placement, about teaching and about you.

Did you know?

A *supervising teacher, host teacher* or *mentor teacher* is the teacher who works with a pre-service teacher to provide mentoring, guidance and supervision, ensuring that key requirements of the field experience placement are met and professional growth learning is supported. The supervising teacher is responsible for completing the field experience report to assess the pre-service student.

In conversation

I remember one prac that I did in a country town. The only place 'to go' was the pub and as my host teacher and I were not into drinking I went along with her Friday afternoon 'down time' and would join her in her kitchen to bake cakes. While baking, we would have great conversations about her journey into teaching, my role on prac, future possibilities for me as an early childhood teacher, children, families. I didn't know it at the time, but these chats ensured that our relationship was open, honest and trusting. It was simple, though pertinent—making time to connect and talk kept my prac on track. (Lucy, practising teacher with four years' experience, 2011)

Ideally, defer to your supervising teacher and the arrangements that best suit them for this reflecting time. Sometimes it might be easier if you and your supervising teacher have a starting point for your extended conversations. The 'On track on prac' pages are designed to 'break the ice' and help build a relationship of mutual trust and respect between you and your supervising teacher. If you think it is appropriate, photocopy one of the 'On track on prac' pages and propose that you 'interview each other', then share your views on the prompt questions.

You might use these more than once or you might use one for each different context. You could also document the conversations as a teacher/researcher, and keep them for your journal reflections—even add them to your portfolio. Remember that these are designed as a way to start the conversation. It will be your judgement that guides you on how best to use them.

Activities

There are also some suggested tasks that are designed to be useful when you are back on campus, or working through lecture materials, tutorials and your own reading and learning. You might use these reflective prompts in this book to make connections across the various other components of your program of study.

Teacher as researcher

There are also parts of this book that you will find useful during your first years as a registered teacher. Sometimes, some parts of teaching don't begin to make sense until you have graduated and begun to accumulate a variety of experiences—then, you may find that you want to go back and think over some of your earlier ideas. Good teachers are always inquirers, always researchers, not simply providers.

Think about it

Cara, who was quoted earlier in this section, is adamant that she has learned more on prac than during all of her other studies. Why might she feel this? What might be another way of thinking about this notion?

To do

In these sections, you will find ideas and suggestions for preparing for prac, developing relationships, understanding professionalism and identity, building your portfolio and getting a job.

In conversation: Real people and their real words

We have included words and opinions from real teachers as they share their experiences of hosting student teachers on prac. You will also find some stories of real pre-service teachers and some common 'mistakes' that student teachers make when on prac, and ideas for remedying these. Be prepared—things will go wrong. Despite this, stick with it!

'Tricks of the trade'

Experienced teachers use methods and strategies automatically, and often they are unaware that they are using 'tricks of their trade' that not everyone knows about. The tips and advice we provide will go a long way towards ensuring a successful prac—helping you to not just 'survive prac' but be successful on prac and become a good teacher.

Portfolio tasks

Your employability will depend on a lot of factors, not just the grade point average achieved in your studies (although some employers consider this a solid indicator of attributes and potential). Over the course of your studies, you need to be generating evidence of your performance—at university, on prac and beyond (e.g. volunteer work, experience in the workforce). If you create a space to store this evidence, and update it regularly with your latest and best evidence, you will have a portfolio that is an accurate indicator of your skills, knowledge, attributes and capacities. Throughout this book, we make suggestions for items you might create and include in your developing portfolio. As a practising professional educator, you will also be required to use your portfolio to track your ongoing professional development.

Professional library

Every teacher accumulates 'favourite' books to which they return again and again, and to which they refer on different occasions because they know what they need. In this book you will find recommendations for books and resources as you begin to build your own professional library—something you will continue to develop throughout your career. You may even use *this* book later, when you become a mentor to new student teachers who look to you for guidance. What kind of a mentor will you be?

A palimpsest

The ancient Egyptians wrote messages on papyrus. When a message was no longer needed, they erased the message and used the same papyrus to overlay new messages. Sometimes the erasure was not complete, and new messages were read around the old messages that remained. This overlaying, with parts of the underlying layers remaining and showing through, is termed a palimpsest. Artists use this technique to produce images that are built on underlying images. As you use this book throughout your preparation for teaching and early teaching career, you will build a palimpsest of ideas, knowledge, practices and skills, all of which will go to make up the kind of teacher you are becoming. Some of the ideas with which you begin will change and shift as you accumulate more knowledge, more experience and more ideas.

Most importantly, while we hope you work on answers we also want you to come to love the questions. Always consider the 'why' questions. Think critically, inquire, wonder and ask more questions. There is no one single 'recipe' for what makes a good teacher. You will be a unique teacher, with your own unique identity.

This is not to say that 'anything goes'. As a professional, there is a body of knowledge, and a set of professional attributes, that you will be expected to acquire, develop and demonstrate. You will be accountable to your community and society, and you will be required to be responsible for the choices you make, and need to be able to articulate why you made them.

You will also become a member of a universally respected profession with a long tradition. While education is not a cure for poverty, it is an important key to social justice and equity. Success for all is the goal of all good teaching. Measures of success are diverse and ever changing. This book aims to prepare teachers for change, not for the status quo.

Educators' practices are influenced by how they understand learning and teaching, children and relationships. Throughout this book, you will meet many provocations for thinking about your images of children, teachers and pedagogies. Keeping a reflective journal and building a portfolio will help you construct a dynamic, ever-changing and developing representation of the kind of teacher you are becoming.

This preparation will not end with your graduation, but will be a lifelong process of learning, teaching, relationships, questions and reflections. A good teacher is always learning.

Activity 0.1

Research palimpsests. Go beyond education. Some contemporary visual artists have created intriguing palimpsests. Create your own palimpsest that tells the stories of how you came to this career path, what kind of teacher you want to be, perhaps the memories you have of your own teachers . . . anything else that makes up the layers of your palimpsest. Keep this somewhere safe as you progress though this course, and add to it as you learn.

Seen on a free postcard in a café

What is education for?
What are you for in education?

Most students experience some degree of uncertainty around prac:

- What will prac be like?
- How will I know what to do? Where to go? How to act?
- Am I assigned a teacher? A class? A group of children?
- How do I pass? Who assesses me?
- What are the requirements?
- What if I don't know what to do?
- What if things go wrong?
- What if the children don't listen to me?

If we can provide one starting point that will help you to respond to these or other concerns you have, it is this: make the rest of this book work for you. Build your confidence and competence, and experience success through your prac experiences as you make every effort to become the quality teacher you want to be.

Your prac experience is yours.

Every prac experience will be different.

You will be responsible for the success of your prac.

Further reading

Blaise, M. & Nuttall, J. (2011). *Learning To Teach in the Early Years Classroom*. Melbourne: Oxford University Press.

McArdle, F. & Wong, K.-M.B. (2010). What young children say about art: A comparative study. *International Art in Early Childhood Research Journal*, 2(1), <http://artinearlychildhood.org/artec/images/article/ARTEC_2010_Research_Journal_1_Article_4.pdf>. Accessed 20 December 2014.

MacNaughton, G. & Williams, G. (2008). *Techniques for Teaching Young Children: Choices for theory and practice*. Sydney: Pearson Education.

Malaguzzi, L. (1998). History, ideas and basic philosophy: An interview with Lella Gandini. In C. Edwards, L. Gandini & G. Forman (eds), *The Hundred Languages of Children: The Reggio Emilia approach—advanced reflections* (2nd ed..). Greenwich: Ablex.

Moss, P. (2014). *Transformative Change and Real Utopias in Early Childhood Education*. Abingdon: Routledge.

Phillips, J. (2011). Resisting contradictions: Non-Indigenous pre-service teacher responses to critical Indigenous studies. PhD thesis, Queensland University of Technology.

Rinaldi, C. (2006). *In Dialogue with Reggio Emilia: Listening, researching and learning*. Abingdon: Routledge Falmer.

1

Becoming, being, belonging: So you want to be an early childhood teacher?

In this chapter you will find:

- 'big picture' mapping of your program of study
- brief descriptions of the various types of settings and services in the field of early childhood care and education
- some histories of how the early years have come to be defined
- worldviews and standpoints
- information about starting your portfolio.

Penny wants to be a teacher so she can make a difference. She still remembers her preschool teacher, Miss Honey, who used to hold her hand and help her say goodbye to her mum when she dropped her at preschool on her way to work. Penny also recalls a teacher she had in Year 8, who really made his students think; on reflection, she remembers that teacher as being scrupulously fair to all students. Penny wants to become a teacher who is kind, helps children to learn and is fair and just.

Henny doesn't really know why she has enrolled in a teacher preparation course. She hasn't really thought about it actually. The choice was more from a lack of any other idea than from a deliberate decision. People have told her that the hours are good, the holidays are great— and how hard can it be? She knows all about education, since she has just been through twelve years of it herself, so she's hoping the study is not too demanding . . . actually, it's young children, not rocket science, so she pretty much knows what they need to learn anyway.

A supervising teacher's thoughts

Who do you think will do better on prac: Henny or Penny?

Well, it's a bit early to say . . . I was a bit like Henny myself when I started . . . I hadn't really given it much thought, and it seemed like a good idea at the time.

But, I can tell you this . . . I must have had close to a hundred student teachers in my classrooms over the years, and I would much rather Penny any day. She sounds like she is more thoughtful, more reflective and she cares about children. That's all I expect really. It's more of an attitude than what they've actually learned at uni. When I have a student who is keen, and cares about the work . . . then that's a help. If I have a student who I have to keep my eye on the whole time, and who never does anything without being asked/told, then it makes my work harder . . . and that's not always fair to the children.

—Joanne, Head of Curriculum, 2010

Research and experience both tell us that a teacher *can* make a difference. This book does not contain 'all you need to know to become a good teacher', nor does it reduce the task down to a 'Teaching for Dummies' instruction book. Instead, it will be a companion to all the other learning you do about teaching.

Look at Figure 1.1, and consider the 'big picture' of what it takes to be a good teacher. According to theories of teacher preparation, teachers need to know and be able to do a number of things.

Activity 1.1

Make a list of all the things you think good teachers need to know and be able to do.

As you make your way through your teacher preparation program, whether you are enrolled in a one-, two-, three- or four-year program, this book can act as a map, guiding you towards the goal of graduation and transition to a teaching career. Like any good travel guide, this book offers choices in routes, with a number of pathways weaving their way through to the destination . . . and beyond. We suggest that at the beginning of

Figure 1.1: A map of what teachers need to know and be able to do

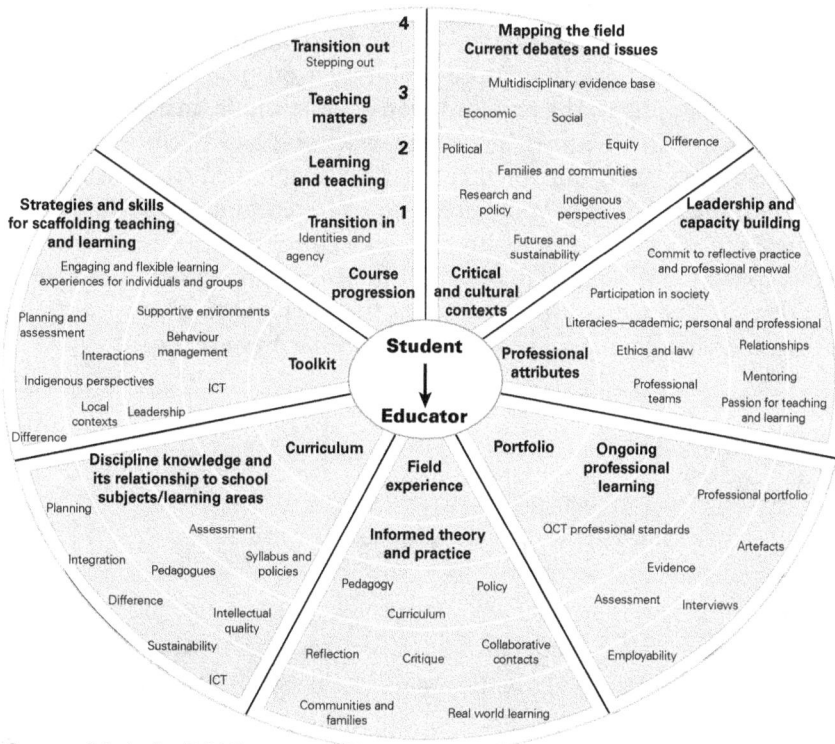

Source: McArdle (2010).

Taking it further

Place a large box within your study space. Every time you experience success as a teacher, collect an artefact and keep a collection in the box—take a photo, make a copy of a child's work with their permission, keep a copy of positive feedback from your supervising teacher. If you prefer, do this electronically, and keep all the material in a file on your desktop.

your course, you study the 'map' in Figure 1.1, work out where you are going and what you need in order to get there, then chart your progress as you make your way through the many roads, side tracks, and loops and turns. Find out what you need to know, and discover how you can acquire the skills, knowledge and attributes you need. Keep records of your milestones so you can *show* what you can do. You will need an impressive portfolio of your achievements when you eventually graduate and take the next step: seeking employment.

A common view of teacher preparation programs is that students learn 'theory' at university, then spend some intensive time in classrooms or other educational settings 'practising' their skills. In more recent times, teacher preparation programs have become more complex, with opportunities for 'practice' beyond the so-called 'prac' periods, and building partnerships through which universities and schools and centres work together with shared goals of preparing quality professionals for the field. Becoming a teacher is not a simple question of 'balance' between theory and practice. Many students say they want more 'prac' in their programs, but an apprenticeship model alone is not the answer.

From a reading of the map in Figure 1.1, it is possible to see that there is both an art and a craft to teaching. The craft requires teachers to develop a 'toolbox' of 'never-fail' strategies that help manage behaviour, plan and stage learning, assess and evaluate. When on prac, additions to the 'toolkit' are specific to the prac situation—for example, managing behaviour when you are a visiting 'practising' teacher is a different proposition from managing behaviour when you have an established relationship over time with the children in your care. The art of teaching is knowing when and what to do, based on a depth of knowledge of theories, reading situations, contexts and people, making informed decisions and 'bringing it all together' in a way that supports success for all children. This is complex, difficult, demanding and pleasurable, rewarding and exciting!

Activity 1.2

I wish there was more prac in our course. I learned more on prac than I ever did at university. (Madeline, student teacher, 2011)

Consider Madeline's statement. Why do you think she says this? Do you agree? What part do you think the university program plays in teacher preparation? What would your prac experience be like without any university input? Where does 'prac' fit in the map shown in Figure 1.1?

Becoming an early childhood teacher

In Australia, the early childhood years are taken to span a child's life from birth to 8 years. This means that early childhood education and care (ECEC) encompasses contexts prior to school and the early years of primary school. Within this age range, a number of different ECEC contexts offer programs and services for children and families. While the terminology used for these contexts varies, there are some common shared understandings, both within Australia and internationally. Some of the different contexts that operate within ECEC are outlined in Table 1.1, and key elements of the programs and the operational features are listed. While not all contexts are included, this table provides a good overview of programs and services. These contexts are clustered as prior-to-school contexts (up to approximately 5 years of age) and school contexts (the lower years of primary school, encompassing up to 8 years of age, or Year 3).

Activity 1.3

Legal definitions of ages and stages can vary from state to state. Research the age at which a person is no longer considered to be a child, and is tried as an adult in the various states of Australia. Conduct a similar inquiry into other countries.

In this chapter, we go into more detail for kindergarten/preschool and child care/long day care. These contexts provide the largest number of ECEC programs in Australia, and this is where you will most likely be placed for at least one prac, or find yourself working after graduation. It is important for you to understand the differences, including the models of ECEC provision, including community-based/not-for-profit and for-profit.

You will be required to complete a prac placement in two of the key ECEC contexts—kindergarten/preschool and child care/long day care—which are the largest providers of prior-to-school programs. In the coursework component of your studies, you will have learned about children's developmental ages and stages. This will prove one useful starting point for preparing for your prac. In addition to the developmental psychology frameworks, there are many other factors that are equally important for you to understand if you are to experience success in each prac. Relationships, environments, cultures and policies all play out differently, and contribute to some of the complexities that are part of this field.

You will develop more knowledge of all these factors throughout your coursework. Your prac experience will be one space where you can read the differences in action.

Table 1.1: ECEC contexts at a glance

Prior-to-school context	Operation
Child care/long day care/ early childhood education and care centres	Terms used interchangeably. Centre-based education and care for children from birth to 5 years, though may also include outside school hours care for children up to 12 years of age. Operate for a minimum 48 weeks a year, and open up to 12 hours per day.
Kindergarten/preschool	Program offered the year prior to primary school—children generally aged 3–5 years (some variation of ages between states and territories). The program usually operates during school hours and during school terms. The name may vary across states and territories e.g. in Queensland it is kindergarten, while in New South Wales it is preschool. These programs generally operate from 9.00 a.m. until 2.30 p.m., and some may include sessional kindergarten for shorter days (for example, 9.00 a.m.–12.00 p.m.). Children generally attend for two to three days per week. Increasingly, kindergartens are offering 'after' or 'before' care to meet the needs of working parents.
Family day care	Home-based care for children aged from birth to 12 years provided by a carer who is registered with a family day care coordination scheme. Generally, three to five children attend at the same time and hours are flexible.
Private home-based care	Private or informal care that is operated independently by babysitters or nannies. It is generally offered in a child's own home.

Mobile children's services	These services operate across rural and remote parts of Australia, providing ECEC programs to children and families. Typically, these programs are provided out of a bus, equipped with resources.
Multifunctional Aboriginal Children's Services (MACS)	MACS provide flexible services for Aboriginal and Torres Strait Islander children and their families. MACS offer care for children under school age and for school-age children, including long day care, playgroups, before- and after-school care, vacation care and cultural programs.
Integrated child and family centres	Integrated ECEC centres provide education and care, through kindergarten/preschool and long day care. The key to their operation is support services that are available to families; these may include, for example, a focus on health, child protection and early intervention.
Occasional care	Provides short-term centre based programs to children from birth to school age.
Playgroups	Provide coordinated activities and experiences for children from birth to school-age accompanied by an adult. Operate under a number of different management structures.
Outside school hours care (OSHC)	Programs that operate outside school hours—for example, before-school care from 6.30 a.m.; after-school care until 6.00 p.m. and vacation care during the school holidays.
School contexts	**Operation**
Non-compulsory schooling (Foundation year/Prep)	Each state/territory has a non-compulsory, full-time school year prior to Year 1, often referred to as a preparatory year (also known in some states as kindergarten, reception, pre-primary and transition).

Non-compulsory schooling (Foundation year/Prep) *continued*	Referred to as the 'foundation' year, these programs are generally not compulsory; however, most children do access this year, with almost 100 per cent attendance.
Compulsory schooling	School-based programs that offer education based on the Australian Curriculum, along with state/territory-based curriculum documents. School-entry age ranges from 4.5 to 6 years across various states/territories. Schools typically operate from 9.00 a.m. to 3.00 p.m.

Some history: kindergarten

Kindergarten provides an ECEC program for children in the 2–5 years age group prior to the commencement of formal schooling. It is sometimes referred to as preschool. Historically, the German pedagogue Fröebel (see Wollons, 2000) focused on children learning through play, and the name literally translates to 'garden for children'. This can conjure up delightful images and analogies of young children growing freely, naturally and beautifully like flowers in a garden, with the 'gardener' tending, nurturing and caring. A kindergarten program is generally planned for children aged between 3 and 5 years. A notable feature of kindergarten/preschool programs is a focus on learning through play. The idea that young children 'learn through play' is an enduring mantra of early childhood education, and 'play' is considered a way of learning (see DEEWR, 2009). Play-based learning has its roots in kindergarten, but the importance of play has infiltrated a wider range of ECEC contexts.

Partly as a result of the Early Years Reform Agenda (EYRA), there have been changes in ECEC in Australia. Kindergarten/preschool programs are increasingly now offered within long day care centre programs. Previously, they were mainly half-day programs. More and more kindergartens are now co-located on school grounds—either state/government schools or independent/private schools.

Child care

Participation in child care in Australia has increased significantly over the past two decades (ABS, 2011b), with over a million children attending prior-to-school early childhood services (Department of Education,

2013). With increased child care use, the most significant growth area has been for children aged 0 to 4 years (ABS, 2011b). In 1996, 13 per cent of children aged 0 to 4 accessed child care or long day care in any one week (ABS, 2011b). In 2011, 31 per cent of children in this age group were in child care, with child care usage continuing to grow.

The substantial increase in child care usage has been attributed largely to changing patterns of women's engagement in paid work (ABS, 2011a), with women more likely to remain in or re-enter paid work after having a child. Patterns of child care usage have changed at different points in time. For example, during the Second World War there was an increase in the numbers of women in paid work, and a commensurate rise in both the number of children seeking child care and the number of child care places. In recent years, the expansion in the number of child care centres, alongside the changes to government policy in early childhood, has seen issues pertaining to workforce and quality of care as central to reform in early childhood (COAG, 2008).

Despite the ongoing substantial increase in the demand for and utilisation of child care, arguments for and against it continue. Brain research and other empirical evidence supports reasons put forward for the expansion of child care, including the benefits for children, society and government (OECD, 2006). In addition, the focus on addressing poverty and disadvantage, as well as the benefits for children's wellbeing and social development, has particularly been highlighted, especially for children aged over 3. At the same time, children's participation in child care has been cautioned against, with some popular parenting books challenging child care use (Biddulph, 2006, 2008; Manne, 2005).

Child care centres historically have provided care and education for young children from birth to school age, so that parents are able to participate in paid employment. With their roots in the provision of care, moves in recent years to shift some of the dominant constructions of child care as 'care' have seen child care centres renamed 'Early Learning Centres' or 'Early Years Centres'. While child care has operated quite distinctly from kindergarten/preschool, this delineation is not a tidy one, and arguments are increasingly being made that child care does indeed include education (and, conversely, that kindergarten includes care).

The distinction of purpose between education and care is not a new discussion in the early childhood field. For some time, early years educators have grappled with the competing discourses of care and/or education. Historically, one consequence of the delineation has been the allocation of hierarchical status, with the marginalisation of professionals who work with younger children. Their working conditions (hours), remuneration and status have been consistently lower than those of their colleagues who work with older children. In part, this is due to an underlying belief that, with younger children, the work is *just* care, or *babysitting*—as opposed to work with older children, where *learning* and *education* are paramount, requiring a more skilled and qualified workforce. More recently, a case has been made for the integration of education and care, and the phrase 'early childhood education and care'—key to this text and central to this chapter—has emerged.

The early years

The map in Figure 1.1 shows field experience carrying across all four years of this particular program. Your early years prac experiences are different each time—unique to the local setting, but also different because of the age of the children, and the policies and practices that are deemed appropriate for each age group. The differences in settings become less pronounced when children are older. In general, the primary school years all take place in the one type of setting—a school. The younger the children, the more pronounced the growth, development and change over time.

For many young children and their families, attending child care is the young child's first sustained encounter with people from outside the family. Furthermore, for many young Indigenous children, and children of recently arrived immigrant or refugee families, attendance at child care may represent their first lengthy encounter with people outside the culture of their birth. The way in which they are welcomed, and the feelings of belonging that all children should have when they enter an early childhood centre, can have profound effects on their wellbeing and development. If children and their families cannot see themselves represented and reflected in the setting, what message does this send? What will they come to understand about themselves?

For at least part of your prac experiences, you will be placed in a setting where babies are cared for. Another prac block will involve children aged 2 or 3. Another prac experience will be with children aged 4 and 5. Yet another will be in the early years of primary school. With each prac, you will need to master the culture and context of the setting, and 'read' this as you develop your skills and build your knowledge—of children, relationships and pedagogies. In other parts of this book, you will find some important information about each of these settings, and what you might expect to learn from each of your pracs. Be sure to find out all you can in preparation for commencing any prac in any of the settings. This also applies if you are a graduate teacher taking up your first appointment.

Throughout this book, we constantly challenge you to reflect and revisit your developing ideas, experiences and identity as a teacher. In each of your pracs, we challenge you to:

- think like a teacher (see Chapter 3)
- act like a teacher (see Chapter 4)
- work like a teacher (see Chapter 5).

In the field of early childhood, any number of titles and nomenclatures are used to describe the people who care for and teach young children— educators, group leaders, lead educators, directors, assistants and so on. We use the term 'teacher' to refer to all of these people, whom we define not by their qualifications, but by their identities and their work.

Think about it

Garth Boomer (1981), an eminent scholar of teacher education from South Australia, said: 'Enduringly, when all the surfaces of the curriculum are stripped away, teachers teach what they are . . .'

What meaning do you take from Boomer's words? What will you teach your young children? Can you think of a teacher you know and how Boomer's idea fits with your understanding of them?

The nature of teaching

Whether you have just completed twelve years of education yourself, or you have children of your own, or you have worked in other career choices and arrived at this point after some years of experience, the complexities in a teacher's daily work are rarely visible to those who do not teach.

You may, for instance, know a lot about your own children, but this does not mean you know a lot about children who have different backgrounds, cultures, lifeworlds, circumstances, histories, abilities or ethnicities. You may have just finished your initial twelve years of schooling, and feel you are very close to what makes a good teacher— and the kind of teacher you *never* want to become. But your experience of the process of pedagogy—what happens when teaching and learning occur—is from one perspective and one position: your own.

Another thread in this book relates to the kind of teacher you want to be, and we provide some pointers for getting there. They include the essential processes of your thoughtful consideration of values and ethics. Looking further ahead, we suggest some steps you might begin with immediately, which could eventually help towards your successful graduation and employability. Your experiences on prac are important for all of these reasons, and more.

What is early childhood education for?

According to the National Early Childhood Development Strategy (COAG, 2009), early childhood education and care are important for enabling every child to have the best start in life. Quality ECEC does this by:

- supporting parents as the child's most influential educators
- promoting early learning and successful transition to school
- addressing disadvantage and vulnerability early
- building human capital and economic prosperity.

Such claims are a long way from the traditional beginnings of nursery schools, kindergartens and similar institutions, which were started either to help improve the lot of poor children and keep them safe from life on the streets, or to provide a means by which women could participate in the workforce. Recent reforms in the field of early childhood education and care have been informed by a growing body of empirical evidence and research that provides evidence underlining the importance of a child's early growth and development for establishing the foundations of their health, learning, and social and cultural outcomes into the future. New policies also point to the benefits that accrue to society as a whole as a result of quality ECEC, through enhanced human capital and capability, increased productivity, greater social inclusion and reduced public expenditure on health, welfare and combating crime.

Activity 1.4

Do you agree with the claims that early childhood education benefits society as a whole? Can you add to this list of common understandings and principles that have been applied across any ECEC context?

What are some of the consequences of these claims? Can you think of any negative effects such claims might have on early childhood educators and the wider workforce?

Where in the world might you find employment in the early childhood field?

One of the unique features of the field of early childhood education is its diverse workforce. Early childhood educators are variously qualified, perform various roles and deliver a variety of programs and curricula. There are differences in settings, funding sources, staffing and programs:

- family day care
- outside school-hours care
- long day care
- secondary schools
- kindergartens
- hospitals, art galleries, museums
- prep classes
- community organisations
- lower primary schooling (Years 1–3)
- policy and/or curriculum
- state-run, privately owned, corporate, religious, independent, local, national, international.

Differences occur at the national and international levels, and more locally at the state, regional, district, city, town and suburban level—there will even be differences between two settings that might be a very small distance apart. At the same time, a number of common understandings and principles underpin all early childhood programs.

Did you know?

A *curriculum* is planned learning that is guided by educators. Curriculum documents provide frameworks and guidelines, or may even prescribe content in subject areas.

Think about it

Consider how versatile you will be when you become a good early years teacher. How will you demonstrate this in your portfolio? In an interview? What will you say?

Worldviews and philosophies, standpoints

Our philosophy base is informed and developed by our ways of seeing.

Taking it further

For more about the importance of recognising differences, see the work of Miriam Giugni, *Exploring Multiculturalism, Anti-bias and Social Justice in Children's Services* (n.d.) and Jean Phillips, Indigenous Knowledge Perspectives (2012).

Think about it

Philosophy asks you to think about your beliefs. What do you believe? Why do you believe this? What are the implications for these beliefs in terms of your working relationships, your teaching program, your actions?

Consider:

- How would you describe your 'worldview'?
- How does your worldview shape your practices with children and their families?
- How have we come to a 'common language' in children's services and ECEC?
- Whose ideas are privileged? How? Why?
- Whose ideas are silenced? How? Why?

Who do we mean by 'we'?

When you are becoming a teacher, there are many influences on your interactions and practices. And when you have graduated and are practising as a teacher, you will continue to be influenced by many factors. At the base of all your actions and practices is your philosophy: how you understand the world, how you understand knowledge and learning, your ways of seeing. Your philosophy of teaching shapes, and is shaped by, the ways you see and understand children, families, teachers, childhood, colleagues, education, research, theories, kindergartens, long day care centres, schools, the community and expectations. Can you add more items to this list?

Our ways of seeing inform our philosophies, which inform our teaching programs and the actions and practices that we adopt/enact.

Think about it

The purpose of the curriculum framework is to ensure that the philosophy of the service is reflected in everything that happens within the program. The task is to find a framework that assists you to do this. In Australia, for the first time, there is now a national framework: the Early Years Learning Framework (EYLF).

Think about it

Consider how the worldview of an early childhood educator might be the same as, and different from, the worldview of:

- a CEO of a multinational corporation
- a principal of a secondary school
- a principal of a primary school
- an elder of a local Indigenous community.

Before beginning your prac block, during the block and after you have completed it, it is important to share philosophies with others and discuss how others might see things differently. In order to become a good teacher, you need to challenge your own views. To be able to do this, you need to research, and you can benefit from confrontation. Revisit, revise and reconceptualise. Always be aware of and open to possibilities for change.

Early childhood professionals who work together in teams collaborate to co-construct a philosophy for their setting. They work to ensure that this philosophy embraces all the participants (staff, children and families) and reflects the community context.

But if you have your own standpoint, based on and influenced by the way you see the world, your images of children and teachers, is it possible for you to understand and accommodate the standpoint of another?

How do we define difference? Different from what?

Cultural competence is an essential capacity for all teachers, and these concepts are directly connected with images of children, relationships and pedagogies. We suggest that a pedagogy is needed that requires listening as much as talking, in order to genuinely recognise and celebrate differences.

Educators who are culturally competent are aware of the multiple ways in which others see the world, and the beliefs and practices that shape how they live and act in the world. This is not simply a matter of recognising multiple cultural ways of knowing, seeing and living, but also respecting and celebrating the benefits of diversity. For early childhood educators, their work is defined by their ability to interact respectfully, constructively and positively with children, families, staff and the community. A good early childhood teacher has an ability to understand and honour differences.

> What does it mean to 'belong'?
> How do we know we belong?
> How do we identify those who belong with 'us'?
> Who do we mean by 'us'?
> How do we identify those who are 'other?'
> Who do we mean by 'other'?
> (Giugni, 2011)

Taking it further

- Revisit
- Revise
- Reconceptualise

Be aware of, and open to, the possibilities of change.

When young children and their families first encounter a caring/learning institution, outside their family and their familiar environments, what is involved for them to feel like they 'fit in' and belong?

Consider:

- What are your experiences of having to change the way you do things in order to 'fit in'?
- What does it take to 'see' someone else's point of view?
- How many diversities and differences are we open to?
- Can we know them all?

Where would you have to stand in order not to see someone as 'other', but simply as another person?

Think about it

- What do you believe?
- Why do you believe this?
- Where did your beliefs come from?
- Are you likely to change your beliefs?
- What would make you change your beliefs?

To do

- Consider how versatile you will be when you become a good early years teacher, or how much more versatile you could be as a graduate teacher. How can you demonstrate this in your portfolio? In an interview? What should you say? Practise for a job interview in any of these settings, and 'sell' your versatility and many abilities that are a feature of quality early years teachers.
- Ask others what they think about teachers and teaching.
- Make a poster with your top ten qualities of a good teacher, and post it in your study area. Revisit every year.
- Make a self-portrait. Make a new self-portrait ever year.
- Start collecting drawings of teachers. Ask children, your friends, your parents, your grandparents, people with whom you work—everyone. Analyse your collection. Sort the drawings into categories. Then change the categories and sort them differently.
- What do children say about teachers? About learning?

- What do teachers say about children? About learning?
- What is said in the media? In the community? By politicians?

To think about

- What is a futures perspective on the profession of teaching?
- What is your own ideal learning experience for young children?
- What will early childhood education and care look like in five years? Ten years? Twenty years?
- How will you teach in this future?
- Have you encountered teachers who refuse to change? Why do you think they make that choice?
- Do you think there are aspects of education that you will never change? Why?
- Will you be a teacher for change, or a teacher for the status quo?
- 'Anyone can teach.' Do you agree? Why? Why not?
- How does your way of seeing teachers change in relation to culture, race, gender, age, socioeconomic contexts, geography, religion, physicality, psychology . . . any other factors?

Start to construct a portfolio

The portfolio is a tool that helps you to gather evidence of your skills, reflect on your experiences and recognise your improvement and development over time. Through active reflection, you can come to:

- recognise the variety, depth, and ongoing development of your knowledge and abilities
- increase your confidence in yourself as an emerging professional
- identify skill areas in need of improvement.

In addition to encouraging reflective thinking and the development of lifelong learning skills, a portfolio enables you to build a comprehensive repository of information. This will provide you with a valuable resource for demonstrating your skills, knowledge and achievements to prospective employers.

Time-poor students might find it difficult to see the point in 'wasting time' on work that is not assessed. Building a portfolio is a task that connects directly with your own experiences, and the purpose of a portfolio is obvious and real.

Taking it further

Principles of assessment *for* and *as* learning (Hargreaves, 1997; James, McInnis & Devlin, 2002) are modelled through a portfolio approach to curriculum.

As you progress through the years of your teacher preparation program, you will map your own learning by building a portfolio. Upon graduation, the final portfolio contains the latest and best evidence of your student achievements, knowledge, capacities and reflective practice. In addition, you can make real connections between this personal experience for you, and the purposes and quality of assessment strategies you use with your own students in the classroom or early childhood setting.

Think about it

How and what might you learn as you compile your portfolio? How could your portfolio be of use as evidence to others of what you have learned?

Employment

When prospective employers ask you for evidence of the skills and attributes for which they're looking, you'll be able to draw on the examples documented in your portfolio to answer interview questions and respond to selection criteria. Having this information ready and organised will make the job application process easier and much less daunting. The wide variety of information in your portfolio will convey a far clearer and more complete impression of you than your résumé or academic history could alone.

Lifelong learning: Professional development

After you have graduated and qualified, and begin working as a teacher, your commitment to professional development and learning (PDL) continues to shape who you are and the kind of teacher you will become. Teacher registration requirements currently require that you document your professional learning experiences. It is also personally beneficial for your ongoing learning that you keep records of your teaching and learning experiences, and how these have worked to inform and challenge your philosophy and practices. These practices will enable you—as a good teacher—to continue to evolve and grow.

On prac, you may be offered opportunities to engage in PDL sessions—teachers are expected to regularly engage with these learning opportunities. If you are able to attend and participate, the in-service sessions will provide you with insights into a range of topics and different modes of PDL. Your participation in these activities will enable you to 'act/talk' like a teacher, where you are building relationships and forming connections with other teachers.

> ### Think about it
>
> My prac teacher told me she has been using the same teaching templates for fifteen years. (Student teacher, 2012)
>
> Why is this a concern? Under what circumstances could this be a positive?

Your portfolio is one way to capture the seminars, conferences, symposiums and meetings you attend. However, professional development and learning extends beyond these experiences, and contemporary conceptions of PDL encourage thinking more broadly about what shapes professional knowledge, including inside, outside and beyond the immediate workplace.

> ### Activity 1.5
>
> Keep an up-to-date record of courses, programs and activities you undertake to strengthen your professional learning. Document the purpose, nature of the activity and learning outcomes, and also keep certificates of attendance. Maintain a chronological history of learning activities—showing your commitment to ongoing learning. Complement this with some priorities and plans for future learning.

To do

Start to develop a learning and teaching portfolio. Think about how you will set this up: format, layout, sections and artefacts. Framing your portfolio around current National Teacher Standards is a useful starting point. Ensure you create a portfolio that enables you to modify and change it over time as your teaching develops. You might decide to develop a different portfolio for every prac setting. This will give you a range of artefacts and evidence from which to select when you graduate and apply for different teaching positions, or move to a new position if you are a graduate teacher.

Taking it further

For further reading about conceptions of PDL see Bredeson (2003).

To research

- What qualifications do teachers need in:
  - Finland
  - India
  - Sweden
  - Brazil
  - Kenya?

  What differences do you see? What similarities?

- Research your community:
  - What ECEC services are available in your community?
  - Who makes up the workforce?
  - What is the history of ECEC in your community?

Further reading

Ball, S. (2003). The teacher's soul and the terrors of performativity. *Journal of Education Policy*, 18(2): 215–28.

Darling-Hammond, L. (2007). A good teacher in every classroom: Preparing the highly qualified teachers our children deserve. *Educational Horizons,* 85(2): 111–32.

Department of Education Employment and Workplace Relations (DEEWR) (2009). *Belonging, Being and Becoming: The Early Years Learning Framework for Australia.* <www.deewr.gov.au/EarlyChildhood/Policy_Agenda/Quality/Pages/EarlyYearsLearningFramework.aspx>. Accessed 20 November 2014.

Giugni, M. (n.d.). *Exploring Multiculturalism, Anti-bias and Social Justice in Children's Services.* <www.cscentral.org.au/Resources/Exploring_Multiculturalism.pdf>. Accessed 20 November 2014.

Giugni, M. & Mundine, K. (2012). *Talkin' Up and Speakin' Out: Aboriginal and multicultural voices in early childhood.* Sydney: Pademelon Press.

McArdle, F. (2010). Preparing quality teachers: Making learning visible. *Australian Journal of Teacher Education,* 35(8): 60–78.

MacNaughton, G. (2003). *Shaping Early Childhood: Learners, curriculum and contexts.* Maidenhead: Open University Press.

Phillips, J. (2012). Indigenous Knowledge Perspectives: Making space in the Australian centre. In J. Phillips & J. Lampert (eds), *Introductory Indigenous Studies in Education: Reflection and the importance of knowing.* Sydney: Pearson Education, pp. 9–25.

—— & Lampert, J. (eds) (2012). *Introductory Indigenous Studies in Education: Reflection and the importance of knowing.* Sydney: Pearson Education.

2

What is prac? Preparing for success across different settings

In this chapter you will find:
- connections between prac and the other components of your studies
- assistance with preparing for success across different settings
- evidence and artefacts for your portfolio
- details about a triad—important relationships that make prac work for you
- your health plan for prac.

Arthur is having a hard time of it with this prac. Last prac was great and he really enjoyed it. He had a Year 2 class and the teacher, Mrs Johnson, told him he was a 'natural' with the children. He really enjoyed being with the children, and they seemed to take notice of everything he said. He even organised a game of football with them at lunchtime, and he really felt like a teacher. This time, he is with the kindy children, and things don't seem to be doing so well. He gets on well with the teaching assistant, Helen, but his mentor teacher, Mrs Taylor, doesn't seem so pleased with him. Helen says she can be a bit hard to please.

And yesterday he was reading a story to the children and they kept getting up and walking away. Eventually, there were only three children still listening to him. He felt very awkward and didn't know what to do, except carry on. He thinks that maybe he is better suited to the older children, and he will try to get a job in a primary school when he graduates. Mrs Johnson will probably write him a good reference.

When Martha was told her placement was in a long day care centre, she drove there to see what the place looked like. She looked up their website, and worked out the best way to get there in the mornings. The only experience she has had with babies is minding her sister's children, so she revisited what they had covered in her child development unit last year. She realised that the teaching strategies she used last year with the primary children would not always be as successful with these younger children, but she was not confident of her ability to communicate with the babies. It all seemed a bit 'random'. The first thing she wanted to do was watch closely how the staff worked with the babies, and see what she could learn from observing them, and asking them questions. She thought she might ask whether she could spend a few hours there one afternoon, before her prac started.

A supervising teacher's thoughts

Arthur or Martha?

Martha has some very good professional attitudes, and there is no problem with her admitting that she doesn't know what she is going to do. Prac is the very place where you can try out, practise and learn. It's great that she is thinking ahead, and will not arrive late on the first day because she 'got lost' or 'didn't allow for the traffic'.

Her idea of visiting early is good, although sometimes that's just not convenient. She should be sure to check first, and be prepared that they might not have the time for her before her prac starts. But to begin by observing is always good, whenever you are entering a new situation.

It would be good if she discussed this with her mentor first, so that they both know she is observing closely, and with a purpose.

Arthur? It's possible he will turn around his attitudes with time, as long as he is open to learning
about what he does not know. It's up to him, really.
—Meta, classroom teacher, 2010

Where does prac fit?

Practical and hands-on experience is important for effective learning, as
John Dewey (2010) pointed out over a century ago. However, Dewey also
insisted on a sound theoretical platform to inform that practical experience. Put simply, both theory and practice are important and, more often
than not, they go hand in hand. Ideally, when you are on prac, you should
make this a time for testing theories, trying out strategies and practising
skills—while all along learning about children and about teaching and
learning. Take every opportunity to ask questions, watch, listen, try again,
reflect and rethink.

Prac is not the only opportunity for combining theory with practice.
Broader contexts for work-integrated learning include opportunities for
volunteering in community services. Many students realise the benefits
in seeking opportunities to work with children, aged people, the under-
privileged and communities. This means they gain extra experience with a
range of people and organisations, and can include evidence of this work
in their portfolios and CVs. In addition, the establishing and maintaining
of relationships helps them to build their own identities as well as experience the intrinsic rewards of helping others.

Prac and other forms of field experience are directly connected with the
other components of your teacher preparation program. When you take an
integrated approach to field experiences, you continually make connections
across your school experiences, your time in early childhood centres, your
dialogues with other professionals in the field, families and community
members, and your engagement with the various theories you are encounter-
ing—including cultural, political, critical, psychological and social theories.
There are those who refer to the theory–practice gap and make distinctions
between what you learn at university and what happens in the 'real world'.
We see university and centres and schools as existing in the same 'real world'.
Part of the work for you as a reflective thinker is to make connections, see
where theory informs practice, and where practice informs theory.

The map in Chapter 1 (Figure 1.1) shows how all of the elements of becoming a teacher are interconnected. The connections you make between theory and practice during your first prac will be different from those you are able to make later in your program, as you build on your experiences, and also build on your understandings and theories.

Make your own map of where and when in your course you actively work to integrate theory and practice, and reflect on each of these instances. See Figure 2.1 for some of the possibilities afforded in a four-year program. Your portfolio could include evidence of your volunteer work, any work-integrated learning experiences and prac, as well as the connections you make between these experiences and your developing attributes and capacities as a professional teacher.

Figure 2.1: Opportunities for integrating theory and practice across a teacher-preparation program

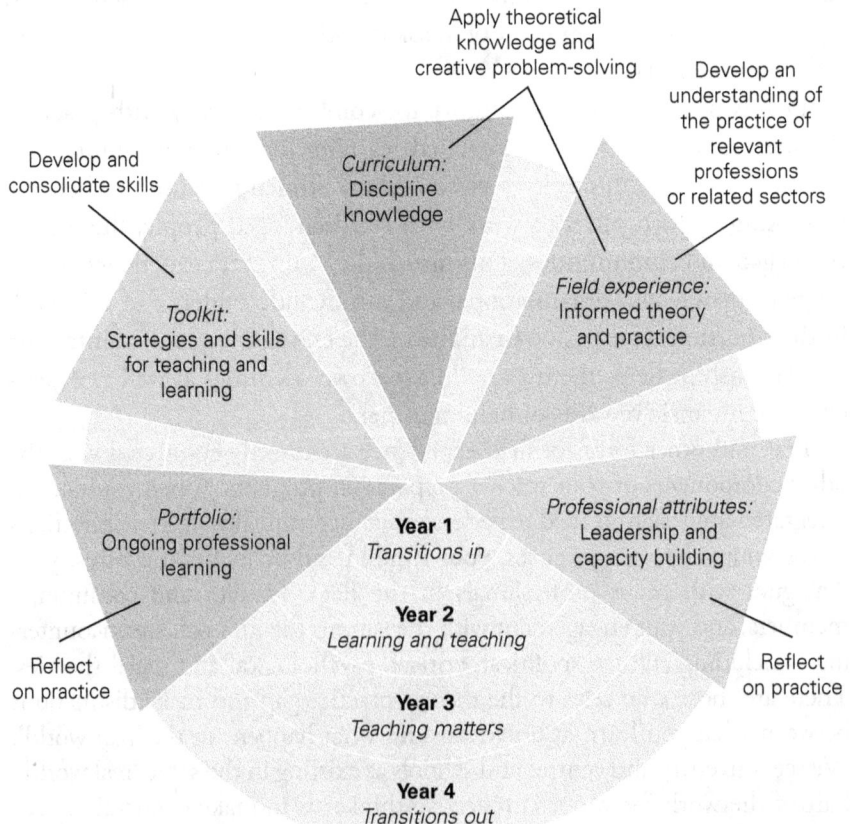

Source: McArdle (2010).

Different settings

Across the years of your program of study, you will be placed in different settings for your pracs. As discussed in Chapter 1, each setting will differ according to any number of factors—including the age of the children, the regulatory bodies, the jurisdiction, policies, traditions, histories, and local and national legislation.

The diversity of contexts within the early childhood years encompasses newborn babies through to children who are 8 years old, and who attend all day or part of the day, every day or some days, at child care, kindergarten, preschool and lower primary. In order to prepare for this profession, early childhood pre-service teachers are required to engage in a range of field experience placements. Your career choices/pathways are exciting and challenging.

An emerging body of research identifies lower primary as the preferred career option of most early childhood graduates (e.g. see Gibson, 2013a). Why do you suppose this is? Do you think Arthur (whose story begins this chapter) is typical? When you are considering career options beyond university, what shapes your thinking? When you prepare for field experience placements across a range of contexts, what do you need to consider? It is important to attend to the nuances/unique features of the different contexts. Each context calls for approaches to pedagogies that are appropriate for the children in those settings.

Think about it

Does an early childhood teacher work in the same way in a child care centre and in a lower primary school?

Early childhood contexts historically have reflected differences in their purposes. Kindergarten/preschool programs traditionally have emphasised learning through play. In addition, preschool has also focused on early intervention and targeting children who are socially disadvantaged. In child care, the purposes have traditionally been to ameliorate poverty and disadvantage and increase rates of parental (particularly mothers') workforce participation. Both education and care contexts have also had their origins in philanthropy, where (mostly) women cared for other women's children. The delineation of preschool/kindergarten as *education* and child care as *care* has thus been constructed through historical origins, and in many cases these original beliefs and attitudes prevail.

Integrated early childhood centres

Like elsewhere in the world (there are examples in United Kingdom, the United States and Finland), Australia has attempted to bring education and care together through models of integrated early childhood centres (for more on this, see Tayler, 2011). Integrated early childhood models blur the traditional distinctions by bringing together what might otherwise be constituted as education/preschool and care/child care contexts. Integrated early childhood centres offer child care and kindergarten/preschool concurrently, along with other programs and services.

The benefits of this operational model extend to families, who are able to access programs that genuinely engage with elements of caring for children and at the same time offer educational programs. Additionally, integrated early childhood programs bring immense benefits for children, where previously they may have been moved from one context to another. When kindergarten/preschool and child care are offered concurrently in one centre, the distinctions between these two contexts and the associated operational features become intertwined. An integrated service may incorporate operational features of both kindergarten/preschool and child care—for example, opening hours, adherence to school terms, qualified staff—while at the same time including programs that actively address and support children's health and wellbeing.

In the integrated early childhood model, staff work across teams. These teams include staff with a range of qualifications and experiences, working with a broad range of children and ages. An early childhood teacher who works in a kindergarten/preschool program will work with children in this particular age range (typically 3–5 years). An early childhood teacher working within an integrated early childhood model would have the opportunity to work across a broader age range, including children aged from birth to 5 years. Additionally, educators working in an integrated model of ECEC are afforded professional opportunities to work with other professionals (for example, social workers, psychologists, dieticians) in cross-disciplinary teams. This model provides possibilities for staff to be enriched in their own professional role, status and expertise.

Community-based/not-for-profit and private/for-profit

Another factor that makes a difference to the setting in which you will conduct your prac is the model for provision—or how the centre or setting is operated. The increase in the number of child care centres in Australia has also seen the emergence of different models of child care operations. Three distinct business models of child care provision have developed:

- not-for-profit/community-based
- for-profit/private
- corporate child care.

A model of not-for-profit/community-based child care has been prominent in early childhood programs in Australia and internationally. Not-for-profit/community-based centres are driven by principles of working with families and are committed to the highest quality. The link between quality and not-for-profit principles has seen the not-for-profit/community-based business model touted as the most appropriate for children and for families. In Australia, such centres are under the governance of organisations such as the Crèche and Kindergarten Association in Queensland, Lady Gowrie Centres (nationally) and the Kindergarten Union of New South Wales (KU). Other jurisdictions have their similar governance mechanisms.

Think about it

In Australia, the provision of for-profit and not-for-profit ECEC care is the result, to an extent, of child care policy—who can provide it, how it is funded and how it should operate (Penn, 2011).

For-profit/private child care centres operate under two related business models: privately owned and operated child care, and corporate child care. Private/for-profit centres are owned by individuals or small businesses, and operate independently. The corporate child care model includes a larger operation in which a number of centres are centrally managed by a company (e.g. in Australia, Guardian Early Learning Group). In recent years, the emergence of social enterprises has seen a reshaping of the ECEC provision in Australia. In Australia during the 1980s, nearly all centres were based on the not-for-profit model. From the mid-1990s, the corporate child care model gained an increased stronghold in the marketplace.

In addition, there will be subtle and nuanced differences between one kindergarten, say, and another. Each institution and setting will have its own 'culture', set of 'rules', routines, ways of doing and ways of being.

Think about it

Recent changes have seen strong cases made for integrated services where children, from an early age, are encouraged to learn, develop and grow in a healthy and safe environment, with increased chances for success. Yet the distinction between education and care has been reinforced, to an extent, through government organisation of early childhood, its funding, its regulatory systems and its structures (for more on this, see OECD, 2006).

Why do you think this is so?

In conversation

At first I didn't realise that the tea and coffee and milk was paid for by the staff. I thought it was supplied. Eventually, my host teacher asked me to contribute to the fund. I was embarrassed. I should have asked first up. (Robert, pre-service teacher, 2011)

At the same time, there will be some commonalities across all early childhood settings. You will be called upon to read each setting and context and make adjustments as appropriate, informed by your knowledge, theories and experiences. This is challenging, but it is also rewarding.

In conversation

I didn't know to pack a lunch. There was nowhere nearby to buy lunch and we could not leave the premises. The first day I almost fainted from hunger! After that, I made sure I took a good lunch! (Lara, exchange student, 2010)

You might like to know that many students who are filled with trepidation at the beginning of prac proclaim loudly at the end of their prac that they do not want to return to university, and they wish they could stay longer at their placement.

> **Think about it**
>
> Investigate possibilities for volunteering at your centre after your prac ends, if this is possible and your teacher is able to accommodate it. You can make a sustained and valued contribution to the community as you benefit from further learning and experience. Professionally, this is an excellent opportunity for development.

How will I succeed on prac?

This book is aimed primarily at supporting you to have a successful prac experience. It will also help for you to revisit when you transition to your career as a graduate teacher. Your prac experience will prove to be a powerful lifelong influence on the kind of teacher you become. Some students take the strategies they see and learn while on prac with them into their own careers, and sometimes they pass these on to those whom they later mentor.

For some student teachers, this returning to a school setting brings back their personal memories and experiences of schooling. But while it is important to position yourself as a learner, you are no longer a child/student in the classroom. Try to be clear about your position, and understand that you are learning alongside the teacher.

> **Think about it**
>
> Why is it important to be clear about your position? Can you think of circumstances where confusion might arise? How can this be addressed?

A sense of your own agency is important to your success. You are becoming a teacher, and are in the process of being inducted into the profession. Take ownership of your prac, and make it a successful learning experience.

What will you contribute?

- What are your strengths, and how will these benefit the setting and the children?

Did you know?

In feedback sessions, teachers have praised the following qualities and skills demonstrated by pre-service teachers during prac: enthusiasm, asking questions, initiative, organisation, relationship-building, reflections, collaboration, teaching style.

- How will the school or setting perceive you?
- What will you bring with you to the setting that will add to the workplace and context?

Take responsibility for your performance

- How will you prepare for prac?
- Will you contribute to the teachers' work, their goals, their efforts?
- Will you receive feedback thoughtfully and responsively?
- What will you do when something goes wrong? (And things *will* go wrong!)

Many students are overwhelmed at the thought of prac, and think about all their needs and everyone's expectations of them. But we have talked with many mentors over the years, and the students who are most valued on prac are those who take some ownership of their learning and development, take responsibility and treat their learning as an ongoing process. How might you demonstrate and develop these traits? Try to think in terms of what you will gain from *your* prac.

It is not possible for you to experience and learn *all* you need to know. You are entering a profession that requires you to respond and react to different events almost every day. What you can do is to become a 'reader' of your field. If you are to succeed on prac, and become a good teacher, you will need to be able to 'read' your placement. By this we mean:

- read the culture of the school/centre
- read the organisational structure of the team/staff
- read the social and power relationships existing in the context you are entering.

We can't tell you everything that you will face, but we do know that you will need to make informed decisions. You will need to read curriculum, policy, children and their behaviours, and your environment.

Before you begin each practicum, consider the checklist in Table 2.1. Make every effort to think through your preparation for, and contributions to, each of the elements. Take the first item, 'Identities'. You might design and prepare a poster for the welcome area in your prac centre. The poster might communicate who you are and your goals for this time spent with the children. What will this say about your identity? How will you prepare to appreciate and understand others' identities and show respect for differences? If you address each of these, then you might tick the 'Yours and others' box. Then, what other items might you add under 'Identities'? We have made a start with one item under each element. Can you add more to make this list your own?

Table 2.1: Prac checklist

Identities: • Yours and others • •	Theory and practice: • Making connections • •	Relationships and listening: • Mutual respect • •
Learning and responsibilities: • Position and agency • •	Planning and preparation: • Professionalism • •	Children, families, communities: • Celebrate differences • •

What happens on prac? Who will I be working with?

Traditional models of prac in teacher education programs have remained virtually unchanged for the best part of a century. The taken-for-granted belief is that students spend time engaging with 'theory' on campus and with 'applications' in classrooms and settings on their prac placements. However, there is no evidence to show that the more time a student spends in one classroom with one teacher, the better prepared they will be for their profession (for more on this, see Zeichner, 2006). Approaches to prac vary from university to university, and system to system, but generally during prac, you will be part of a 'triad' in some form (see Figure 2.2).

You are the first member of the triad: the pre-service teacher. The second member of the triad is a supervising teacher (who might have another title, such as host teacher or mentor teacher), and for the most part you will work alongside this teacher. Sometimes—particularly in a long day care setting—you may work alongside any number of other staff members. But there will be one qualified teacher who will be charged with inducting you into the work of teaching.

The third member of the triad will be a representative from the university. This person may be referred to as your university mentor, liaison academic or by a similar title. In general, the role of this person is to support you throughout your prac, be available to deal with you and any individual needs that might arise and, if needed, liaise with your host teacher. Sometimes you might need the liaison academic to advocate on your behalf, providing some clarity about university systems or expectations. On occasion, a host teacher has asked the liaison academic to communicate with the pre-service teacher if there is a need for intervention.

?

Did you know?

A *university mentor* or *liaison academic* is a university-based academic who oversees the field experience and provides guidance and support, often online or over the phone.

Figure 2.2: Triad for prac

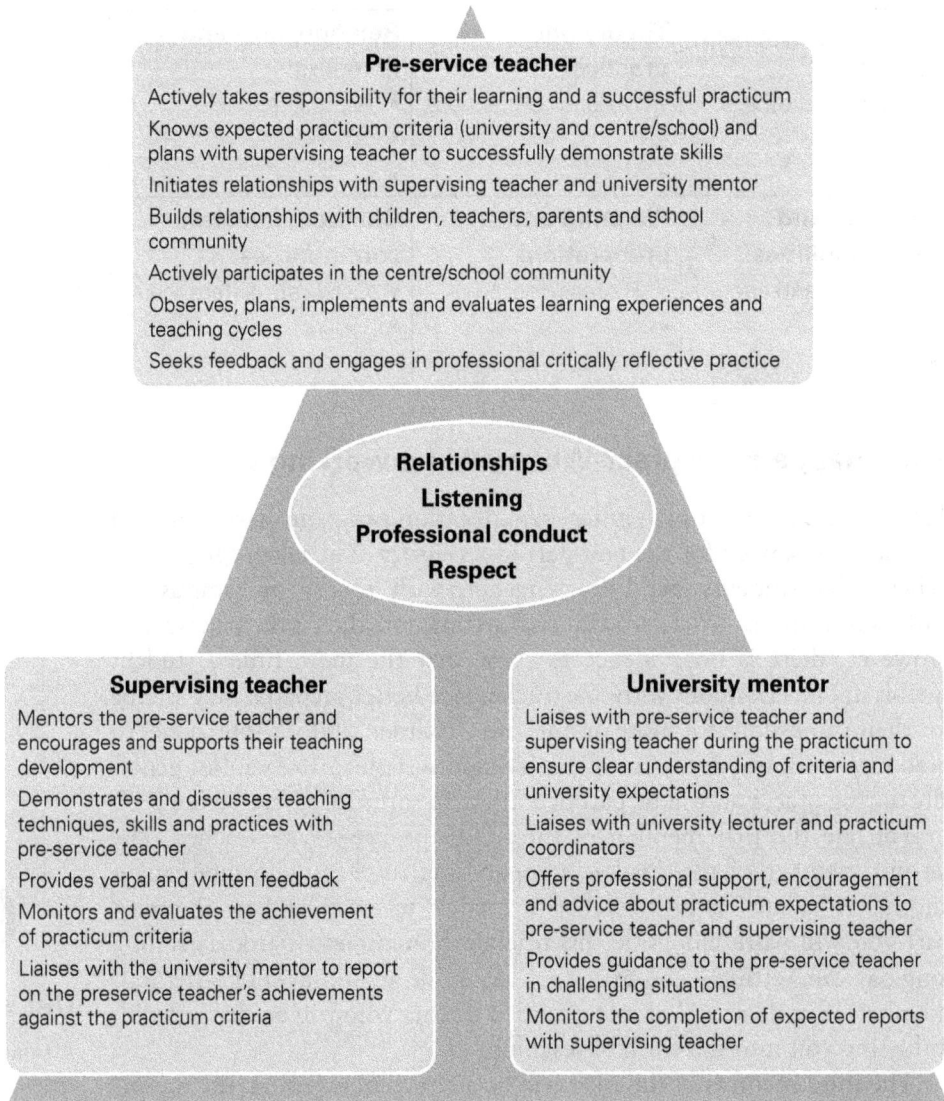

Pre-service teacher

Actively takes responsibility for their learning and a successful practicum

Knows expected practicum criteria (university and centre/school) and plans with supervising teacher to successfully demonstrate skills

Initiates relationships with supervising teacher and university mentor

Builds relationships with children, teachers, parents and school community

Actively participates in the centre/school community

Observes, plans, implements and evaluates learning experiences and teaching cycles

Seeks feedback and engages in professional critically reflective practice

Relationships
Listening
Professional conduct
Respect

Supervising teacher

Mentors the pre-service teacher and encourages and supports their teaching development

Demonstrates and discusses teaching techniques, skills and practices with pre-service teacher

Provides verbal and written feedback

Monitors and evaluates the achievement of practicum criteria

Liaises with the university mentor to report on the preservice teacher's achievements against the practicum criteria

University mentor

Liaises with pre-service teacher and supervising teacher during the practicum to ensure clear understanding of criteria and university expectations

Liaises with university lecturer and practicum coordinators

Offers professional support, encouragement and advice about practicum expectations to pre-service teacher and supervising teacher

Provides guidance to the pre-service teacher in challenging situations

Monitors the completion of expected reports with supervising teacher

Think about it

Find out on prac: Who reports to whom? What is the line of management? What are the organisational structures? Where do you fit in all of the relationships?

Your key mentor will be your host teacher. In some larger schools and organisations, there may also be a member of staff who oversees all the prac students, sometimes organising your experiences, meetings and rosters. This person will be referred to as the site coordinator, or some-thing similar. Primarily, you will be working most intensively with your host teacher or mentor.

Over the course of your prac, your host teacher will provide support, advice, feedback and modelling, and eventually will complete an evaluation of your performance. It is very important to understand that prac is not an assessment exercise from beginning to end; rather, you are assessed on your learning, your development and your performance. You are not expected to perform at the level of a professional and experienced teacher. A number of factors will affect your achievements on prac, and although this is as close as you can come to the 'real thing', it is still very different from being a graduate teacher.

Did you know?

A *Site coordinator* is the person at the school or setting who provides broader-level support for the pre-service teacher, with a focus on key school/ centre policies and procedures.

Activity 2.1

Find a copy of the assessment form that your host teacher will be required to complete. Refer to this throughout your prac to remind yourself of your goals and expectations. (Figure 4.1 shows a mock-up prac report template to give you an idea of what this form will look like.)

Relationships

It should be obvious at this point that relationships will play a large part in the success of your prac. The important relationships will include those with staff, families, community members and children. First you will need to develop and maintain positive and respectful relationships with the children in your care. If you are to manage behaviour, listen to children, and come to know their interests, needs and capacities, you will first need to establish relationships of mutual trust and respect.

You also need to understand the existing relationships that are part of the 'culture' of the setting. Power resides in all relationships, and can be both powerful and 'slippery'. It is important to your success on prac to understand where the power lies in all the relationships you will be required to maintain. Sometimes in your relationships with children, for instance, the balance of the power will reside within the child. Can you think of an example of when this might be the case? Is this a positive or a negative situation? When would it be important for you to ensure that the balance of the power rests with you?

Think about it

When you are on prac, check in with this question: In your particular placement setting, who holds the most power? How? Why? Is this a good thing? What are the effects of power in each relationship?

Power can also reside with regulatory bodies. As professionals, early childhood educators are awarded a degree of autonomy in order to interpret curriculum according to the needs of the specific children in their care. Nevertheless, teachers are not free to ignore policy, or regulatory and curriculum documents that are mandated. Teachers remain accountable for their performance and, increasingly, for demonstrated outcomes.

Listening is important in all relationships. The Chinese character for the verb 'to listen' contains characters for heart, eye and ear (see Figure 2.3). This implies both a deeper understanding and shared learning.

Figure 2.3: The Chinese characters that make up the verb 'to listen'

Ears 聽 Eyes

Undivided attention

Heart

Standard 7 in the Australian *National Professional Standards for Teachers* (Education Services Australia, 2011a) requires that teachers '*Engage professionally with colleagues, parents/carers and the community*'. Learning to establish and maintain relationships is an important part of your professional identity as a teacher. Take every opportunity to practise the necessary skills, and ask for guidance and support if you need them. If possible, gather evidence of your success with managing and maintaining relationships, and add this to your portfolio to demonstrate your attainments against Standard 7.

> ### Think about it
>
> What kind of listener are you? When you listen, do you show:
> - genuineness: you really want to hear and understand what the other person is saying
> - curiosity: you are interested and want to hear and find out more about the person
> - responsiveness: you respond to the person in a sensitive and appropriate manner?
>
> Practise these qualities, and observe as you practise. Make notes in your journal.

Taking it further

For the *National Professional Standards for Teachers*, see the website for Education Services Australia (2011b).

Throughout your time on prac, you will be constantly involved in both personal and interpersonal interactions. Remind yourself to:

- be respectful
- listen carefully
- communicate well
- be proactive—it is important to remember that this is *your* prac, and it is up to you to make it work.

Knowledge about, with and for Indigenous and non-Indigenous peoples occurs within a 'cultural interface' that requires critical reflection on the 'self' (for more on this, see Nakata, 2002, 2007). Relationships between oneself and others require negotiated understandings that can take time, and can also change. Community engagement and relationships, for instance, will differ when populations include Aboriginal or Torres Strait Islander people, and may require particular protocols to be observed. Protocols may also differ across communities, and between urban, rural and remote locales. Authentic embracing of Indigenous leadership can prove crucial to the effectiveness of sustained relationships that benefit teachers, students, parents and community (for more on this, see Luke, Woods & Weir, 2013).

Taking it further

For more on embracing cultural ways of knowing, see Grace and Trudgett, It's not rocket science: The perspectives of Indigenous early childhood workers on supporting the engagement of Indigenous families in early childhood settings (2012).

> ### Think about it
>
> - How will you know about the protocols within communities in which you will be working?
> - Where can you find the necessary information?
> - Does the university offer support for this?

Consider the relationships listed below, as they will be important to the success of your prac. Remind yourself of your responsibilities and the part you will play in establishing and maintaining these important relationships. The more you are aware of your own perspectives, assumptions, beliefs, attitudes, and cultural and social experiences, and particularly how these shape your identity, the more sensitive and responsive you can be to others in the relationships you build.

Relationship with your early childhood centre/school

- Create a relationships map of the centre/school personnel and include everyone's roles and responsibilities.
- Get to know your site coordinator (meet, greet, review).
- Seek invitations to, and take part in, meetings, events and professional development opportunities (in and out of 'work' hours).
- Spend time with specialists, librarians and other teachers to extend your skills and knowledge.
- Explore a day in the life of a teacher assistant.
- Network with the other pre-service teachers at the school.
- Make a plan for what you do in your 'break' times—meet other teachers, go to the staff room, explore the library and so on.

Relationship with your supervising teacher/mentor

- If possible, visit your prac site before you start. Make an appointment and introduce yourself.
- Clarify in your own mind what the university's expectations and requirements are for your prac. Prepare well for a discussion with your supervising teacher so that, together, you can plan how you will meet the expectations and demonstrate the required skills.
- Visit the centre/school's website to find out about its priorities, behaviour-management strategy and other relevant policies that you will need to follow (or ask about).
- Copy for your host teacher (1) the field experience information provided by the university and (2) the schedule of responsibilities. They may already have a copy, but make them a copy to have at hand in case they don't. Be prepared to talk about your responsibilities as outlined in these documents. How does your host teacher interpret the responsibilities?
- Ask your host teacher to share with you the characteristics of the best pre-service teacher they ever had. Use the 'On track on prac' pages in Chapter 8 to frame such a conversation.

Taking it further

Use the 'On track on prac' pages at the end of this book to support conversations.

Relationship with your university mentors

- Introduce yourself via email to your allocated university mentor—who might be different from your lecturer or tutor.
- Pass on the details of the university mentor to your host teacher, and pass on contact details for your host teacher to your university mentor.
- Make regular contact with your university mentor throughout your field placement, with reflective comments about your progress. They are there to support you and advocate on your behalf. It is your responsibility to engage with and sustain this relationship as part of your professional practice.

Relationship with children's parents

- This can be challenging for many prac students, as you are taking on a new aspect of your identity, and this professional role may be new to you. Understand that this relationship always requires sensitivity and professionalism—like all the relationships connected with prac.

Think about it

Imagine that you are the parent of a child beginning Year 3. What are some of the priorities that you have for your child in that year of school?

An important factor here is where you *see* parents:

At school or at the centre

- An 'open-door' policy means parents are welcome to come into the setting any time with their children. Does your school/centre have this practice? Why or why not? What do you think will be your policy about this in the future?
- There might be differences between preschool and school, or between Year 1 and Year 3. You might not see the parents at school.
- Parents are sometimes invited to meet, particularly in relation to conflict situations, or to relay something negative. It is important to prepare well for such conversations, and seek guidance from your host teacher before making negative observations to a child's parents or family. If you are not sufficiently prepared, delay the conversation, and make another time when you will be ready (see Whitton et al., 2006, p. 201).
- 'Listen' to body language. Be aware of other ways of communicating, i.e. non-verbal cues.

Did you know?

If you need to have a difficult conversation with a child's parent, prepare what you will say. 'Sandwich' the negative issue between positive observations of the child's capacities.

At the shops

- Avoid spontaneous parent–teacher interviews in the supermarket.
- This can be tricky in small communities. Think about your professional identity and reputation.

At social events

- Be aware of confidentiality issues. Ethics are always important. Never discuss other people's children.

In the staffroom

- You may need to consider your management of the parent who is also a colleague.

Think about it

- How much of your personal life, beliefs and thoughts will you reveal in the classroom?
- Will you act differently in the playground?
- How will you act when you meet students in informal situations?
- Will you behave differently in different roles?

In conversation

I am finding it a bit hard to get examples to show my relationships with different people. I feel as though I get along really well with other staff members and I talk to the parents in the morning as well as collaborating with my host teacher about the coming days. I was just wondering if you had any ideas as to how I could show this in my portfolio? (Elizabeth, pre-service teacher, in an email to her liaison academic, 2012)

For the relationship section of my field portfolio, does writing about me attending meetings with my teacher, such as staff meetings, meetings with Learn Support Staff and attending planning day with the other Grade 2 teacher count toward relationships? If I added them to my field folder would I just state the meeting I went to who was there and why it was helpful and how it helped with building relationships? (Elizabeth, pre-service teacher, in an email to her liaison academic, 2012)

Teacher as researcher

Good teachers are researchers, and learn to ask the 'why' questions. They are not just consumers of other people's research, but consider and weigh up options, and generate and analyse evidence. They use their analysis of the evidence to make informed decisions about their developing practices.

Think about it

Martha prepared for a new prac placement by revisiting her learning in her child development unit. In what ways will this knowledge enable her to build relationships with the children with whom she will be working? In what ways might this knowledge constrain her in the relationships she builds? What else could she do to prepare?

Reflective practice and critical inquiry are two important tools that good teachers use to examine their own practice and conduct their own research. Reflective practice helps teachers to generate questions and to hypothesise about what is and is not working. According to the EYLF, there are three dimensions of teachers' work about which they might generate reflective questions. First, they might reflect on the technical level of their pedagogies—for example, developing ways in which they might plan, interact, monitor, document and assess. Second, they might reflect on the practical dimension of their work—such as finding ways to more effectively promote learning, either in an individual child's progress, or all the children's learning. Third, teachers might reflect critically—for instance, identifying whose views are dominating, and whose views are regularly overlooked or overshadowed.

This questioning of their practices can then be taken up as a form of critical inquiry. Teachers purposively examine their practices by collecting data and then analysing them to develop deeper awareness or gain further insight into what might be happening. Data might be in the form of observing what learning strategies children are using to solve challenging tasks. Or perhaps teachers might plan to keep a tally of the types of questions they most often ask children. Analysing the data can provide a basis for further reflection and the development of strategies. This often leads to further and ongoing inquiry.

Taking it further

For more on this, see *Belonging, Being and Becoming*, usually called the *Early Years Learning Framework* (DEEWR, 2009), on reflective practitioners.

> **Activity 2.2**
>
> Plan for artefacts and other evidence you can select for your portfolio that will be evidence of your many skills and abilities.

Critical reflection does not mean 'criticising'. In the arts, the term 'critique' is used to refer to an experience of intense discussion, feedback and thinking, as the artist shows their work for others to view. In education, it means reconsidering sometimes taken-for-granted beliefs and practices, and looking at them in the light of what we all know now about the differences that are produced by factors such as race, gender, ethnicity and culture. When you are reflecting on experiences during and after prac, which lenses will you use:

- an autobiographical lens
- your eyes as a student
- the experience of peers
- your experience of school as a child, as you now recall it
- the theories, literature and research about children and education
- the policy agendas and frameworks about assessment, accountability and reporting?

Taking it further

For more on critical reflection, see Latham et al., *Learning to Teach: New times, new practices* (2006, pp. xvi–xviii).

To do

Consider your philosophy of early childhood education. Here are some questions you might ask yourself:

- What do I believe about young children and how will this affect my teaching?
- How will I negotiate dilemmas?
- Who will be the deciding factor in how time is controlled: teacher or child?
- Is knowledge content or is it process?
- Which is more important: intrinsic or extrinsic motivation?
- Do I plan based on the belief that each child is unique, or do I plan based on a belief in universal patterns of learning?

Being a reflective practitioner is not always about coming to the 'correct' answer. Sometimes it is the questions that are important. Think about the questions you ask of the children and of your colleagues. Spend time planning your questions: they are important to your own learning and teaching. There may be an expectation that teachers have all the answers. Try to change your thinking about this, and celebrate your questions and your curiosity. Wonder and imagination are just as important as 'solutions'.

While it is important to keep abreast of evolving research findings and debates, it is also desirable to invest time and skill in developing the mindset and disposition of the 'teacher as researcher'. When you create a space for regular reflective practice, you provide the opportunity for pausing and thinking about how teaching and learning are working in the classroom. This sense of inquiry is also something you want to nurture in children.

Teachers of inquiring classrooms:

- carefully and thoughtfully observe and reflect on life in the classroom
- work together with children to pursue their questions
- follow children's ideas, interests and hypotheses.

> "" Be patient toward all that is unsolved in your heart and try to love the questions themselves. (Hill, Stremmel & Fu, 2005, p. 43)

Ethics and professionalism

Teachers are expected to behave ethically at all times. Young children are among the most vulnerable people in our population, and those who are charged with their care are awarded an enormous privilege and, along with this, carry a weighty responsibility—for children's safety and protection, under all circumstances. Besides the legislative measures and requirements, such as criminal checks and Blue Cards, you must give serious thought to this side of the profession you are preparing to enter. In preparation for your first prac, you should become familiar with the relevant regulatory and governance bodies that have jurisdiction over your placement setting. Find out about the professional bodies for early childhood educators, and any memberships of professional organisations that your host teacher maintains.

For more on ethics, see Chapter 3.

Your health on prac

We conclude this chapter by highlighting that your success on prac will also depend on being healthy, in mind and body. You will probably be coming into contact with many people, and this includes larger numbers of young children than you would usually encounter. Not only do you need to be aware of personal hygiene, and care for young children's health and hygiene, but you also need to manage your stress—both physical and emotional.

Physically, you will be required to be fit, active and energetic throughout the day. Emotionally, you will maintain a sense of control if you are organised, allow sufficient time for all that is required of you, and actively cultivate a positive and willing attitude to each aspect of your day.

In conversation

I have a health plan which maps out my weekly activities for exercise, meditation and down time. If I don't put these into my work diary, time gets taken up with other work tasks. Just setting aside five minutes at the end of my lunch break for a short meditation makes a huge difference in my day. I wasn't always this proactive. It was only after I was introduced to stress reduction and its benefits for teachers at a great seminar I went to that my attitudes changed. (Kim, director of long day care centre with twelve years' experience)

Consider the six dimensions of wellness, as developed by Dr Bill Hettler (1976), co-founder of the National Wellness Institute (NWI) (see Table 2.2). Make yourself a health plan for prac, and use this framework to check in daily on your own wellbeing.

Table 2.2: The six dimensions of wellness

Emotional:	Occupational:
Self-esteem	Work satisfaction
Stress management	Work attitudes
Managing emotions	Work development
Social relationships:	**Intellectual:**
Family	Creativity
Community	Mental stimulation
Environment	Utilisation of resources
Physical:	**Spiritual:**
Fitness	Morals
Healthy eating habits	Ethics
Healthy medical practices	Values
	Beliefs

Your wellbeing on prac will play a large part in your successful completion of the prac block. Like Kim, make a weekly plan and take action to attend to:

- physical health, exercise, back care
- happiness, self-esteem, stress levels
- management of hygiene and potential for disease, infection
- work attitudes, work satisfaction, handling trauma
- relationships: at work, home and in the environment
- nutrition and rest.

Taking it further

Read the following documents:
- *Code of Ethics*, Early Childhood Australia (ECA) (2006)
- *National Professional Standards for Teachers* (Education Services Australia, 2011).

In conversation

I just had to call in all my favours when prac was on. My parents came and stayed with us to mind the kids. My playgroup mates came and got Ruby and took her with them to playgroup. We had frozen dinners quite a bit. And on the weekend, Barry took the kids out so that I could get my planning done. I don't think I would have survived without all that. We had a roster and everyone had to help. (Kathy, undergraduate student, mother of two children, 2012)

Activity 2.3

What are you going to do once you get out there, on your prac placement? Think about the following questions.
- How will I use what I have been learning at university?
- What do the various theories I have studied mean to me?
- How do I want to teach?
- What are my ideas and opinions about school, child care, kindergarten, prep?
- What relationship do I want with the children?
- What relationship do I want with parents?
- How can children's opinions be heard and valued, and their questions researched and investigated?

Discuss your answers with someone studying along with you.

Activity 2.4

Think about current international, national and state education agendas. What is being promoted? Is it an agenda of:

- accountability?
- reporting?
- a focus on achievement?
- assessment?

Teacher as researcher

What does a classroom with early childhood approaches/perspectives look, feel and sound like from the perspective of:

- children
- you, the teacher
- parents/families
- other teachers?

How and why might it be the same as and/or different from other educational settings?

For your portfolio

Develop a one-page statement about building positive relationships.

Look back through many of the ideas that have been explored in this chapter, and in particular consider ways of demonstrating:

- occasions when you are an active listener
- specific examples of respectful relationships you have built and maintained
- your performance in the different roles and responsibilities in your field experience
- your performance in different roles and with different responsibilities beyond university, in your workplace or as a volunteer.

For this, you may find it valuable to start with a paragraph that provides your overview, then use bullet points to capture what is important to you and how you go about building positive relationships.

Further reading

Early Childhood Australia (ECA). (2006). *Code of Ethics*, <www.earlychildhood australia.org.au/our-publications/eca-code-ethics>. Accessed 20 November 2014.

Education Services Australia (2011). *National Professional Standards for Teachers*, <www.aitsl.edu.au/docs/default-source/default-document-library/national_ professional_standards_for_teachers.pdf?sfvrsn=4>. Accessed 25 March 2014.

Grace, R. & Trudgett, M. (2012). It's not rocket science: The perspectives of Indigenous early childhood workers on supporting the engagement of Indigenous families in early childhood settings. *Australasian Journal of Early Childhood*, 37(2): 10.

Hettler, B. (1976). *Six Dimensions of Wellness Model*, <www.nationalwellness. org/?page=Six_Dimensions>. Accessed 20 November 2014.

Hill, L.T., Stremmel, A.J. & Fu, V.R. (2005). *Teaching as Inquiry: Rethinking curriculum in early childhood education*. Boston: Pearson Education.

Latham, G., Blaise, M., Dole, S., Faulkner, J. & Malone, K. (2006). *Learning to Teach: New times, new practices*. New York: Oxford University Press.

Luke, A., Cazden, C., Coopes, R. et al. (2013). *A Summative Evaluation of the Stronger Smarter Learning Communities Project: Vol. 1 and Vol. 2*. Brisbane: Queensland University of Technology.

Nakata, M. (2002). Indigenous knowledge and the cultural interface: Underlying issues at the intersection of knowledge and information systems. *International Federation of Library Associations and Institutions*, 28(5): 281–91.

—— (2007). The cultural interface. *Australian Journal of Indigenous Education*, 36(5): 2–14.

Whitton, D., Sinclair, C., Barker, K., Nunlohy, P. & Nosworthy, M. (2006). *Learning for Teaching: Teaching for learning*. Melbourne: Cengage.

3

Think like a teacher: Pedagogies, values and ethics

In this chapter you will find:

- images of teachers
- images of children
- information about why you should form relationships and which relationships you should form
- knowledge about embedding Indigenous perspectives
- details of how to construct a personal statement for your portfolio
- some understandings of ethics and values.

Mihalia does not understand why there is so much assessment in her course. It causes her so much stress. At the end of each semester, she finds herself doing 'all-nighters', trying to get her essays handed in on time. More often than not, she has to ask for an extension, and it's not her fault. She is also working three shifts a week at a café in order to pay her bills. Why do they have to do all these tasks anyway? She just wants to be a teacher, not an academic. And it's not fair that they have group work assignments. What is the point of that? It would be much easier if she could just get on with her own assignments. But they all have to meet up in their group, and sort out who will do which parts of the task. And she always seems to be the last to get her bit done. It's just all extra stress.

Darlia likes to keep a study diary. At the beginning of each semester, she notes when each assignment is due. She also makes a note in her diary three weeks before each assignment, so she can plan ahead and won't realise at the last minute that something is due. She knows that if she leaves things until the last minute, they will be rushed and not as good as they might be. She also knows it will cause her stress and, again, she will not do as well as she knows she can. The group work assignments take more time because the team needs to get organised, and if the members work smart, they can pool their resources and help each other out. At Darlia's part-time job, they try to do things this way too. If someone has a lot of exams coming up, then the others will cover their shifts. Coming up to prac, Darlia tries to do a few extra shifts if they are available so she might be able to manage better on prac, and not have to do too much.

A supervising teacher's thoughts

Look, I know that students have a lot on their plates, and I think they have a lot of assignments and they work and some of them are juggling families. But, honestly? That is not really my problem. I am busy too.

What is expected of the students when they are on prac?

I'm not heartless, and I am willing to cut them some slack sometimes, and I understand things can go wrong with the best of plans.

But I like to see them at least trying their best, planning ahead, giving it their all while they are here, and having a go.

I'm always glad of an extra hand in the room. But if they are like an extra child in the group, and I have to look out for them all the time, then it gets hard . . . and I lose my patience a bit.

—Liu, kindergarten teacher, 2013

As recently as 20 years ago, initial teacher training included a number of 'rules' for teaching. One was 'don't smile until Easter' (please note, this was situated within the southern hemisphere school year). Later, teachers could relax more and have some fun with the children, but first they needed to establish their authority. Other 'rules' included: don't talk until every child is looking at you and listening; always be sure that you are able to see every child in the room; silence is golden.

Activity 3.1

Can you think of the 'truths' that might underpin some of these 'rules'?
Can you imagine when you might apply similar rules?
Under what circumstances might these be appropriate?
Under what circumstances might they be inappropriate?

Like much folkloric knowledge, these 'rules' may contain some 'truths', but they also invite critical reflection. A simple web search will locate any number of lists of 'rules for good teaching'. There are also other sets of 'rules', such as a code of ethics, which we will discuss later in this chapter. The point is that it is possible to learn all the techniques, teaching strategies and methods available, and still remain unfit for teaching. Becoming a teacher requires something that cannot be packaged and sequenced and staged: thoughtful and reflective pedagogies.

Becoming a teacher—being a lifelong learner

When it comes to teaching, there is a lot to learn. Becoming a teacher marks an important transition in your life, whatever stage you have reached. You will have many preconceived ideas about what it means to be a teacher, and these will be shaped by any number of influences—movies, books, newspaper reports, your own personal experience as a student, others' experiences. As you progress towards graduation, and experience a number of different prac settings, and as you begin teaching after graduation, you will be building a knowledge base that will become part of your thinking. Some of this will be part of a body of knowledge shared by all professional teachers. And some will be your own understandings, arrived at through your own experiences and reflections.

It is important that you think like a teacher, and then act and work like a teacher. In this chapter, we explore thoughtful, critical, reflective pedagogies. Ethics and values are critical for your actions while on prac and in your early teaching career. And we prompt you to engage with ideas, theories, critiques and rules—to think like a teacher.

There is much to learn as you prepare to teach. Some of this is content, pedagogical knowledge, skills and techniques. Some involves attitudes and attributes. See the map in Figure 1.1, and trace all the different knowledges that you will acquire as you become a professional teacher. You will add to your knowledge of teaching and learning throughout your life. Graduation is another beginning. The process of learning to drive a car works as a popular analogy. After you have learned enough to be granted your licence, you learn more as you drive.

Images of teachers

Our ways of seeing the world shape and produce our approaches, actions, interactions and responses. In everything we do, we bring with us our beliefs and attitudes—there are many ways of seeing: children, childhoods, families, cultures, gender, ethnicities, disabilities, teachers, education, kindergartens, long day care centres, the teaching profession, colleagues, workplaces and the community.

What is your image of a teacher? Naturally, every pre-service and beginning teacher wants to be a 'good teacher', but what does that mean? What makes a good teacher? For some, the answer is simple: qualifications. For others, answering this question might be based more on personal experiences and perceptions: a good teacher is kind, caring, helps you, never shouts, is fair, funny, smart, tough, friendly, not too friendly, never sarcastic, organised, interesting, interested.

Think about it

What do you know about teaching? How do you know this:
- personal experience
- movies
- media
- cultural
- social?

Debates about teaching shift over time. A maxim for 'good teaching' (and parenting) was once 'Spare the rod and spoil the child'. What do you understand this to mean? Is this considered 'good practice' today?

❝❞

'Anyone can teach'—do you agree? Why? Why not?

What are the current 'maxims' of which you have become aware when it comes to 'good teaching'? What are the debates? What are the points of contention? For example, should teachers be rewarded through their salary and bonuses according to their 'performance'? If so, how is teacher performance measured? Are students' test scores an indicator of the quality of teaching? What are the arguments for this position? What are the arguments against this position?

Be aware of the lens through which you are viewing the teacher's practice at your prac placement, and your own developing teaching practice. The lens you use can affect how you view and interpret relationships, organisation, teaching and learning, assessment and reporting. Consider the following quotations about teachers, and how the words affect you. You might like to revisit these quotes as reminders of why you have chosen this profession.

> *The fundamental message of the teacher is this: You can change your life. Whoever you are, wherever you've been, whatever you've done, the teacher invites you to a second chance, another round, perhaps a different conclusion . . .* (Ayers, 2004, p. 13)

> *it is excellence in teachers that make the greatest differences, not just teachers.* (Hattie, 2003, p. 4)

> *We are not what we are; we are who we can become . . .* (Caldwell, 2007, p. 782)

How do you see yourself as a teacher?

Good teachers make teaching look easy. Effective teaching leads to learning, and learning is such a powerful and transformative experience that it is the learning that is memorable, not always the teaching. What makes a teacher a professional?

Activity 3.2

Make a note of the kind of teacher you want to be. Post it somewhere where you will look at it regularly. Note any changes you make over time.

Table 3.1: Thinking about being a good teacher

What is your image of a good teacher?	What teachers stand out for you in your memory of your own experiences?	Which teachers do you want to be like?
How do your friends talk about teachers?	How do members of your family see teachers?	Which teachers do you *not* want to be like?
What do children say about teachers?	What do politicians say about teachers?	How do members of the community view teachers?

Taking it further

Make some statements that begin:
- A teacher . . .
- This teacher . . .
- Teachers . . .

Qualifications

In Finland, all teacher candidates are required to write a research-based dissertation as the final requirement for their master's degree. In some places and in some circumstances (such as the United States, Australia and Scotland), you can become an early childhood teacher with six weeks' formal training. In some places, teaching is learned through an apprenticeship model, not a university degree.

Names and titles for teachers can sometimes denote differences in roles, responsibilities, qualifications, status and hierarchies. For instance, in Australia, what is the difference between a teacher aide and a teacher? Between a teacher and a group leader? Between a teacher and a lead teacher? Between a teacher and a principal and a deputy principal and a director? What cultural information do you need in order to be able to distinguish the differences here?

The notion of doing it 'properly' is not simply a matter of settling on current 'rules' for being a good teacher and refining one's skills and knowledge. There are always examples of teachers who are simultaneously 'good' and 'bad'.

Parents, carers, grandparents, uncles and aunts can all teach children—perhaps to fish, cook or ride a bike. There are those who say 'parents are the child's *best* teachers'. Others disagree. What do you think about this? Why? Is it possible that, in some circumstances, parents are *not* good teachers? It is, of course, possible that a parent may be a child's first teacher, but this is not to say that parents are always the *best* teachers.

Are teaching and learning the same?

Activity 3.3

Do some reading and research. Where in the world are the teachers who are doing it 'properly'? What are the qualifications, skills, and other requirements for becoming a teacher in:

- China (Beijing, and elsewhere in regional China)
- Japan
- the district of Reggio Emilia in Italy
- Kenya
- South Africa
- Brazil
- Mongolia

and any other place you select to investigate?

The trouble with the profession of teaching is that everyone has experienced learning, and many people consider that this means they know about teaching. When people experience being treated by the medical profession, or being serviced by a tradesperson, does this lead to patients advising about health matters or clients taking up plumbing? So why is education different? Is teaching a profession or a trade or something else?

Consider the different ways of being a teacher in the following contexts: the teacher interacting with children in the classroom and the teacher meeting children at the supermarket; teachers who supervise teams of young children playing Kanga Cricket in front of crowds of thousands at the lunch break at an international cricket match; the teacher after school; the teacher in the playground at lunch break; the teacher on school camp; the teacher talking with children; the teacher talking with families; the teacher talking with friends at the weekend.

Think about it

How does your way of seeing teachers change in relation to culture, race, gender, age, socioeconomic contexts, geography, religion, physicality, psychology . . . any other factors?

When all other variables are accounted for, it is teacher knowledge that has been shown to be the single greatest factor that can make a difference in children's chances of success (Timperly & Alton-Lee, 2008). What is the body of knowledge that teachers need to know?

Think about it

How else do children learn?
Is there always a teacher involved?
Is the 'teacher' always an adult? Always a person?
What makes a teacher?

Watch any of the movies or dramas about teachers in Table 3.2, or others you know of, and consider the questions posed.

Think about it

Can you think of examples of teachers who are 'good' and 'bad'? Think of fictional characters who are heroic teachers, and who 'break the rules'—for example, Mr Keating in the film *Dead Poets Society*.
Is there a role model of a teacher from a television show or film you would like to emulate? Or a model of a teacher you definitely do not want to become?
How will you become/avoid becoming this kind of teacher?

Teachers for change

In the Introduction to this book, we presented Phillips' (2011) framework for reflecting on your position as a teacher. There are four possibilities when it comes to this particular aspect of your identities:

- non-Indigenous teacher, teaching Indigenous children
- non-Indigenous teacher, teaching non-Indigenous children
- Indigenous teacher, teaching non-Indigenous children
- Indigenous teacher, teaching Indigenous children.

Table 3.2: Movies and TV drama series about teachers

TV series: *Summer Heights High* Who are the 'good' teachers? Why?
TV series: *Seven Periods with Mr Gormsby* Mr Gormsby does not fit the mould of a 'good teacher'. Do you think he is a 'good teacher'?
Movie: *Dead Poets Society* When this movie was released, enrolments in American teacher education institutions rose by a remarkable percentage. Why do you think this happened?
Movie: *Stand and Deliver* **Movie:** *Freedom Writers* **Movie:** *Kindergarten Cop* How do you think these teachers see their roles? How do you think they became the teachers they are? How might others see these teachers differently? What do you think the movie's producer wanted to say about teachers and teaching?

Taking it further

For more on valuing Indigenous knowledge, see McLaughlin, Whatman & Nielson (2013).

The *Melbourne Declaration on Educational Goals for Young Australians* (MCEECDYA, 2008) identifies the central role that education plays in building equity and social justice for all Australians. It explicitly points to the importance of Australia's Aboriginal and Torres Strait Islander cultures to the nation's history, and the nation's present and future directions. In 2013, the design of the Australian Curriculum positioned Aboriginal and Torres Strait Islander histories and cultures as important as a cross-curriculum priority, to be embedded across all key learning areas for all students. In 2009, the EYLF recognised the importance of ensuring cultural security for Aboriginal and Torres Strait Islander children and their families.

The Australian *National Professional Standards for Teachers* explicitly articulate the expectation that all teachers are experienced in and competent to include Indigenous knowledge and perspectives in their teaching for all students. This is not only to cater for Aboriginal and Torres Strait Islander children, but also to meet curriculum requirements around all children's understanding, appreciation and valuing of, and respect for, Indigenous knowledge.

Defining and demonstrating the embedding of Indigenous knowledge is in the early stages in many contexts, and as a pre-service or graduate teacher you may be called upon to lead the way in this important aspect of education. The challenges involved when attempting to bring what is perhaps new knowledge and innovations on practice to your prac setting or classroom can be testing. You could well be called upon to negotiate complex intersections of expectations, knowledge and practice. Any attempts to demonstrate your knowledge and expertise in embedding Indigenous knowledge will hopefully be affirmed and supported.

In conversation

I didn't want to come off as one of those 'pushy prac students'. You hear these horror stories about students who walk in and want to do whatever they want, and they take control of the class, and the teacher is left going, 'These are my students'. I don't want her to feel like she has to take a step backward. (Vanessa, 2012, in McLaughlin, Whatman & Nielson, 2013, p. 31)

Relationships are crucial here, and developing your capacity to negotiate and sustain effective professional respect and understandings is one of the key elements in this book. You may be the leader in this aspect of relationships, and may be called on to introduce this initiative.

One of the major findings of a large inquiry into Indigenous education was that:

> *There is broad community support for the embedding of Indigenous knowledges in the curriculum, but Indigenous students and staff report significant problems with non-Indigenous teacher knowledge and inter-cultural sensitivity.* (Luke et al., 2013, p. 415)

Successful embedding is possible when pre-service teachers are supported through role modelling, affirmation and being afforded flexibility to accommodate Indigenous knowledge in the curriculum (McLaughlin et al., 2013). This represents an opportunity for you to be a teacher for change, not the status quo, and to make a real contribution to the setting and the children.

Taking it further

For more on accommodating Indigenous knowledge in the curriculum, see Rigney, *Indigenous Education: The challenge of change* (2010).

Did you know?

Things do not always go to plan, and your ideal placement, ideal supervising teacher and ideal group of children may not (ever) occur. A willingness to create the best possible outcomes will enable you to get the most out of every prac. Be open to the unexpected.

Think about it

How will you be a teacher for change?
What knowledge will you need to be able to negotiate this task?
What support will you need? How will you access this support?
What could go wrong?

What can go wrong?

Things *will* go wrong on prac. You can prepare and plan for every step of your prac, but you are entering a profession that deals with people—and very young children at that. It is impossible to predict everything that will eventuate, as interruptions are normal in a typical day spent with young children. You are at the beginning of your induction into the profession, so you will probably make mistakes. The important thing is how you react and respond to your mistakes.

Think about it

'It's not my fault!'

Whenever possible, try to act with 'grace' and the quality of accepting that things don't always go to plan. Sometimes, as a pre-service student or graduate teacher, you will need to accept blame/responsibility rather than looking to blame others—this is not a desirable or attractive quality.

You don't need to labour the point that you made a mistake—acknowledge your mistake/misunderstanding, apologise and—most importantly—convey that you have reflected and that this has a provided a learning experience for you to grow as a professional.

Artists think of mistakes as a path to something better. You can learn from mistakes, and in the process add to your growing repertoire of knowledge and experiences. When you are tempted to blame someone or something—the institution, colleagues, parents, children—pause and ask whether there is another way in which you might read a situation. Is it that these children are 'naughty', or is it that 'children these days are not taught to . . .'? Or is it that you have not found a way to effectively engage their interest and engagement? In any case, take responsibility for what you do next, and take your position as a teacher seriously.

At the very least, teachers need to lead by example. Theoretical understandings are important, and it is also important for student teachers to have opportunities to build capacity, to develop and practise personal attributes like resilience and reliability. Programs of volunteer work may not 'count' directly in your program or your assessment, but the processes required for performing at your work or as a volunteer will enrich your learning about teachers and learners, and add depth to your understandings—of teamwork, responsibility, reliability, community and diversity.

Your group assignments can appear to be antithetical to a university system that measures performance by grade point average. Mihalia's comment that begins this chapter is a frequently heard complaint. But learning to work as a productive member of a team is important in any school. Leadership and management are important to your development as a quality teacher. Such attributes do not come 'naturally' to all students, and it is important to build your capacities.

Activity 3.4

List five values or characteristics that you believe are important for a teacher working with young children.

The successful completion of assessment tasks also requires the development of skills and attributes such as time management, meeting deadlines, mentoring and capacity-building—although the reason and purpose for such requirements might sometimes be lost! You will be judged on prac for your performance with curriculum and pedagogy, but equally important will be the personal attributes you demonstrate, like punctuality, reliability and resilience.

While you are undertaking prac, keep a look-out for opportunities to be actively engaged by talking to your teacher and reading information in staffrooms. As a pre-service or graduate teacher, you can actively engage with the profession by looking for opportunities to join networks, become a member of professional organisations, subscribe to journals and newsletters (including online), attend conferences and provide input into policy development by contributing to forums and inquiries.

Did you know?

Children today love luxury. They have bad manners, contempt for authority; they show disrespect for elders and love chatter in place of exercise.

This quote is commonly attributed to Socrates, born c. 470 BCE. It seems that complaints about children have not changed much since ancient times!

Part of being a professional is the use of professional language and professional knowledge. While education is soundly focused on teaching and learning, the term 'pedagogy' has become popular, since it goes beyond simply the teaching or the learning, and refers to all that occurs between the teacher and the learner, including the interactions, resources and environment.

Think about it

Make notes to yourself in response to the questions below. Keep coming back to these questions each year.

- What do I expect of myself as a teacher and what do others expect of me?
- What are my career aspirations?
- What goals will I set for this work period to support these aspirations?
- What support and/or professional development do I need to build my capabilities to meet these expectations, undertake key work tasks and achieve my career goals?

To do

- Make a poster that you will use to introduce yourself at your next prac. What information should this poster communicate? Who is the audience?
- Tell a graphic story about teaching, showing what a difference a teacher can make

For your portfolio

Your portfolio will be read by others as an indicator of your identity. What kind of a teacher will your portfolio show you are?

Compose your personal teaching statement (600–1000 words). Clearly and succinctly articulate your beliefs, values and attitudes about:

- the personal and professional qualities you bring to teaching (your strengths and 'selling points')
- your perspectives on current ECEC reforms and initiatives (e.g. the importance of ECEC)
- your values and beliefs about children, learning and early education

- your knowledge and understanding of effective teaching and learning in the early years (linking to contemporary ECEC curricula)
- your commitment to reflective practice and ongoing professional learning.

Activity 3.5

Consider these questions:

- What is your image of a teacher?
- What are your beliefs and values about effective teaching and learning?
- Can you articulate these clearly and concisely to children, families, colleagues and future employers?
- Has your teacher education course influenced your thinking about teaching? How?
- What is your image of people who teach?
- What experiences have you had in education?
- What do you see as important qualities of people who teach?
- Do you think these qualities are reflected in community images and thinking about teachers?
- What is the professional expectation of conduct for teachers?
- Would it be possible for a 'good teacher' to have 'bad practices'?
- Why did you choose to become an early childhood teacher?
- What do you believe to be most important principles and practices for ensuring effective teaching and learning in the early years?
- Why do you believe these principles and practices are particularly important?
- How do your beliefs and values 'fit' with contemporary curriculum?

Record your responses to these questions in a space where you can revisit and add to your notes over the years.

Teacher as researcher

If you are to start thinking like a teacher, and you recognise the factors that have shaped your beliefs to date (e.g. media, memories, individual experiences, other people's opinions, 'myths'), how can you take a different approach and see through other lenses? When teachers are researchers, they add depth to their understandings, and bring these new understandings to their work.

For example, when Georgia was completing her final prac in a kindergarten, she noticed that the boys in the group very rarely chose to sit in the book corner and read quietly, like a number of the girls did. Georgie used the framework shown in Figure 3.1 to look into this observation, with the aim of improving her own capacities as a teacher of young children.

Figure 3.1: Teacher as researcher design framework

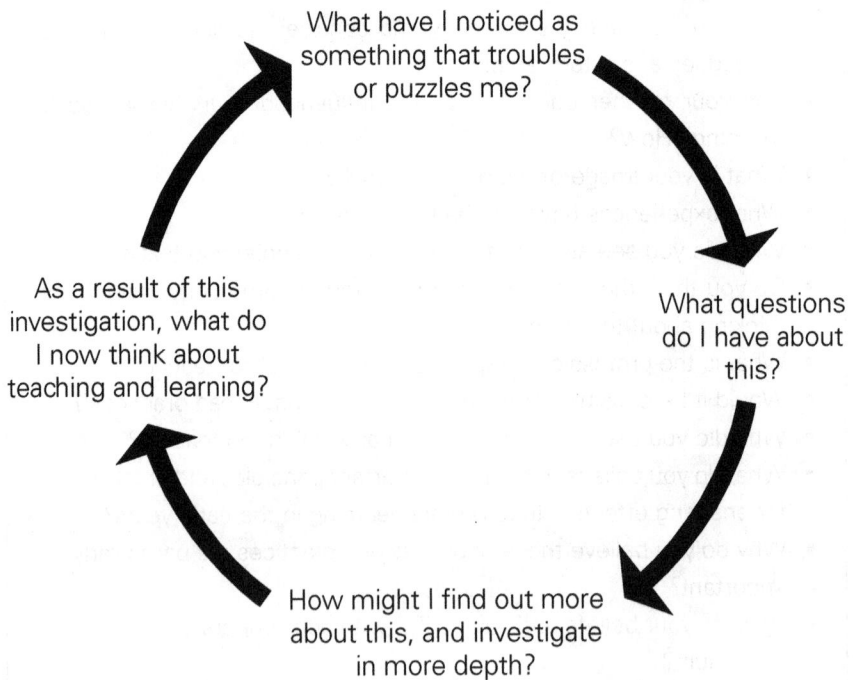

What have I noticed as something that troubles or puzzles me?

What questions do I have about this?

As a result of this investigation, what do I now think about teaching and learning?

How might I find out more about this, and investigate in more depth?

Think about it

There are a number of 'frameworks' for design and conducting research as a teacher, and you might develop an approach based on similar principles to Georgia's. (For more on this, see Fleer et al., 2006, p. 229.)

Georgia first documented her observations, and then took some time to think about good questions that might add to her knowledge about teaching and learning in relation to this difference in behaviours that was intriguing her. She spoke with her literacy lecturer at the university, who gave her some readings on gender and the early years. She also talked with the children at various times, and asked them some carefully designed questions. Together with her host teacher and some other interested pre-service teachers, Georgia analysed her data, and proposed some 'findings', or 'readings' of the behaviours and patterns she was observing. As a result of her research project, Georgia made some recommendations, and implemented some carefully thought-through changes to the environment and to some of the classroom routines. Later, she evaluated how effective her changes were, and whether these had resulted in any improved outcomes for the children. This research project made an impressive addition to Georgia's portfolio, and she was invited to present her findings to the next parent meeting at the kindergarten.

When you are reflecting at the end of each day of your prac, think like a teacher:

- What am I noticing about the children and their learning?
- What is the important research in this area? Make connections here with your units of study at university. Refer to Figure 1.1 as a reminder of how different knowledges are connected.
- Who are the recognised 'experts' in the field, and what are they saying?
- What research is being conducted in this area? What projects do you know of? What are the findings?
- Who is advantaged by these teaching strategies? Who is disadvantaged?
- Will this approach to pedagogy help support all children?

What could you research at this point?

Images of children

The kind of teacher you are becoming depends on how you see children. The way we view children is shaped by politics, cultural values, history, social factors, research, individual beliefs and experiences.

- How do you see children?
- What do you know about them? How do you know this?
- What are your images of children? Where did these images come from?
- What are your beliefs and values when it comes to young children? How did you form these beliefs? How do these beliefs about children shape the way you will teach?
- Can you articulate these beliefs clearly and concisely to children, families, colleagues and future employers?
- What do you think is important in early childhood education?

Taking it further

Make statements that begin:
- A child . . .
- This child . . .
- Children . . .

- Who would or do you prefer to teach? Young children, babies, toddlers, kindergarten, prep, primary? Why or why not?

Activity 3.6

Spend time visualising your day in your preferred early childhood context as a workplace. What would your day look like? What would your role be?

If you are a pre-service teacher, fast forward to post-graduation. You are at a barbecue with a new group of friends and in the course of conversation the question comes up, 'What do you do?'

Write a script that (hypothetically) answers this question, outlining where you work (the early childhood context), your role, the positives/ what you love about the job and the challenges/what really annoys you.

In your script, include responses from your new friends, who may or may not know much about early childhood teaching.

The ways in which you see children, or the construction of a particular image of a child, involve making choices, *but also* taking responsibility for those choices. Are your choices considered, or are they simply based on folkloric opinions that are passed down, or taken-for-granted 'truths' that go unquestioned?

Challenge your choices. Stand in the shoes of another who disagrees with you. How have you arrived at your choices?

Consider your assumptions, perceptions, values, beliefs, and ideals

Draw a quick sketch of a child. Now, what changes will you make to your drawing if you are asked to show specifically race, gender, culture, class, religion, ethnicity, developmental age/stage, time, geography, physicality, psychology. Are there any other circumstances that call for changes to your initial idea of 'a child'?

?

Did you know?

Influences on ways of seeing children and teachers include history, media, family, culture and contexts, community, life experiences, professional development, theory, curriculum documents and support materials, readings and research.

Activity 3.7

List five characteristics or things you know about young children. How do you know these things? Record in your professional learning journal.

It is widely advocated in many countries that early childhood education is based on child-centred practice—that is, the child is at the centre of curriculum practices and decision-making. Teachers plan learning experiences that are based on what they know about the child, and the child's interests and abilities, as well as what they know and anticipate about how young children behave and what is considered appropriate.

It is important, then, to consider our understanding of childhood and children, and how the decisions we make about curriculum are shaped by the ways we see and speak about children:

- child as pure and innocent
- child as naughty/cute
- child as 'empty slate'
- child as imminent
- child as competent
- child with rights.

For more on this, see James, Jenks and Prout (1998) and Woodrow (1999).

> How we nurture our babies and young children is universally recognised as fundamental to our humanity.

To do

Collect some images of children in art and popular culture—paintings, movies, advertising, music, television. How is the artist seeing children if they are depicted as 'fairies' asleep under a leaf in a pumpkin patch? What about the image of the child as portrayed by Macaulay Culkin in the *Home Alone* films? How are children depicted in *Kindergarten Cop*? If you had a child like Bart Simpson in your group, how would you teach him? What about Lisa Simpson?

Make a 'blueprint' that maps the complexities and diversities of the construction of children. This blueprint provides the underpinning for a teacher's planning, and should inform your working, interacting and pedagogical approaches with a group of children. The capacity to adjust and change for individuals will have to be a feature of the blueprint.

Does our image of children require us to make their remarkable thinking visible to others? Or does our notion of children allow us to display to others what we have taught them rather than what they know?

Relationships

How are images of children connected with the key idea of relationships? Why are these links important for teachers?

One way of seeing the work of the teacher is not simply as a transmitter of knowledge and information, but rather as creator of relationships.

- What does this mean for you as an educator?
- What does this mean when you are working with young children who are babies; just walking; aged 3 years; older?
- How will you enact this role of creating relationships?

Consider your assumptions, perceptions, values, beliefs and ideals

Why relationships? And how many?

Just because something is 'taught', it does not follow automatically that children have learned it. Children's own experiences, activities and resources play a large part in what is learned. Your relationship with a particular child will shape, and be shaped by, your images of children. Teachers' expectations are considered by many to have a direct effect on all children's success—whether through improving self-esteem, building confidence or raising standards of achievement.

What types of relationships are there between learner and teacher? Where does power reside when a teacher and student are together? Is it always with the teacher? Can you think of times when the power resides with the young child? What does a secure, respectful and reciprocal relationship with children look like in practice?

And remember that each place of learning is unique—shaped by the children, their families, their teachers and their communities, policies and societal expectations. When you are next at a shopping centre or a public gathering, watch the young children, and be mindful of what you see and how you see them. First, you will notice that very young children are not alone—they are always part of a relationship.

What is your image of families?

From birth, children are in continuous relationships. Children are born into families, and your relationships with children connect you with their families. How do you think about families? Do some of the following terms apply:

- parents
- diverse
- unique
- partners
- collaborators
- rights?

There are hundreds of different images of the child. Each one of you has inside yourself an image of the child that directs you as you begin to relate to a child. This theory within you pushes you to behave in certain ways, it orients you as you talk to the child, listen to the child, observe the child . . . The environment you construct around you and the children reflects this image you have about the child . . . The quality and quality of relationships among you as adults and educators also reflects your image of the child. (Malaguzzi, 1994, p. 52)

What is your image of communities?

Note the connections between your prac placement location and the community. The relationship between the teacher and the child's community is shaped by the way you see children—as individuals and as members of a broader community. Good early childhood teachers work to see the community as a critical, key component of education and care, and a relationship with the community as essential to the quality of children's education. When teachers have knowledge of the community, join in some experiences, form relationships and build partnerships with community members, they find a wealth of learning opportunities. They can also often gain access to additional resources and support.

Often, early childhood centres are embedded within a school community. This brings particular roles and responsibilities for the early childhood teacher. Opportunities for both advocacy and activism can also be part of the relationships with young children's communities.

- Does our image of children embed them within the family and community, or does it contextually alienate them?
- Does our image of children see them as desirous of relationships from birth, or do we have an image of children who need to be taught how to relate, and a belief that this will happen as part of their development?
- Is our image of children as individuals within the group or is it of children as a group of individuals?
- Does our image of children see them as having rights from birth, and as citizens and community members in the here and now or only as citizens of the future?

Identifying your values

Take a moment to think about anything that may come to mind associated with values. Values are what you feel, think or enact through your heart, mind and body. They may be to do with your work ethic, religion, family or even education. For instance, you might value 'a fair day's wage for a fair day's work'. In Chapter 6, you will find a list of values, grouped around the categories of relationships, personal and work.

There are any number of issue that you might 'value', and that you could be called on to explain and defend. For instance, racism might be under discussion, and in response you might insist that it is important that 'all people are treated equally'. With a particular issue in mind, answer the following seven questions about your valuing of that. Place a tick in the box if your answer is 'yes'. The suggestion is that if you are able

Taking it further

Reflect on the UN Convention on the Rights of the Child, which can be found at <www.unicef.org.au/Discover/What-we-do/Convention-on-the-Rights-of-the-Child.aspx>.

Taking it further

Make statements that begin:
- A community . . .
- This community . . .
- Communities . . .

to answer 'yes' to all of these questions, you can be certain that the matter is something you find valuable.

1. Have I chosen this value freely (i.e. not had it imposed on me by external pressures)? ☐
2. Have I chosen this value after considering other alternatives? ☐
3. Have I thought about the consequences of expressing this value? ☐
4. Am I proud of or do I prize and cherish this value? ☐
5. Would I publicly affirm this value (i.e. defend it openly before others)? ☐
6. Have I acted on this value? ☐
7. Have I acted with repetition or consistency, or repeated a pattern of behaviour regarding this value? ☐

These seven questions have applied the work of Louis Raths (1966). He studied the process of values and proposed seven standards for constructing a value. An integral part of thinking like a teacher is to thinking about your values—what is important to you, and how you enact this is your daily life.

Your values and your profession

Knowing your work values is a fundamental part of career planning. If you are able to express your values in your work life, then this helps you to achieve a sense of fulfilment and satisfaction with your work. Your work takes on meaning and purpose.

An alignment between your values and your work can also play a functional role in work-related outcomes, such as greater motivation, organisational commitment and work performance. You will sometimes see employers hiring individuals who have compatible values with the organisation. Therefore, to avoid future conflicts, it is important to ensure that there is a good match between your values and your professional life.

Stop for a moment and consider these questions:

• What is important to you?
• Why do you work or study?
• What motivates you to work?
• What motivates you to study?
• What do you want work to provide you with?

Mismatch between your values and the values of your workplace

There are a variety of factors that can cause disharmony in a workplace. One is a variance between your values and those of the organisation.

Tensions can arise when certain values that are important to you are missing in your occupation. For instance, some occupations and employers make more demands on your time and dedication than others. If you are someone who places a high value on family time, then you may face a dilemma. Rather than your work bringing you joy, it provides you with little personal satisfaction, causing you to become unmotivated and bored.

Make sure you are clear about what is significant to you in order to make consistent decisions and actions. This also helps you to avoid constantly acting in response to what others want. To know whether your values match those of the organisation, you need to know your own values and understand those of your work environment.

In order to work out what the organisation believes is important:

- Take a look at its mission statement or vision.
- Visit the work environment to see whether it follows through on what it says is important to the organisation.

Think about it

Why is it important to understand your core values, especially on prac?

Understanding your values can:

- give you a greater understanding of your own behaviour, actions and reactions
- give a greater sense of direction and purpose to your life and career choices
- help you make decisions that are worthwhile and true for you
- help you identify what motivates you to accomplish the important goals you set in your life
- help you know what type of activities, people and environments you most desire in your work
- help you focus on career objectives that are important to you and potential employers
- help you achieve success and satisfaction in your career if you are doing something you value.

In conversation

I was a bit frustrated with my course because I didn't see the point of a lot of what we were expected to do. But as soon as I started my first prac, I knew that this was what I wanted to do, and I wanted to be the best teacher that children could have. Now that I have seen what it's like to be a teacher, I want to learn all I can. (Theresa, student teacher, 2011)

When I did my first prac, I learned something really important. I learned that I didn't really like schools, and I was never going to be able to fit in and do the things that are expected of a good teacher. I just don't have the 'personality' that's required. I'm glad I realised this on my first prac. I talked with the career counsellor back at university, and they helped me rethink my career choices. I couldn't be happier. I don't think I ever would have made a good teacher. I just don't have the patience required to deal with all those people! (Ruth, lawyer, 2010)

Ethics

When a group of professionals share a process of critical reflection in order to determine their obligations as professionals, they attempt to define some of the values and expectations of their field. Rather than leaving these crucial matters to 'chance', or to the individual and their own personal decisions about values, professional ethics involves shared understandings about appropriate actions and behaviours.

At the same time as early childhood educators celebrate young children's remarkable capacities and competence, it is equally true that young children are among the most vulnerable and powerless people in our society. Early childhood professionals have a special responsibility: to always act in the highest ethical manner.

Ethical behaviour involves professionals making informed, responsible decisions and acting with discretion. Whenever people interact and form relationships—whether personal or professional—it is inevitable that obligations will develop.

While you are on prac, you must ensure that you act honestly and fairly at all times. You will have access to a lot of privileged information, both in relation to the young children and to your host teacher and other staff. You will be privy to details about the organisation/institution, and you will be part of relationships that are built on trust and mutual respect. You will need to honour these principles. If you are seeking any information that you will use beyond your own personal knowledge-building, you are expected to obtain informed consent and maintain confidentiality.

There are a number of places where you can clarify expectations and requirements. For early childhood teachers, these are specified in:

- education legislation
- quality standards
- professional teaching standards
- funding guidelines
- school and ECEC service policies
- a code of ethics.

In Australia, the professional organisation Early Childhood Australia (ECA) first developed a code of ethics in 1990. It was compiled by a national working party. This code is now in its second iteration, which was also compiled by a national working party (see <www.earlychildhood australia.org.au/our-publications/eca-code-ethics/>). The ECA Code of Ethics:

- defines core professional values
- explicates professional responsibilities
- was developed by the profession for the profession
- is aspirational.

In the most recent version of the ECA Code of Ethics, it is possible to understand the current 'rules' that define the actions and behaviours of early childhood teachers from the underpinning values. These serve as an important guide for all your actions and behaviours, both on prac and in your work as a graduate and professional teacher.

The application of these values shapes your ethical standards. In relation to children, you could undertake to:

- act in the best interests of all children
- respect the rights of children and advocate these rights
- recognise children as active citizens
- respect the special relationship between children and their families
- create and maintain safe, healthy environments that enhance children's learning
- acknowledge the uniqueness and potential of all children

As a guiding principle, undertake to always act in the best interests of children, families and communities.

Did you know?

The underpinning values in the ECA Code of Ethics are respect, democracy, honesty and integrity, justice, courage, inclusivity, social and cultural responsiveness, and education.

- work to ensure children are not discriminated against
- acknowledge children as competent learners, and build active communities of engagement and inquiry
- honour children's right to play, as both a process and context for learning. (Early Childhood Australia, 2006)

To treat the Code of Ethics as a 'set of rules' can be helpful in many circumstances. However, this approach to ethics is also problematic. Many situations are seldom a simple matter of right or wrong. Coming to decisions about how to act cannot always be determined by a code written by people far removed from the immediacy of situations, contexts and people, in all their complexities. No matter how thorough, it is more than likely that any code of ethics will have shortcomings. No collation of 'rulings' can be expected to be the only basis for judgement about ethical practice.

Ethical analysis involves higher-order thinking and inquiry. Over-reliance on someone else's 'rules' will at some time lead to frustration and confusion. Students of ethics are often presented with classic 'ethical dilemmas', where no 'recipe' for procedure suffices, and there is no clear-cut 'right' or 'wrong' way to proceed. A better way to think of ethics, rather than as contained in a 'set of rules', is to frame ethics as ranging along a continual and uncertain process of relations (Dahlberg & Moss, 2005).

Activity 3.8

Ethical behaviour is supported by certain professional dispositions, including shared inquiry, collaborative reflective practice and a commitment to ongoing learning.

Make a note of any ethical matters that you observe on prac. Reflect and, where appropriate, discuss with others—your host teacher, your peers, your university support academic.

The fundamental obligation while you are on prac is to keep children safe. One way of promoting and supporting ethical behaviour is to have a thorough understanding about your *duty of care*. This can be a highly legalistic term, and subject to fine-grained interpretations. Duty of care is about professional judgement, and reasonable and ethical behaviour. A well-informed professional teacher will ensure they have an accurate understanding of this principle in order to understand their limits, and also their capacities, when working with young children.

In conversation

I was told that you are not allowed to cuddle children, even if they fall over and hurt themselves. Turns out that this is one of those 'myths'. I went to the source and read up on child protection policies. There are a lot of 'myths' and rumours, and at each prac, I am told something different. (Melallie, pre-service teacher, 2012)

The best supports to sustaining your duty of care include:

- ongoing discussion and critique of practice
- informed policies and procedures
- professional development
- trusting and open relationships with parents.

Activity 3.9

Reflect on these terms. Record your initial responses to these terms in one or two words. Revisit this exercise each year.

- inclusion
- additional needs
- families
- culture
- special needs
- child
- children
- teacher
- relationships
- learner
- babies
- child care
- toddler
- disability
- Early Years Learning Framework.

To think about

- What are teacher standards, virtues, ethics and personal values? How do they apply to me now?
- Personal values—what are my guiding values in life and as a teacher? Where do they fit into my teaching philosophy?

To do

- In some countries, a child's right to participate in key policy decisions is taken very seriously. See if you can find countries where children have a say in policy, and even parliament.
- It is essential to reflect continuously on your ways of seeing. While on prac, you are constantly accessing new information, experiences, contexts, ideas, interactions, observations, situations, research, ideas, relationships and people. All of these factors influence and shape your ideas, values, beliefs, lifeworld and standpoint.

Further reading

Dahlberg, G. & Moss, P. (2005). *Ethics and Politics in Early Childhood Education*. London: Routledge.

Early Childhood Australia (2006). *Code of Ethics*, <www.earlychildhoodaustralia.org.au/wp-content/uploads/2014/07/code_of_ethics_-brochure_screen web_2010.pdf>. Accessed 20 November 2014.

Fleer, M., Edwards, S., Hammer, M., Kennedy, A., Ridgway, A., Robbins, J. & Surman, L. (2006). *Early Childhood Learning Communities: Sociocultural research in practice*. Sydney: Pearson Education.

McLaughlin, J., Whatman, S.L. & Nielson, C. (2013). *Supporting Future Curriculum Leaders in Embedding Indigenous Knowledge on Teaching Practicum*. Brisbane: Queensland University of Technology.

Malaguzzi, L. (1993). For an education based on relationships. *Young Children*, 49(1): 9–12.

—— (1994). Your image of the child: Where teaching begins. *Child Care Information Exchange*, 96: 52–61.

Rigney, L.-I. (2010). Indigenous education: The challenge of change. *Every Child*, 16(4): 10–11.

United Nations (1989). *United Nations Convention on the Rights of the Child*, <www.unicef.org/crc>.

Woodrow, C. (1999). Revisiting images of the child in early childhood education: Reflections and considerations. *Australian Journal of Early Childhood*, 24(4): 7.

4

Act like a teacher: Being professional

In this chapter you will find:

- professional identities and performativities
- professional relationships
- suggestions about how to become a 'reader' of curriculum, cultures and workplaces
- information about making a good impression on your prac
- advice about professional expectations
- information about what to include in a portfolio
- tips about the nature of a prac report.

Laura checked out her placement, had a 'practice run' and made contact with the school on three occasions prior to commencing prac. Before starting prac, she carefully selects her clothes for each day of the first week, ensuring that they meet the expectations that she has clarified with the deputy principal. She wants to make a good first impressions, as she knows they count. She has never been late to prac, and spends a couple of hours each evening at home, writing up, reflecting and preparing for the next day. Laura takes every opportunity on prac to gather samples of children's work, photos (with permission) and any positive feedback or notes from families or others. This means she has tangible records of her participation, her achievements—anything that will show her in a good light to future employers.

Sarah is a good talker, and forms relationships easily. She was never one to worry too much about the details. It wasn't until her first prac that she realised this was not going to be enough. It didn't help that she was pulled into the director's office on day two and asked to cover her midriff. The wheels started to really fall off when, after the fifth day, she couldn't keep up with the written requirements. The hours were not what she had expected—early starts and late finishes. And the staff meeting in week two (she had missed the first one, which didn't seem to go over too well with her supervising teacher) went until 6.00 pm. Despite trying to maintain her social life during prac (which was usually all-nighters Friday, Saturday and Sunday), she had to curtailed her outings to just one all-nighter. Even then, she ran into one of the parents from the centre. They had a few laughs over Sarah's funny stories about the children.

Luke is an Indigenous pre-service teacher, and before his first prac his university mentor, Jill, insisted that he consider what he was going to wear to school on the first day. Because he was mainly studying physical education, he had planned to wear his sports gear. Jill was insistent that he dress more formally, in long sleeves and a tie. Her advice was, 'Even if, after the first day, you are told it is OK to "dress down", first impressions are important.' Luke took her advice. On the first day, when he walked into the classroom, the teacher had all the children stand and say, 'Good morning, Mr Patterson'. Luke tells the story: 'That is the first time anyone ever called me Mr Patterson.' This was a profound moment for him. He had a very successful prac, and the school principal has expressed his interest in employing Luke after graduation. (Thanks to the research of Julie McLaughlin for Luke's story.)

A supervising teacher's thoughts

Sometimes I have a student teacher who is just a 'natural', and they have a way with the children, and get on with everyone. This puts them ahead from the start. The trouble is, with some of those students, they don't try so hard, and they think they can get by 'winging it'. Sooner or later, the wheels start to fall off, unless they realise just how much work is involved, and that they need to make the time. Some things just can't be left until the last minute. I am much happier if they show me they are willing to put in the 'hard yards'. I want to see planning, and I want to see that they are thinking about it all, not just 'hanging out' with the children.

– Chloe, classroom teacher, 2013

What do good teachers need to know and be able to do?

In this chapter, we look at more of the complexities of what it takes to be a good teacher. In Chapter 3, we referred to the knowledges that underpin the work of teaching. In this chapter, we turn to the actions and ways of being of a good teacher. Here we are following some of the rhizomatic threads to which we referred in the Introduction, and you may find yourself revisiting this chapter before and after every prac and once you begin your teaching career.

While you are on prac, you are expected to act like a professional at all times. As you will see in what follows, professional identities are both enabling and constraining—when you act like a teacher, there are 'rules' of behaviour. Some might be obvious, while some are unspoken. Some are local, some are more over-arching. This chapter will provide support in your efforts to navigate how to act and talk like a teacher.

Everybody has a stake in education. From policy-makers to politicians to the wider society, there are always calls for changes to education and schools. If teachers are to resist bouncing from one government reform to another, they need a strong sense of what education is for, and what *they* are for in education. We know that a good teacher makes a difference. As discussed previously, evidence-based research has shown that a good teacher is a significant factor in improving the chances of success for all students. While there are many life situations where we might teach and learn from each other, not everyone has the knowledge and skills it takes to be a professional teacher.

Taking it further

The question of what good teachers need to know and be able to do is asked by many who are interested in preparing quality teachers. See Darling-Hammond (2005), Duncum (1999), Feiman-Nemsar (2003) and Zeichner (2006, 2009). Do your own research and read more about this.

Think about it

Do you agree that not everyone has the knowledge and skills it takes to be a good teacher? What about those who say 'parents are a child's first teacher'? If everyone can teach, why do we need qualifications? Consider that parents/carers also tend to their children when they are unwell. Does this mean everyone is a nurse or a doctor?

The belief that teachers matter is not new to many parents, who know all too well the importance of their child's teacher. But ideas about what is needed to make a good teacher can be part of folklore, and often stem from our partial and imperfect memories of our own schooling. The complexities of the work of teaching are not easy to articulate, and good teachers make it look easy, both to their students and to onlookers.

What constitutes a professional? And what makes an early childhood teacher a professional?

Identities

Each early childhood teacher will have identities, shaped by their own experiences, their studies, and the people and circumstances around them. One way to think about *professional* identities of early childhood teachers is to see identities as fluid rather than fixed. Instead of a single 'true self', who you are emerges, evolves and changes over time—depending on what is happening, where you are, who you are with and what is required of you.

In your working life as an early childhood teacher, there are policies, mandated curricula, and regulations that shape the profession and the identities of the people working in it. Consider how work identities can be indicated by the words used to describe the work: child care worker, carer, educator, teacher, professional. Through the use of particular words, importance and power can be assigned to the work of the early childhood professional.

Organisations assign various titles to members of the workforce, and these titles define roles, but they often do more than this. In his book *The Pleasures and Sorrows of Work*, Alain de Botton (2009) visits a biscuit factory to meet with the design director, who is assigned importance and status by this position title. For the work he does, he could just as well be titled the biscuit maker. Similarly, early childhood teachers working in child care are assigned various titles.

Currently, if you work in a long day care centre, you might work alongside a teacher, an educational leader, a supervisor or someone with the position title of carer. It is important to the success of your prac that you are aware of 'who is who'—each person's role/position/responsibilities—and how these roles fit with those of others within the early childhood setting (the child care centre, kindergarten or school). This knowledge provides you with insights and understandings about how the organisation functions and operates. This helps you to locate your role/place within the team.

When you tell your friends and others that you are studying to become an early childhood teacher, what are the reactions? Some students tell of disbelief, and wonder why you would need to study because 'it's just playing isn't it?' or, worse, 'it's just babysitting'.

A study of history will show that those who work with young children have long struggled with the issue of recognition and status. Consider the following points about acting like a professional while on prac:

- You will encounter many different, multiple and changing professional identities.
- There is an ongoing and contested debate within the early years community regarding the development of an early childhood professional identity that respects all aspects of practice and areas of knowledge.
- There are historical and artificial divisions between care and education that have allowed a concept of professionalism to emerge that values some areas of expertise and work more than others.

Following on from this, think about what being professional means to you.

In recent years, the workforce in early childhood education and care has come under increasing scrutiny, both in Australia and internationally, with various systemic inquiries (e.g. see Productivity Commission, 2014). Where once early childhood workers were simply thought of as babysitters, more recently a considerable agenda for 'professionalising' the early childhood workforce has resulted in a number of developments, including:

- a national agenda for defining and regulating 'quality', which includes improving child outcomes
- increased requirements for formal qualifications and expectations of knowledge
- improved pay and conditions
- professional status, including lists of professional attributes

Taking it further

For more on teachers' identities, see Gibson (2013a, 2013b).

- development of leadership and interpersonal skills
- belonging to a professional group—a collective professional identity and a cohesive group with a shared vision and a strong collective voice.

It seems that sometimes it is more common to draw attention to professional behaviours and attributes by their absence—as in behaviours clearly considered 'unprofessional'. According to Sumsion (2005), the key characteristics of early childhood professionalism include:

- putting the interests of the client (child/family) first
- a focus on relationships
- valuing a non-hierarchical workplace.

Relationships and professionalism

Most people expect an early childhood professional to be able to:

- establish and maintain secure, respectful and reciprocal relationships
- work in partnership
- collaborate with their colleagues.

Safe, supportive and reciprocal relationships underpin genuine partnerships with parents, and there are clear expectations around what teachers need to do in order to establish and maintain these relationships. Consider the following extract from a code of ethics (Early Childhood Australia, 2006, p. 3):

In relation to families, I will:

- Listen to and learn from families
- Assist each family to develop a sense of belonging and inclusion
- Develop positive relationships based on mutual trust and open communication
- Develop partnerships with families and engage in shared decision-making where appropriate
- Acknowledge the rights of families to make decisions about their children
- Respect the uniqueness of each family and strive to learn about their culture, structure, lifestyle, customs, language, beliefs and kinship systems
- Develop shared planning, monitoring and assessment practices and communicate in ways that families understand
- Acknowledge that each family is affected by community contexts

When you reflect on your 'image' of an early childhood professional at work, what types of qualities, practices and interactions come to mind?

- Be sensitive to the vulnerabilities of families and respond in ways that empower and maintain the dignity of children and families
- Maintain confidentiality and respect family privacy.

Think about it

- What particular personal and professional qualities define you as an early childhood teacher?
- What professional experience do you have? (Think broadly)
- What are your strengths?
- How do these contribute to your success as a teacher?
- What knowledge, skills and/or qualities do you want to develop further?

Secure, respectful and reciprocal relationships provide strong foundations for children's learning and development. (DEEWR, 2009)

Becoming a 'reader': Curriculum documents

Curriculum documents support educators to implement programs that meet the mandated requirements for particular contexts, and are required reading for all professional educators. As a prac student, you need to be familiar with the relevant documents, which will vary across the age groups with which you will be working. They also vary from country to country, and sometimes from region to region. One of your first tasks, when notified of your prac placement, should be to identify the mandated curriculum framework and read it.

In Australia, the Early Years Learning Framework is the first national learning framework mandated for educators who work with children up to the age of 5 years. Before this, each jurisdiction had developed and implemented its own curriculum frameworks and documents, to varying degrees of detail and regulations. In New Zealand, the *Te Whāriki* document (Ministry of Education (NZ), 1996) is a similar national policy document. Learning frameworks have similarly been developed in the United Kingdom, Finland, Norway, Sweden, Hong Kong and elsewhere.

There are also additional documents that accompany and/or extend these practice frameworks. For example, each state in Australia has developed a set of curriculum guidelines for the kindergarten year—aligned with, but not the same as, the EYLF. Foundations for Success also aligns with the EYLF, but is specifically targeted for extending and enriching Aboriginal and Torres Strait Islander children in their kindergarten year in Queensland. The Australian Curriculum is the first national curriculum for schools in all states and territories in Australia. My Time, Our Place is a framework that supports the ongoing development of children in school-age care services.

No single curriculum document captures all there is to teaching—and nor should it. According to Luke et al. (2013), curriculum documents are ideally low on prescription and high on professionalism. Thoughtful and reflective teachers—teachers for change—do not 'slavishly' follow along with the pages of a curriculum document without making it their own 'map'. With every framework, it is essential for a professional teacher that the content is considered alongside a philosophy of teaching, theories of learning, ethics and values. In order to use frameworks in this way, it is important to understand the components of a curriculum design (rationale, outcomes and so on), as well as the context for which it was written—and how and why.

Reading: Places, people, workplace cultures

But being a 'reader' of mandated curriculum documents is just a starting point for success on prac. Each early childhood context is unique. Each setting has its own ways of operating that make it different from others. As a prac student, you will encounter a range of different types of contexts (e.g. child care, kindergarten, preschool, primary school). In order for you to build strong relationships with the setting, and the staff within it, it is important that you understand how that setting works, or the culture of the place. As a 'reader' of the culture of the organisation, you will be well positioned to see how you fit, and how best to engage with this setting.

Being an effective reader of the setting will enable you to make wise decisions—the right decisions for that setting. One way to become an effective reader of your prac placement setting is to think about the organisation's culture.

If you understand the organisational culture of your placement setting, you will have a framework for understanding its features. The culture of an organisation can be 'read' by attending to three areas: artefacts, values and basic assumptions (Schein, 2010).

- *The artefacts* are the visible structures (e.g. buildings, equipment, resources, clothes staff wear) and the processes (e.g. policies, how decisions are made).
- *Values* are usually shared, and shape ways of working. Examples of values that you may see in an educational setting are care, authenticity, respect and rights.

- *Basic assumptions* are the essence of the setting—the taken-for-granted practices that may be invisible to the outside eye. For example, that staff return books to the library after use may not be stated anywhere, but it is a practice that is adhered to. It is important to know how to read these basic assumptions, as they are the practices that may not be written down anywhere.

It is these shared elements that amalgamate to eventually become a culture. For you as a prac student, it is important to observe carefully and ask the right questions. If you know the organisational culture, and spend time getting to know what makes the setting work, then you will be well positioned to build relationships and will have a more successful prac placement.

What can I do to get off to a good start with this prac?

First, make this *your* experience. Understand that things can and do go wrong, and that you will need to fix things when this happens. There will not always be another person to help with this. It is therefore essential to be prepared, and to be in a mindset that you will ensure your success.

Performativities

Luke's story at the beginning of this chapter works as an illustration of the power and importance of performativity. This is not about Luke's 'identity', or the notion of a 'real' Luke. Rather, his dress and introduction to the children was performative, and had direct effects not only on the children, but on Luke himself. The performative nature of being an early childhood teacher is something that people enact or do, rather than something they are. Here we differentiate between 'performance' and 'performative'. A *performance* is akin to acting or role-play, or what we show to the world. *Performativity* is more to do with cultural norms, and repetition is key to performativity. The children greeted Luke in a manner that spoke a particular 'identity' into being, and in turn Luke 'became' the 'Mr Patterson' that the children and the teacher 'read'. Likewise, a strict dress code can work to both enable and constrain teachers' performativity.

In some early childhood settings, there is an increasing trend towards having a work uniform. The dress code and practice in a local private school where Diana completed her prac was for women to wear a skirt and jacket. Diana found that this affected the ways in which she was able to connect with and relate to people, especially the children in

Think about the 'culture' of your prac placement. Using Schein's (2010) three elements of organisational culture, create a diagram to capture the artefacts, values and basic assumptions of the setting.

**Taking it
further**

For more on
the concept of
performativity,
see Butler (2011);
Osgood (2006);
Robinson & Davies
(2008).
    For more on
professionalism
and the transition
to the workplace
see Ailwood et al.
(2006).

her daily work. She found herself controlling her activities to suit the
restricted movement of her skirt, and needing to avoid snagging her
tights and dirtying clothes that required dry cleaning. Currently, in early
years contexts, it is more common to have a polo shirt bearing the logo
of the childcare centre, school or employer. Again, these uniforms can
work to both enable and constrain—the practicality allows for a more
active approach to pedagogy and activities; however, culturally, the
professional status of the wearer might be read differently from, say, a
skirt and jacket.

Think about it

Consider the following list of 'personal qualities':
- confidence
- commitment
- independence
- initiative
- a positive outlook
- a sense of humour
- strength and energy
- persistence and determination
- warmth and compassion
- the ability to take risks
- effective time management
- resilience and the ability to accept change
- adaptability and flexibility.

How might understandings of performativity provide a useful lens for
considering this list?

Anticipating situations on prac

Consider the 'what if' scenarios in Table 4.1. Read through the possible
solution to circumvent the problem. Then think about how you would
manage this situation.

Table 4.1: 'What if' scenarios

What if?	Possible solution	My solution
I arrive late?	Do a trial run beforehand, catch an earlier train/bus on your first day.	
I don't wear the appropriate clothes?	Prior to prac or your first day in the workplace, contact the school or centre and ask whether there is a dress code.	
I can't remember people's names?	There are a number of strategies to remember names—you don't need to know each person's name from day one, but at least know your supervising teacher's name and those of the key people in the centre/school (such as the director, principal, deputy principal).	
I can't find the workplace?	Prior to commencing prac or your first job, do a couple of 'practice runs' so you know how to get there—which public transport to catch/where to park.	
I don't fit in?	Part of being on prac and starting a new job is building relationships with staff—get involved, take opportunities and ask to be included.	
I don't understand the role?	Take the time to clarify your role during prac—and look over your university's expectations so you understand how these fit with your teacher's expectations.	
I don't know what time to start, finish or take my lunch break?	Ask questions and seek clarification.	
I don't like it?	Teaching is hard work—rewarding and dynamic, but hard work. It is not unusual to have at least one very challenging prac, where you question whether this is the job for you. Take time to reflect, write and learn from each and every experience.	

> ## Activity 4.1
>
> Now think of three other possible 'what ifs' that may come up during prac or in your early days in the workforce, and write some possible solutions.

First impressions in the workplace

Create a positive first impression, then develop the attitude and skills to maintain it. First impressions are formed immediately, and can then be very difficult to change. It takes between thirty seconds and two minutes to form a first impression, so how you begin your first day at your workplace is very important. First impressions count—be on time, organised and enthusiastic from day one. Be prepared and ready to speak up and ask questions. All these factors provide your supervising teacher with perceptions about you.

Here are some essentials to help you to create and maintain a positive first impression:

- *Dress to impress.* Consider the work environment that you will be entering. If you are at all unsure of the dress code, call the organisation and ask about their standard attire. The way you dress indicates how you want an employer to think of you. The golden rule is to be clean, neat and fit in with the environment. (If on prac, check with your university lecturer beforehand if you are unsure, or if you have nothing suitable to wear.) Op shops (second-hand clothing stores) can be a great source of appropriate clothing and other resources. It is better to dress 'up' on the first day, rather than dressing too casually. It is preferable to be told to dress down after you begin in the workplace than to make a poor impression to begin with.
- *Stay off your mobile phone* and don't send text messages unless you are on lunch or break. Even if other co-workers are on their personal phones, it's best to avoid such practices, especially in the beginning when you are still unsure of policies. If you have to have your mobile phone at work, it shouldn't ring. Set it to silent/vibrate, as the sounds of different ring tones going off all the time can be very annoying to others.
- *Be open-minded and show respect towards others*—even if you don't necessarily like a particular person. They may be your mentor or supervisor in the future.

- *Keep your voice at an acceptable level.* A loud voice that is noticeable in a particular work environment can not only be counterproductive for others who are trying to get on with their work, but can be extremely irritating.
- *Show flexibility and offer to help others.* You are there to learn, so take advantage of opportunities to observe and contribute.
- *Make sure you understand the rules surrounding email etiquette.*
- *Stay positive and upbeat—and smile!* Showing a sense of humour helps to create a positive feeling in the workplace. Nothing works better than having and expressing a positive attitude. Let your enthusiasm for being part of the team and the organisation show to everyone with whom you interact.
- *Be receptive to feedback and listen to constructive criticism.*
- *Develop a habit of reflection.* Stop and reflect on the day's learning and consider how you could have handled things differently.

Often, it's a simple matter of using your common sense and behaving in a manner that shows courtesy and respect for others, but there are numerous things that you should obviously not get involved with or encourage. Below is a list of some of the most commonly cited examples of behaviour that is often frowned upon, and even not tolerated, by most employers, regardless of type:

- *Don't* engage in idle gossip about other colleagues or your boss, or 'bad mouth' them to others.
- *Don't* get involved in any banter that might have sexual, racial or any discriminatory overtones.
- *Be modest*, and don't harp on about any of your previous achievements or be an attention-seeker.
- *Don't* try to court favour with your boss or immediate supervisors. Just doing your job in the best way you can is the most productive way of impressing those higher up the ladder.
- *Avoid* using your mobile phone during work hours. Use breaks to network and find out information rather than spending them on your phone.
- *Don't* just assume something is acceptable practice. Establish the rules first.

Dress for success

There is no need to purchase school/centre-based uniforms or a fancy new wardrobe while you are on prac, and you can do this gradually once you begin work. Well-presented attire that is clean, in good condition, practical and fit for purpose is all that you need.

- *Clothing.* This should be freshly cleaned and pressed. You are likely to be spending much of your time at the level of the children: bending, squatting, sitting on small chairs. Take this into account when you dress. Here is a good test. Take a look in the mirror before you leave. Check that the clothing fabric is not too transparent. Stretch up, lean forward, squat down and also turn around. If you can manage those movements without over-exposing flesh or underwear, you are off to a good start. Make sure skirts and shorts (if appropriate in the workplace) are of an appropriate length. Too short will not make a good impression. Clothing emblazoned with slogans is best avoided.
- *Sun safety.* This is a big issue. No matter what your personal practices are outside the education context, while on prac or in the workplace you will be expected to model this for the children. So that you are not exposed to the sun's damaging rays, always use sunscreen, wear a hat and keep your shoulders covered when outside on playground duty.
- *Hair.* Your hair should be clean, tidy and off your face as much as possible. It is wise to tie longer hair back, especially if you are working with young children. In some schools, there are particular cultures around hairstyles— for example, coloured hair and punk styles are not welcome. It is best to check the workplace's websites and policies for this before you start prac.
- *Face.* Your face should be clean and fresh. If you wear makeup, keep it simple and light.
- *Accessories.* Keep these to a minimum so as to eliminate distractions. Dangly earrings are often not practical when working with very young children. Remove any other piercings until you know the policy and attitudes within the setting.
- *Shoes.* Check for workplace requirements regarding footwear. You may be required to wear closed-toe shoes. Think practical business shoes that will suit playgrounds, sandpits and obstacles as opposed to fashion shoes.
- *Bags.* If carrying a bag, make sure it is in keeping with your business attire. It needs to be clean and practical. If using a backpack to carry lunch and shoes, be mindful of its condition.
- *Nails.* Long nails can inadvertently scratch young children or make handling resources such as outdoor equipment difficult. If choosing adornments such as nail polish, clear or subtle is best.
- *Perfumes and other fragrances.* Fragrances such as perfume, after-shave and cologne should not be too overpowering. Remember to wear deodorant, as most people perspire when anxious. If you are a smoker, there should be no evidence of smoking on you or your clothing. Smoking would not be appropriate at any time during your working day, nor in any place near young children.

Remember, the most important accessory is a confident attitude (even if you are feeling like a fish out of water) and an enthusiastic smile.

Anticipation

What do I need to know before I start?

As much as you will be looking forward to your work placement or starting work, you will also probably be feeling anxious about your first day—this is normal. Think back to times when you were in a similar situation. How did you feel on your first day at high school, your first week at uni, the first day at your part-time job? Were you nervous and anxious? How did you cope with these feelings?

Anticipation when entering the workplace may be influenced by:

- other students who have completed a work placement, and knowledge about whether their experiences were positive or negative
- your 'personality type'—especially if you are a 'a worrier'
- your knowledge of the workplace
- your past experiences.

In order to manage your anxiety you will need to gain a sense of what is expected of you and have an understanding of what to expect from your workplace.

What is expected of you?

- Make yourself aware of your workplace health and safety policy, procedures and practices.
- Perform in accordance with corporate/centre/school/institution aims.
- Follow accepted attendance patterns and times.
- Report to your supervisor as directed.
- Clarify expectations.

What can you expect from your workplace?

You can expect your workplace to:

- provide you with a safe working environment
- complete an induction program or learning agreement that will help you to familiarise yourself with other staff and understand expectations in relation to the work and working conditions
- provide you with appropriate supervision and support.

Did you know?

The professional qualities expected of you include:
- knowledge (e.g. curriculum, pedagogy, policy and procedure)
- personal professional qualities (e.g. flexibility, commitment, passion, good communication skills, time management)
- lifelong learner qualities (e.g. engaging in continuing professional learning, knowing when to ask for help). (Education Services Australia, 2011a)

What is the average working week?

- Full-time employees worked an average of 39.9 hours per week in 2011 (ABS, 2012).
- In 2009, 15 per cent of employees worked 50 hours or more—that is an average of more than nine hours a day (ABS, 2012).
- A standard working week in the public sector is 37 hours—seven hours and fifteen minutes a day (not including a 45-minute lunch break).
- A teacher's working week includes both face-to-face teaching time and time dedicated to preparation and assessment, professional development (for example, staff meetings, network meetings) and other duties (e.g. playground duty).

Now I'm worried . . .

At first you will be eager to start and get involved at your workplace—after all you didn't take this on just to sit and observe.

We have looked at the things that you need to know before you start. Now that you have worked through some of the expectations of the workplace, let's examine some of the concerns and anxieties that this may have produced. After all, it is perfectly normal to experience these feelings, and to be a little daunted by the prospect of entering a new and unfamiliar workplace.

Your prac (work placement) and your first position in the workplace provide a chance for you to experience and expand your real-world skills in your intended profession and to make a contribution to your employer. Together with eagerness and hope, there will inevitably be some anxiety. You might be worrying about some of the aspects in Table 4.2.

Acknowledging these worries can help you to prepare some response strategies that will give you the confidence to progress. One key response strategy is preparation.

> Clarifying expectations will go a long way towards reducing your anxiety. The more you know, the easier it will be.

Table 4.2: Concerns about prac and beginning work

Self	Supervisor
What will be my role?	What is their expectation?
Do I have the ability?	What is their supervisory style?
Co-workers/colleagues	**Children/families**
Will they accept me?	Will I do/say the right thing?
What are the standards of behaviour?	Will my service be valued?

Your workplace is different from university

It is not uncommon for students to experience some form of disappointment or disillusionment with the workplace. The main reason for this is a
difference between what you anticipated and what you really experience.
This can result in a dip in morale.

It is important to let go of the attitudes and expectations you might
have of university life when entering the workforce. The workplace
operates differently from university. See Table 4.3 for an illustration of
those differences.

Table 4.3: Differences between university and the workplace

At university you may:	In the work environment:
• have control over your time • have specific deadlines or timeframes • have lots of direction • have opportunities to question things • get direct feedback by way of grades • have less of a focus on interpersonal relationships	• things are often not done the way theory may suggest • you must learn to work with colleagues from diverse backgrounds • you will find there is often a clearer understanding of the 'right way' of doing things • you will receive less feedback • you will be given less direction • you will need to respond to others' needs • quality outcomes are a priority

I know nothing!

That's just not true! Go back to the map in Figure 1.1. Look at all you
have learned in your teacher preparation program. And this is in addition
to your learning before and outside university.

But when you are starting a prac, it is easy to have a crisis of confidence. As lifelong learners, we are always returning to the position of
learners, not knowing and needing to learn more. It is important to recognise what this feels like. It is also important to have ways of reminding
ourselves of what we do know, what we have learned, our strengths and
what we bring to any context.

The same applies as you are get ready to graduate and transition to the workforce. After completing your qualifications, you know much more than when you commenced your studies, yet as you prepare to enter the profession as a fully qualified teacher, you may still have those feelings of 'not knowing'. But you will be surprised at how much you *do* know.

Take the time to regularly reflect on your experiences in the workplace and at university. This includes what you have learned, not just what you have done. Reflection and review add to your growth and learning.

Your portfolio will help you with this. When you maintain a robust portfolio, you have a good way to track your learning. This will be both for your own benefit, and to demonstrate your development and learning to others—including employers and potential employers.

On prac: What goes in your portfolio?

Beginning with your very first prac, or workplace experience, you can begin to gather evidence of your performance, your learning, your successes and your reflections. Each year, you will add your latest and best evidence of these. You can replace older artefacts with more recent and more effective demonstrations of you strengths and achievements.

For a list of suggestions about what to collect on prac for your portfolio, see Chapter 8.

If you are rigorous in collecting as many pieces of evidence as you can, you will have a large amount of data available.

There are any number of frameworks you might find useful for the organisation of your portfolio. Your university may have a preferred frame, or an ePortfolio already set up for you. When it comes to seeking employment, you might use the job's selection criteria, and organise your material around them. The National Professional Teacher Standards might provide a useful foundation.

Being qualified as an early childhood teacher does not limit your employment prospects to working in schools, kindergartens, or long day care centres. There are many other employers who value the strengths you can bring to their workplace. Beyond portfolios, a range of different tools can capture your professional engagement, learning and growth. Consider the following as possibilities for demonstrating your growth, capacities and development. Make as many links as possible with any other employment experience you have accumulated:

Aim to make reflection and review deliberate and regular activities.

Did you know?

Keep a large box or file in your study area, and simply put items in there as they are generated. Later, when it comes to compiling your portfolio, you can go through this collection, and make purposeful selections of your latest and best evidence.

- *Training log.* Include date, subject, brief overview, comments. This will help you to track your training and personal development opportunities. It will also help you to build a picture of your career development and assist you in planning.
- *Activities log.* Keep a record of regular activities to refer back to, and to help you to improve.
- *Project planning and progression file.* It is useful to have all relevant documents in one place to enable you to track progress and review the methods used in particular projects.
- *Compliments file.* This can be a 'feel good' file. It is also a useful tool in development reviews with your manager.
- *Useful contacts.* Keep a list of people who are useful contacts so that you can refer to them quickly.
- *Workplace diary/journal.* Some ideas of topics that you could include in your workplace diary/journal are:
  - best/worst thing that happened today
  - compliments/criticism received and how you felt
  - new skills learned
  - contacts made
  - main contribution to the workplace.

> Remember to include in your portfolio evidence of critique and analysis—it is not just a collection of items.
>
> It's a good idea to practise presenting your portfolio. Your verbal presentation adds a layer that analyses, organises and clarifies your work.

At one university, students are required to present their portfolios as an assessment task in their final year, as a practice for their 'real-world' interviews with employers. One student asked in an email, '*I want to start putting my portfolio together . . . I will follow the criteria sheet but how many pieces of documentation do I need for each section?*' Another had concerns over the restriction of the task to 20 pages: '*I'm not sure how to cover all the Professional Teacher Standards in only a 20-page folio because I have plenty of examples to show I have met the different standards.*'

Really, this is a question like 'how long is a piece of string?' You need as many pieces of documentation as are necessary to support your claim. There are no hard and fast rules about how many artefacts you should include. The best principle to follow is to select the latest and the best demonstrations of your strengths. Faced with a portfolio, readers rarely want repetition, so make your point strongly the first time. Sometimes, one very powerful and illustrative example can serve to support a number of your claims.

Figure 4.1: Listen more than you talk

Listening is not easy. In Figure 4.1 above, Luca is certainly doing a lot of talking. But is anyone (any duck) listening? There are moments like this for some educators. Some research conducted in various teaching contexts (e.g. classrooms, art galleries) shows the teachers/guides doing most of the talking. Our provocation here is to think about how a good teacher is also a good listener.

If you are genuinely listening, you need to suspend your judgement, be aware of your prejudices, set aside your assumptions and cultivate a deep awareness of who is talking and what they are communicating. This is an important principle when developing your pedagogies and your relationships. According to the EYLF (2009, p. 12), genuine partnerships, families and early childhood educators:

- value each other's knowledge of each child
- value each other's contributions to and roles in each child's life
- trust each other
- communicate freely and respectfully with each other
- share insights and perspectives about each child
- engage in shared decision-making.

This is also an important practice to cultivate in your position as a pre-service or graduate teacher, particularly in the relationship with your mentor/s.

How to receive feedback: Your prac report

Throughout your career as a teacher, you will regularly receive feedback on your professional performance. On prac, your supervising teacher may provide you with feedback daily, or weekly, or more or less frequently than this. Formal feedback will take the form of a final report, which is usually completed in the last few days of your block prac. In many cases, you will have a scheduled 'interim report' part-way through your block prac, providing you with progressive feedback on your performance. Later in your career, this same process will take the form of a performance review, or something similar.

For more on giving and receiving feedback, see Chapter 5, where we go into more detail about how to handle feedback.

Your prac report: What is it and how it can benefit you

In some ways, a prac report is like a performance review. It is also an assessment strategy. It can be useful for you as a prompt for reflection—on what you have achieved during a set period of time—and it can be viewed as the culmination of your prac block, a work placement or an internship. Later, a performance review can be helpful as a regular career-management activity.

Your prac report does not have to be painful or scary, and there will probably be no surprises for you in the report. Ideally, if you have established good communications with your supervising teacher, you will have been addressing feedback regularly throughout your prac block. Make this review process a tool in your learning and development as a great teacher. You can use such reviews to help you to identify ways to grow personally and to measure your progress.

Like most things to do with becoming a good teacher, there is an art to receiving feedback. Prepare yourself to hear negative feedback, things that surprise you, things that you might not immediately agree with and things you were not expecting. How will you respond? It is 'natural' to be defensive, but try to keep an open mind and listen *actively*, rather than waiting to 'have your turn'. If you are prepared for the negatives, you will be more likely to continue to be active listener. If you are really struggling with what you are hearing, try to take notes so that you can think about it later. If you are finding it difficult to respond, have a rehearsed response ready—for

> Make yourself familiar with the form feedback will take in the particular placement you are about to start. Become familiar with the criteria and all components of the processes.
>
> Make sure you understand who is reporting on you, and to whom. Understand the stakes, and also understand each party's roles and responsibilities.

example, 'I would like some time to think about this some more.' Listen more than you talk. If possible, try to set up a time later in the day, or the next day, to discuss further—after you have had time to reflect.

At the same time, don't be an *idle* listener during this review of your performance. Actively ask for examples of points of improvement or negative statements your supervisor may make. Use common sense and don't challenge everything your supervisor writes or says. There are power distributions in all relationships, and at this point your supervising teacher is 'evaluating' your performance. You should carefully watch your tone as you pose questions. But you do need to come away with an understanding of where there is a need for growth or change, and why.

Upon reflection, evaluate where you are now compared to where you want to be one year, two years, five years and even ten years from now. This can start some serious soul-searching about what you really want to do. Once you feel comfortable with your plan, write it down. Periodically review your career goals list and refine your plan as needed.

After your prac report

This prac report is the primary method for assuring you are meeting your supervising teacher's expectations. If the power distribution feels unfairly balanced, be sure to discuss this with your university liaison academic, whose role it is to support you, and help with communications between you and your supervising teacher. If you are unsure or unclear about any of the feedback, ask for time with your university liaison academic to work through these matters.

An important task after a review is to decide how to implement the suggested improvements. Don't hide your report at the bottom of a drawer. Plan some time in your diary to review the objectives that have been set. Seek out support opportunities early, in order to work on some of the goals that have been agreed upon.

As the time for your next review approaches, read through your last review again. Make sure that you've made strides in the areas you identified as the attributes on which you most needed to work.

Prac report template

Figure 4.2 shows a blank mock-up prac report template. This will give you some idea of how detailed your feedback will be. Try to complete this as an exercise in self-evaluation, and then compare it with the report you receive from your supervising teacher. Ideally, do this exercise with a blank copy of the form used by your university for the same purpose.

Figure 4.2: Sample prac report template

Teaching and learning (Standards 1–5)				
Pre-service teacher is working towards designing and implementing learning experiences for individuals and groups.	Not developing adequately	Developing adequately	Well developed	Supervising teacher comments
• Gathers information about how children aged from birth to 3 years learn, and utilises this to design and implement meaningful learning experiences with individuals and small groups.				
• Exhibits clear understandings of ways to plan, implement and evaluate meaningful programs that are individually, culturally and contextually relevant and that recognise the diverse needs of learners.				
• Understands and uses relevant curriculum framework documents to support planning.				

How do I show initiative? Context, culture, organisation

A degree of artistry is involved when it comes to being a successful prac student. This is not always the same as becoming a good teacher. Success on prac might require a degree of finesse. This reflects your capacity to act with discernment in unique situations.

If in doubt, ask questions—always with the intention of growing and learning as an early childhood professional.

Think about it

Do you agree that being a successful prac student is not always the same as becoming a good teacher? In what ways might this be true?

There are many things that you can do to be prepared for field experience. Taking the initiative means not waiting to be asked to engage in a task. When you assist the teacher without being specifically asked to do so, this can position you favourably and positively as a student teacher. If you find yourself in an ambiguous situation while interacting with the children, always perform as the teacher, not the child/student.

In conversation

Scott arrived early one day (before his supervising teacher) and decided to rearrange the book corner. He took care to include materials that he thought were appropriate, and he displayed them aesthetically. His action was seen as great initiative.

Elsewhere, when he was completing another prac, he did a similar thing, with a different supervising teacher, and he was seen as 'pushy'.

This is tricky. What is considered initiative in one context could be interpreted differently in another. This can come down to the context and the culture, or even to an individual supervising teacher. Always be authentic about who you are (and don't pretend to be something or someone else just to impress). At the same time, be sure to consider the context in which you find yourself.

If you do your best to cultivate open, honest and respectful relationships with key people on your prac or in your first employment situation (i.e. supervising teacher, director or principal), you will be well positioned to 'read' the context and culture of the organisation and gain a sense of how best to take initiative.

At the beginning of this chapter, we referred to 'becoming a reader'—of contexts, cultures, organisational structures and curriculum requirements. Here you need to draw on your professional knowledges, practise skills and use your imagination. You are developing the capacity to make critical yet informed judgements pertinent to each situation. This is what will make you a professional.

Activity 4.2

Think about the following questions and note down your answers:
- How will I use what I have learned at university while on my prac or in my first position as a graduate teacher?
- How do I want to teach?
- What relationship do I want to develop with the children?
- What relationship do I want to develop with my supervising teacher?
- What relationship do I want to develop with other staff at the centre or school?
- What relationship do I want to develop with parents?

Activity 4.3

Practise teaching in front of your fellow students, and film each other. Performativity is an important part of 'being' a good teacher. You will learn from watching yourself and watching each other. For more on this, read about the strategy of 'micro-teaching'.

Teacher as researcher

- Identify and observe a teacher whom you would consider a professional.
- What is your image of an early childhood professional?
- What do you expect of an early childhood professional?
- What particular characteristics and qualities do you admire? Why?
- What has influenced your views and expectations of early childhood professionals?
- How might these views and expectations continue to be shaped and influenced?
- Interview a teacher/teachers about professionalism. What questions will you ask?
- Read about identity theories and performativity to inform your questions.
- What do you think families expect of and from early childhood professionals?

Portfolio task

As you are becoming a teacher, you are in a 'transition' period, and you will face challenges. Remember to gather evidence that will demonstrate how you dealt positively and proactively with challenges you encountered:

- transitioning from student teacher to internship and graduate teacher
- planning and documentation
- establishing a good work relationship with your host teacher
- establishing effective relationships with children
- building relationships with families
- managing time and (realistic) expectations
- managing unrealistic expectations
- making connections with the principal and broader school community
- collaborating with other teachers and school/centre staff
- working with a host teacher with a different educational philosophy
- putting your best foot forward—your professional capabilities
- promoting yourself as a valued asset and team member
- preparing for an interview.

Further reading

Butler, J. (2011). *Your Behaviour Creates Your Gender*, <http://bigthink.com/videos/your-behavior-creates-your-gender>. Accessed 20 November 2014.

Darling-Hammond, L. & Bransford, J. (eds) (2005). *Preparing Teachers for a Changing World: What teachers should learn and be able to do*. San Francisco: Wiley/Jossey-Bass.

Duncum, P. (1999). What elementary generalist teachers need to know to teach art well. *Art Education*, 52(6): 33–7.

Gibson, M. (2013a). 'I want to educate school age children': Producing early childhood teacher professional identities. *Contemporary Issues in Early Childhood*, 14(2): 127–37.

—— (2013b). Producing and Maintaining Professional Identities in Early Childhood. Unpublished PhD thesis, Queensland University of Technology.

McLaughlin, J., Whatman, S.L. & Nielson, C. (2013). *Supporting Future Curriculum Leaders in Embedding Indigenous Knowledge on Teaching Practicum*. Brisbane: Queensland University of Technology.

Osgood, J. (2006). Deconstructing professionalism in early childhood education: Resisting the regulatory gaze. *Contemporary Issues in Early Childhood*, 7(1): 5–14.

Robinson, K. & Davies, C. (2008). Docile bodies and heteronormative moral subjects: Constructing the child and sexual knowledge in schooling. *Sexuality & Culture*, 12: 221–39.

5

Work like a teacher: Understanding curriculum documents, documentation, leadership and mentoring

In this chapter you will find:

- reading and using curriculum documents
- creating curriculum
- planning engaging lessons
- the learning environment
- leadership and mentoring
- managing feedback
- maintaining health and resilience
- professional teacher standards.

Matt has always been surrounded by teachers. He grew up in a teaching household and his father and aunt are both teachers. Matt has already spent time in classrooms as a volunteer, and feels that he has a good understanding of how teachers work. He has already started a teaching portfolio that incorporates the Professional Teacher Standards. He showed this to his supervising teacher, who pointed out possibilities for additions to his growing collection of artefacts. He gets up an hour earlier when doing prac so that he can fit his exercise session in over the time he is on prac. He knows the hours are going to be long, and he needs to stay fit.

Jason is the first of his family to enter into teaching. He is really looking forward to working with young children, and the hours and holidays should suit him since he has a young family himself. Unfortunately he was late on the first day of his prac because he had under-estimated the travel time and had to drop his own children off first. Jason likes to 'go with the flow', and is sure he will make it through his prac. Teaching doesn't look that hard—he manages his own children, so he is fairly confident he knows what to do.

A supervising teacher's thoughts

Q. Do you like having students?

Definitely! If they are good students, I really like having them in my classroom. The children like it too, and I like to hear what is the latest they're learning at uni. I see it as part of my contribution to the profession—to help ensure we have good teachers coming into the job. I like to help them learn the ropes, and pass on a few 'tricks of the trade'.

Q. What makes a 'good' student?

Ah . . . well . . . they're all different, of course. But I like them to be reliable, always on time, prepared to stay back if required. I don't mind if they make mistakes . . . that's how you learn. The best student I ever had started out with not much of a clue . . . but he really listened to my feedback, asked questions, was keen and interested, determined to learn from me, and he never sat down. If he wasn't working with the children, he was watching what I was doing. And he came back to help me with an excursion that happened a week after his prac finished. I am sure he will be a great teacher.

—Elaine, deputy principal,
18 years' experience in classrooms and schools

One way of thinking about the work of teachers is to think about the 'nuts and bolts'. Much of your preparation will involve learning how to design and plan engaging and intellectually challenging learning experiences for a diverse population of learners. This includes learning about assessment, and understanding the role and use of curriculum documents. This is knowledge that is crucial to becoming a professional educator, and while you are on prac you will have many opportunities to practice these skills and refine them.

It's important to know that, although you may spend a large amount of your program learning about the 'nuts and bolts', this alone does not capture what it means to be a good teacher. There is actually much more to the work of teaching than meets the eye.

When you approach your prac wisely, you can develop insights into the many ' less visible' workings of teaching. Watch, listen, observe, ask questions, make notes, reflect. How many relationships do you see your supervising teacher attending to during the day? What is the work of the director/principal/assistant? Are parents and families made to feel welcome? How? When are the 'management committee' (e.g. P&C, school council or board) meetings held? Who attends? How many meetings does your supervising teacher attend? If you were to consider aiming for an administrative or leadership role in the future, how could you find out what is involved?

> Prac experience will not cover everything you need to know about teaching.

In conversation

I wish we had more prac. I learned more on prac than during my four years at university. (Leith, graduating teacher, 2011)

Leith is not the first, and not the only student, to say this. Do you agree with Leith's view? How might someone else experience this? What might be missing with this thinking?

In this chapter, we draw your attention to the complexities of teachers' work, and some of the less obvious aspects that, with your deliberate attention, will support your successful prac and your future teaching appointments. We are not attempting to capture all that you need to be able to do in order to work like a teacher—your teacher preparation program includes many facets of this. Here, we are giving you a sense of the finesse and creativity that will be required of you, above and beyond the more obvious 'nuts and bolts' of your performance as a teacher during prac.

In Chapter 4, we referred to being a 'reader' of curriculum documents. This was in the context of acting like a professional—understanding the mandates, frameworks and expectations that help shape the ways in which teachers are expected to act. We return to curriculum in this chapter, but not in the detail that you will cover elsewhere in your program (see Figure 1.1 as a reminder of the place of curriculum in becoming a teacher). Here we discuss the usefulness of curriculum documents as 'tools' or aids for you while on prac.

We also turn to the environment, and look at how the space in which you are working can directly affect the learning that takes place there. We devote some time to leadership, since it is important to the profession that you understand that your work does not stop in the classroom, school or centre. Every good teacher shows leadership in their immediate setting, in the community and, even more broadly, in the early childhood sector. In Chapter 2, we emphasised the importance of a health plan for your prac. Wellbeing and resilience will be important to the quality of your work throughout your career. As you spend time surrounded by young children and their families, in a workplace that is designed for activity and engaged learning, your sustained health and fitness will be important. Finally, we return to the *National Professional Standards for Teachers*, and suggest how you can use these as a guide during prac.

I have to prepare a lesson for the children—where do I start?

First, it is highly unlikely that your host teacher will give you a task like this unless they feel you are capable. And you will be supported throughout the process. Don't be afraid to ask for clarification if you are unsure of exactly what is expected of you.

Second, be aware of all the possibilities for support and resources. Remember your university liaison academic is available to support you. Remember too your other units of study in your program. You will have learned about planning pro formas, and endless versions of these can be found through a simple web search. The library also has many resources.

Third, whenever possible, plan well in advance, and make your plans available for your host teacher to review before you enact them. This might not always be possible, and your host teacher might not think it is necessary. But it is a good process to follow.

Because early childhood pedagogies are child centred, it is rarely helpful to follow pre-packaged 'lesson plans' or worksheets—any of these would have to be adapted to suit the particular children and contexts. Nevertheless, as a general rule, start with the child.

So take a look at any observations and reflections you might have made, as well as any information you have accumulated about the child/children, their interests, strengths, capacities, cultures and ways of being. You should also draw on your knowledge of child development, sociology, your images of children and your knowledge about learning.

Next, for the 'nuts and bolts' of what to plan, a curriculum document provides a good support—but which one? And where in the document should you look?

Think about it

Discrimination is not the effect of people being different, but the way society is structured which gives the impression that there are 'normal' ways of being. (Giugni, n.d., p. 12)

Reading curriculum

Curriculum documents differ from country to country, and can also differ within countries, depending on the type of educational institution or service, the jurisdiction and the governing bodies. Nevertheless, curriculum documents have many features in common. For success on prac, you need to demonstrate that you are an accomplished 'reader' and user of curriculum documents. (For more on this, see the discussion in Chapter 4).

The number of different curriculum documents used in educational contexts can sometimes seem overwhelming. In early childhood education in Australia, for instance, the EYLF is a national framework (not exactly curriculum) written for all children aged between birth and 5 years. At the same time, teachers will draw on more local, regional or state-mandated documents, and you might also find that your supervising teacher draws on something older, yet 'tried and true', or documents from elsewhere.

Curriculum documents can become a powerful means for articulating and justifying your practice, examining your perspectives and opening up dialogue about teaching and learning. Rather than being a slave to curriculum documents, we encourage you to become:

- a reader
- a critiquer
- an enactor.

Did you know?

Inclusion Support Program target groups include children with disabilities, children from culturally and linguistically diverse backgrounds, children from refugee or humanitarian intervention background and Indigenous children. (DEEWR, 2012, p. 39)

Activity 5.1

Check with your teacher early in your prac, or even on your pre-prac visit. Find out about the curriculum documents the school or centre finds most useful. Which are mandated for this context? Later, when you have built a relationship with your supervising teacher, the 'pros and cons' of various curriculum documents could make a rich topic for a more sustained conversation.

Did you know?

During your pre-service teaching and after graduation, you will hear about many different types of curriculum and approaches to curriculum. Have you heard/read about:

- emergent curriculum
- negotiated curriculum
- technology-enhanced curriculum
- hidden curriculum
- back-to-basics curriculum?

It is essential that you take the time to become familiar with the array of curriculum documents that are relevant to your context. It is only once you know them that you can work out how to put them to work for you.

An effective way of feeling empowered to use curriculum documents to assist your work rather than to 'dictate' your work is to critique them:

- Set aside time before your next prac to carefully read through the relevant curriculum documents.
- Start by examining their layout and how they work.
- Then think more about their purpose:
  - What are the assumptions underpinning the documents?
  - Note the language that is used.
  - What outcomes are expected of both the learners and you?

Don't be afraid to write questions on curriculum documents and add statements or rearrange them in a way that is more user-friendly for you.

In conversation

I remember when I first began working in England I was frustrated by having to understand a whole new set of curriculum documents. At first they just didn't make sense to me—the layout was confusing and you had to flip between different pages and documents to link statements and outcomes together. Eventually I photocopied the documents, cut them up and rearranged them so that I had one user-friendly document. Rearranging the documents made it much easier for me to use them to reference when I was planning. Some of the other early years teachers asked me about this 'new' curriculum document that I was using, and when I explained what I had done they also started using my version. The principal was so interested in my idea that she asked me to do a presentation for all of the teachers in the school from reception through to Year 6. (Lyn, ECEC professional, 2014)

Creating curriculum

There is more to curriculum than is written in curriculum documents. Although definitions of what 'curriculum' means are constantly under debate, thinking about curriculum as a process rather than a static 'object' or 'thing' can be helpful. Creating curriculum thus involves (among other aspects) an intricate weaving together of knowledge about teaching, an understanding of learners, and an understanding of the context and the community in which teachers work. Good teachers don't deliver a 'ready-made' curriculum; they create it with learners—hence the term 'creating curriculum'.

The curriculum that teachers create in practice is shaped by more than teachers and learners alone, however. It is shaped by government agendas, historical practices and evolving educational research. Government mandates such as the scheduling of national tests will shape some curriculum parameters. Local ways of knowing and understanding may shape other curriculum decisions.

As a teacher, your task is to create a curriculum with your learners that meets their needs and is relevant for your context and community. During your prac, you will be expected to engage with the curriculum program that has been designed by your supervising teacher. This might involve delivering learning experiences or 'lessons' that have already been planned by your teacher. At different points, you will also be expected to design and plan your own learning experiences. By doing so, you will have the opportunity to create small parts of the curriculum. Later, when you are a practising educator, creating curriculum will be your responsibility.

Activity 5.2

Do some research to work out which documents will be relevant for your next prac. For example, while *Belonging, Being, Becoming: The early years learning framework for Australia* (DEEWR, 2009) is a national curriculum framework document for the early years, other specific, centre-based curriculum framework documents might also be used.

Look through the curriculum documents that you will need for your next prac, and examine them from the perspective of an early childhood educator. Look for synergies and contrasts in language, perspective, assumptions and expectations with regard to children's learning, families and teachers.

What does your critique of the curriculum documents tell you? Discuss your thoughts with your peers. How might you draw on these documents during your practicum?

Think about it

What shapes the curriculum? Policy, research, public opinion, curriculum writers, political agendas, communities, governments, regulating authorities, colleagues, history, discourses . . . anything else?

The essential building blocks of creating curriculum involve the points listed below. Use them as prompts for your own evaluation and reflection on the learning experiences you plan and implement with the children:

- building relationships with learners, colleagues, families and community
- taking the time to get to know your learners—their interests, ideas, ways of working, existing knowledge, skills and learning preferences
- understanding what is expected of your learners as outlined in school or curriculum framework documents
- understanding what is expected of you as a teacher, and your professional roles and responsibilities in the particular place where you work
- making informed pedagogical decisions that build on your understanding of learners
- understanding the complexities of the particular context and community in which you work
- switching children's learning 'on' by designing and planning engaging and intellectually challenging learning experiences that encourage participation and cater for the diversity of your learners
- creating an engaging environment that is conducive to learning
- managing the speed and pace of the day
- listening to what is happening around you, and continually providing and seeking constructive feedback about children's learning and your teaching.

At different times in your career, we hope you will experiment with different ways of creating curriculum that draw on a variety of theoretical and research insights. You will also build enhanced knowledge of teaching as you gain more experience.

While on prac, and even when you are a new graduate teacher, you are often limited in your scope and opportunities to make significant curriculum decisions. Your future plans for how you might create other aspects of the curriculum can be documented in your reflections during prac. These reflections will provide an avenue for you to record your thinking and ideas about what elements and approaches you would like to adopt for creating curriculum with learners.

One 'tried-and-true' framework for planning

The following framework works very well as a way to organise your thinking and planning, as well as helping you to reflect and evaluate afterwards. It takes into account the key ideas that will always help you with your tasks of creating curriculum—whether in the prac context where you are trying out some of your ideas for the first time or later, when you are able to draw on your accumulating experiences and developing understandings.

Time

The speed and pace of the day, as well as timeslots within it, can affect how learners and teachers feel. Effective teachers work carefully with learners to construct a rhythm to the day that maximises the process of learning, engagement and wellbeing. Both teachers and children benefit from a balance of active and slower paced engagement, focused learning with independent and small-group dynamics, and dedicated time for rest and reflection. Getting the rhythm right takes trial and error, as well as monitoring and adjustment, as the needs of learners and teachers change.

Children get frustrated when they are rushed, and bored when they aren't sufficiently engaged. Learners often like some routine and predictability in the general schedule of the day, but they also like a scattering of the unexpected.

Resources

Resources that enhance learning can be found in any number of places—from the local park to the back of a cluttered centre or school cupboard. Often simple resources work best, as they engage learners without causing too much distraction from the task at hand. Good handmade resources often last for years, and can be adapted to suit different learners and contexts. Think about visual, tactile and auditory resources.

whom they are responsible, Epstein (2007, p. 4) argues that intentional teaching means more than this, noting that:

intentional teachers are intentional with respect to many aspects of the learning environment, beginning with the emotional climate they create. They deliberately select equipment and materials and put them in places where children will notice and want to use them. In planning the program day or week, intentional teachers choose which specific learning activities, contexts and settings to use and when. And they choose when and how much time to spend on specific content areas and how to integrate them. All these teacher decisions and behaviors set the tone and substance of what happens in the [setting].

Ideas

Curriculum documents and textbooks are often full of basic ideas for how to design and present a learning experience. But ideas can be drawn from anywhere:

- visiting a museum or art gallery, attending a concert or performance
- watching a movie
- reading about current events in the newspaper
- talking with an artist
- going for a walk
- starting a collection.

Do things that you find interesting, and just about anything can trigger great ideas that you could adapt and use for learning experiences. If you are having trouble coming up with ideas to make your teaching engaging, why not 'phone a friend' and have a chat about possibilities? Often talking about issues can prompt you to find new solutions.

People

The teacher doesn't always have to be at the centre of learning activities. When children work in small groups and with peers, they can enhance each other's learning. The inclusion of learners or teachers from different class groups, as well as visitors from the community, can also enrich a learning activity. If possible, call in an 'expert', who can share their knowledge and passion with the children.

If visitors can't be there in person, consider setting up a video link, or integrating audio-visual material. Colleagues, friends, families and community members often have specialised skills that you can tap into as well.

Some learners require the assistance of particular support people at different times through the day—check with your supervising teacher.

In conversation

I was watching a football match and the coach had a biscuit tin with magnets inside that he used at half time. Individual magnets had players' names on them, and the coach used the lid of the biscuit tin to show the players where their positions were and what moves he wanted them to make. This magnet idea helped me to design a flexible seating plan that I used with the learners in my class. I also adapted the idea to use for organising enrolments on a central board when I was the director of an early childhood centre. (Lydia, tertiary teacher, 2012)

Spaces

The physical environment has a powerful effect on learning. All the senses are involved when we learn, and there are ways of thinking about learning that consider that we learn just as much with our bodies as with our minds, and that the two are not separate.

A busy, cluttered space sets a particular tone. If the children are presented with predetermined tasks, and 'activities' and 'worksheets', they are given a particular message—about themselves, their capacities and their learning. They understand that in this space they must perform certain tasks, they have little or no choice or control over their learning, and the adult makes most of the decisions for them. A different atmosphere is created when children are welcomed into a carefully and aesthetically constructed space where they can make choices freely, access materials, and their learning has been planned in connection with their interests and your knowledge of them.

Think about how you learn best. Some learners do not always learn when they are inside or sitting at desks. Think about spaces and places that enhance learner engagement. It can often be helpful to draw on your lesson plan a map of the spaces and arrangements that you will use for your learning experience.

" "

Have you considered borrowing resources from organisations such as the local museum or historical society?

Can you access recycling centres, such as 'Reverse Garbage'?

Become a 'scrounger', and let people know that their 'rubbish' could very well be your treasures.

Activity 5.3

The great debate: Effective teaching in the early years requires more 'intentional teaching' and less 'free play'. What do you think? Work with your peers to present arguments for and against.

Draw a diagram of your current understanding of early childhood. Include some representation of your view of the teacher's role as well as your view of children as learners.

Consider the birth to age 3 context. Do you need to change, add or delete anything because of this? What? Why?

Date this diagram and keep revising it each time you undertake prac.

Perhaps add modifications and new ideas in a different colour, to track your developing understanding.

This concept map could be incorporated into your portfolio.

?

Did you know?

Some experts you could consider calling in include scientists, nurses, doctors, engineers, conservationists, artists, architects and musicians.

Environment as the third teacher

For Australian Indigenous peoples, country is a living entity, with a yesterday, today and tomorrow, a consciousness and a will towards life. Such a holistic worldview does not separate the environment from the mind, body and heart. As Deborah Bird Rose (1995, p. 85) explains, for Aboriginal and Torres Strait Islander peoples, the 'earth has Aboriginal culture inside', and 'country is alive with information, for those who have learned to understand':

> *Everything come up out of ground—language, people, emu, kangaroo, grass. That's Law.* (Hobbles Danaiyarri, a Mudbura man of Yarralin, in Rose, 1995, p. 9)

In the framework presented above, the fifth factor was space. It is easy to overlook the importance of the environment to learning. For centuries, students of aesthetics have understood the power of our senses, and how our surrounding environments act on us, shaping our thoughts, feelings and ways of being.

Consider, for instance, how the architecture of a sporting stadium affects those who enter it. Likewise, think about the feelings created when you enter a church, a temple, a doctor's consultancy room, an art gallery, a prison, a forest, a beachside unit. Not everyone will feel the same about each of these spaces, but the space itself will have an effect on you. And you will come to have expectations of each of these spaces. For instance, what would you expect to see in a doctor's surgery? What would you *not* expect to see (e.g. an ashtray)? How did you feel when you entered your prac placement for the first time?

An integral part of curriculum is the environment, and in this section we discuss your use of the environment within the constraints of the placement setting. During your prac and when you begin teaching, you will be expected to consider the environment as an integral aspect of your teaching. The extent of your control over the environment might vary—from incorporating decisions about the environment into your learning experiences to being completely responsible for designing and planning a particular area in the room or outdoor space. Whatever the scope of your input for decision-making while on prac or when you start to teach, you will be able to draw on your experiences to develop your own ideas through your reflections on the environment, how it is used and how it works.

Think about the space from a learner's perspective. Look at which spaces children use and how they use them. Put yourself in those

Who else in your centre or school might be able to contribute to your lesson?

Have you factored in any learning support or teacher aide assistance?

How will learners be enabled in your learning experience?

How can they contribute to learning and teaching?

Will your learning experience work better inside or outside? On the floor or at tables?

What can you do to enhance the learning environment?

What message will be conveyed by the way you organise the environment for your learning experience?

Is this the message you want to convey? Why?

spaces—lie on the ground looking up as babies do, or sit in the back row of a classroom. Seeing from these perspectives can help you to understand much more about the environment and how it is working for learners.

Both the environment in which teachers work and the one they create for learners can significantly impact teaching and learning. Environments have a powerful way of creating an overall atmosphere and setting the tone of a place. Learning environments communicate powerful messages about what is valued, what the expectations for behaviour are and how learners are viewed.

A room that is arranged with a variety of inviting spaces, including interesting displays, resources and areas with clusters of cushions, can send one message. Quite a different message is sent by a room where the walls are covered in stylised images, and the desks are separated from each other and arranged in rows. When teachers make wise decisions about the environment, the space can function to enable and enhance learning. If children can see themselves represented in the environment, they have a sense of belonging. What sort of world do you show to the children with whom you are working? Can they see themselves in that world? What do they learn about themselves? What is the culture 'inside'?

One way of 'reading' how learning environments are functioning is to apply the same framework we featured above. Consider:

- use and organisation of *time*
- selection, use, storage and arrangement of *resources*
- where *ideas* have come from
- the *people* who help with ideas and learning
- use, organisation and aesthetics of *space*.

It is possible to make direct links between what we believe and the opportunities we provide for children and their learning. The environment says a lot about how teachers view and value children.

For example, if we believe children are:

- competent explorers
- imaginative thinkers
- creative problem-solvers
- able to see the wonder and beauty within nature and the environment

then we must give children opportunities to:

- make decisions
- express themselves

Did you know?

When you are asked to plan learning experiences while on prac, your considerations about the environment might include light, layout, furnishings, texture, smell, safety, risk-taking, movement, relationships, time, opportunities, resources.

Taking it further

For more on learning and environment, see Eaton and Shepherd (1998).

- make discoveries
- pose questions
- consider the views of others
- test their hypotheses
- be curious
- take wonder and delight in the unexpected
- work collaboratively with others.

Early childhood learning environments are also workplaces for teachers and colleagues, and places where parents are welcomed. As such they should invite, enable and sustain all of the people that use the space. When families enter the space, do they feel welcome? Can they see themselves represented? Is there a place for them to sit, stay, be with their children, talk with the teacher? How do they know they are welcome?

Leadership

Leadership is an important attribute for all teachers, and a core part of working in early childhood education settings. When you understand about people and how they work together, this helps you to take your place in the placement setting, and make a real contribution to the work of the team. In many ways, the early childhood workforce is unique—members of a team perform in various roles, but all of these roles are directly intertwined and interdependent, all with the common aim of providing quality care and education for the young children involved. It is important to be clear about the responsibilities and structures within an organisation. The way in which the organisation is structured provides insights into the many roles—and particularly how they connect or disconnect.

In the next chapter, we look at your employability, and point out the many career paths available to graduate teachers. Options extend way beyond a job in a classroom or child care centre. One such pathway is into administration and leadership in an educational setting.

While on prac, you will probably spend most of your time with teachers who have chosen not to go down this path. However, we strongly advise that, whenever possible, you make the most of any opportunities while on prac to also build some understandings around the nature of teachers' work when the role becomes one of leadership, management and administration. For this reason, we include some prompts for you to think about leadership. Take these understandings and questions about this important attribute to your prac experiences in each different setting.

Leadership in ECEC settings is unique. For each type of education and care setting (long day care, kindergarten, prep, lower primary school) there are specific nuances that require particular understandings of ways of working together. At the same time, there are some common understandings of leadership in ECEC that provide valuable reference points for working together optimally.

A vision provides shared understandings for ways to promote organisational and individual growth. This provides a framework so that (ideally) all members of staff are 'pulling in the same direction', rather than autonomously working solo. A vision puts the focus on a leader having influence—working to shape, guide and develop people's thinking. In the case of education, this includes team members' approaches to pedagogy and practice. While vision and influence are central to leadership, they are not static attributes; rather, together they constitute a dynamic activity (Rodd, 2013).

For a pre-service teacher on prac, your understandings of leadership—how organisations operate and function—will provide you with important tools for working together with your supervising teacher, and other staff within the setting. An awareness of the organisational culture (values, beliefs, artefacts) and the organisation's structure (roles and responsibilities, lines of reporting) will provide you with important understandings that will empower you to be able to navigate through a successful prac placement. A clear understanding of the culture and structure of your placement setting, including the roles of leadership, will mean you are afforded a degree of agency in managing your own performance and success on prac.

> **"**
>
> Leadership is about vision and influence. (Rodd, 2013, p. 12)

In conversation

Nobody told me that I was supposed to clean up the outside area and pack everything away. I thought the cleaning staff would do that at the end of the day. Later I found out that another staff member had been doing it all week. I felt really bad, and I'm sure it reflected badly on me at the beginning . . . until I worked out that everyone helps out with everything basically. (Tanya, student teacher, 2010)

Each time you undertake prac, it is important to proactively understand how leadership in your prac setting 'works', and what you will need to do to successfully integrate yourself into this setting.

Leadership: An important node where many threads meet

The tricky balance for you on prac is that, according to Fullan (1993), preparing to be a quality teacher requires that you become a teacher for change, not the status quo. At the same time, your prac experience is based on an apprentice model of learning, and your success will be connected with your ability to learn from the modelling and mentoring provided to you by a successful and experienced teacher. The two aims are not necessarily antithetical, but positioning yourself will often call for a degree of finesse and understanding.

Key leadership understandings for you on prac include the managing of your roles in and responsibilities to the prac site, and your roles and responsibilities to your university mentors. Your preparation for prac, and your reflections afterwards, could take into account the factors listed below. Consider your positioning in relation to the following:

- the culture of the setting (values, beliefs, artefacts)
- the context of the setting (primary school/child care/kindergarten, size, number of staff)
- the organisational structure (roles and responsibilities, lines of communication)
- curriculum documents (their philosophical orientation) and planning requirements
- supervising teacher expectations
- mentor expectations (university and prac, lines of reporting)
- field experience requirements (university requirements).

Mentoring

Mentoring is an integral component of professional teaching practice. Mentoring provides the opportunity for teachers to engage with others in order to expand their knowledge, stimulate critical reflection and improve their teaching practice. This involves teachers taking time to watch, listen to and discuss their pedagogical practices in a quest to extend, expand, deepen and sustain effective teaching. Their analysis and reflections are in relation to theory, ongoing research and policy frameworks.

In many schools and early childhood centres, engaging in mentoring is an essential element of being a member of a 'learning community' that operates to support professional practice. Whether it is during the pre-service teaching years or after graduation, connecting with good mentors and supportive learning communities can be a valuable way to enhance teaching and your skills as a teacher.

Mentoring involves work for both the mentor and the mentee, and at times it can be challenging. Good mentors often prompt teachers to identify and then find answers to their own questions, rather than just providing solutions. Mentoring relationships can help to build teaching confidence and improve teaching skills and knowledge by stimulating ideas, providing insight into different perspectives and prompting the exploration of new ways of thinking.

Mentoring comes in many forms. Mentors might:

- offer advice
- act as a role model
- advocate on your behalf
- work alongside you as a colleague
- give constructive feedback on your written work
- ask questions about your practice
- just be a good listener who will help you work through issues and ideas.

However, mentoring doesn't just happen by itself. The development of mentoring relationships takes commitment, time, communication and sustained effort. A sense of shared respect and trust is vital to a good mentoring relationship, as is a willingness by the mentee to be open to the process.

During your pre-service years, you will have mentors both at the university and in the field. Relationships with mentors are an integral component of the prac experience, and pre-service teachers are expected to be proactive in the way they develop these relationships—particularly with their supervising teachers and their university lecturers.

Think about the type of pre-service teacher that you would like to mentor when you graduate—polite, eager to learn, prepared, enthusiastic. You can be proactive in building your mentoring relationships by taking the time to:

- initiate contact
- exchange contact details
- organise meetings in advance
- develop shared understandings
- be clear about what support you would like and why
- establish clear lines of communication and communicate regularly
- use respectful conventions for communication—via email and on the phone
- ask questions and clarify if you don't understand
- follow up on meetings

- be respectful of other people's time—prepare in advance
- acknowledge constructive and supportive comments
- be appreciative.

Receiving feedback

Along with mentoring relationships, constructive feedback is critical for effective learning in education contexts. Constructive feedback is not only essential for children's learning; it is also vitally important for the development and growth of a teacher's professional learning. In a quest to identify the most powerful influences on student achievement, Hattie (2003) undertook a meta-analysis of over half a million studies focused on teaching and student achievement. His findings identified constructive feedback as one of the most significant influences on student learning.

Teachers therefore need skills and techniques in both providing constructive feedback to children and receiving constructive feedback to enhance their own learning about teaching.

The establishment of clear lines of communication and good professional working relationships can foster a positive environment for working with constructive feedback on teaching practices. It is a good idea to clarify expectations for both yourself and the supervising teacher by discussing feedback early on. This discussion should cover the what, how and when of feedback during prac.

For example, prior to a learning experience, you and the supervising teacher might agree that the focus of feedback will be on the way that you use and project your voice during a learning experience. The supervising teacher might suggest audio-recording a section of the learning experience to review together at the end of the day, as a helpful strategy. When the audio is reviewed, you and the supervising teacher can then work together to identify strengths and areas for further focus.

Sometimes you might find it difficult to take on board comments about your teaching performance during prac. This can be exacerbated when you are tired, feeling overwhelmed or don't understand what to do with the feedback. The following strategies can help you to respond to feedback in a professional and constructive manner that will capitalise on possibilities for improving practice:

- Welcome feedback—someone is interested in helping you to be a better teacher.
- Listen carefully to the feedback—it is easy to jump to conclusions and misread messages.

- Ask for clarification—perhaps an example might help you to understand more clearly.
- Take time to think through the feedback before responding—sending your thoughts in late-night emails can be counterproductive.
- Talk the feedback through with a confidant.
- Get help if you need it—sometimes the same comment put another way can be helpful.
- Choose one feedback item to work on initially.
- Develop an action plan for addressing the feedback.
- Share your action plan with your mentor—at university and/or in your prac setting.

Do the best you can until you know better
Then when you know better
Do better
Maya Angelou
(1994)

Reflecting: What to do after you have received feedback

Maintaining a reflective journal during prac can be a helpful tool for unpacking your thinking. Your journal can be a place to record your thoughts, ideas and perspectives. It is important for you to put time aside to enable you to reflect constructively and professionally on multiple perspectives. An action plan linked to your journal also helps you to set goals, target feedback and see your accomplishments.

Some of the questions on which you might reflect when it comes to your own performance, and your becoming the kind of teacher you want to be, could include:

- Were the children engaged from the beginning?
- Was I well prepared?
- Were my instructions clear?
- Did I talk for too long?
- Were any children disengaged?
- Was I scanning effectively?
- Did I use my voice effectively?
- Did the children understand the concepts?
- Was there sufficient challenge?
- Did I assess for learning? What did this tell me?
- Was my feedback effective? What strategies did I use? Who engaged with these? What impact did they have?
- Did children have the opportunity to extend their thinking beyond recall and recount levels?
- What did I learn?

Your reflections are always for your own thinking, and sometimes they are to be shared—with your supervising teacher and/or your university mentor. This is not the same as a personal 'diary'. It is an analytic tool with recognised capacities for improving practices and developing your skills, knowledge, values and attributes as a professional (Ryan & Ryan, 2013). The anticipated audience for which you are writing includes yourself, at various stages of revisiting over a period of time, and sometimes your mentors. Your reflections will do the following:

- It will reveal your thinking about issues associated with teaching and learning, and how your thinking changes/grows over the period of the field experience. Reflecting is more critical than a simple recall and recount of events.
- It will require you to link micro and macro processes. How does what is happening in the room relate to broader issues (e.g. in the media, associated with national bodies, in relation to families, in relations to policy).
- You can include questions that you are asking yourself.
- You might consider how you could be connecting several ideas together

Continue to add to your reflections during prac. They can be centred around a number of key ideas and issues rather than in a dated diary format.

It's not my fault!

Earlier in the book, we referred to the processes of transition and how, as you are becoming a teacher, you are shifting in your positioning and your identity. While on prac, you are at once a student and an educator. It is important to take responsibility for and ownership of your prac experience. This will involve making good decisions, understanding your responsibilities and keeping good lines of communication open with all your mentors. Before blaming others for challenges that happen during prac, stop and think about how you may have contributed to the situation:

- Did you clarify?
- Were you organised?
- Did you ask the right questions?
- Did you ask for help?
- Could you have approached an issue in a different way?

Making mistakes is okay—it is actually an important part of the learning process. Not taking responsibility for those mistakes is often what the issue becomes during a prac challenge. If you are beginning to think like a teacher, act like a teacher and work like a teacher, it is time to step up and take steps to 'fix' it when things go wrong.

According to Guy Claxton (2008), when it comes to learning, teachers need to help students learn to 'welcome error', recognising it as a learning opportunity. The same applies on prac. You will not be the first pre-service teacher to make a mistake. Things *will* go wrong. You will be judged on how you react and respond to errors. Begin to think of yourself as a 'fixer', and work from a position of strength. For some, this will mean a departure from habits of thinking and being, where your response to mistakes is to look elsewhere for resolutions. Now you are working like a teacher—try to fix it yourself. If that is not possible, make sure you know who to turn to for advice, help and support—and ask them.

Wellbeing: Sustaining your health and resilience

Teaching can be an exciting and rewarding career. It can also be emotionally and physically taxing. For the first few days of prac, you will return home exhausted. It gets better, because teachers become 'work fit', and you will build up your strength and resilience for the work. But don't be surprised if you find yourself feeling extremely tired after an entire day with young children. When you think about it, there are not a lot of jobs that require you to build and maintain so many relationships in the course of a day's work. It is important for teachers to consider their wellbeing, health and resilience right throughout their careers—from pre-service teacher through until retirement, and beyond. In the workplace, sustaining your professional wellbeing takes time and proactive thinking.

In conversation

I had to explain to my husband and my son. They didn't realise that every day I attend to over 25 relationships, many of them quite demanding. By this, I mean . . . not only the group of children I work with, but also their families, and the other staff at the centre. No wonder I am exhausted at the end of the day! (Leonie, early childhood teacher, 2013)

There are a number of strategies that can all help to sustain your enthusiasm for teaching:

• building strong collegial relationships
• seeking opportunities for professional development
• exploring new teaching approaches
• being actively involved in networks.

Taking time out is another important strategy for reducing stress and invigorating your health. At the end of the day, it helps if you can take time out to unwind. It also helps if you do something that helps to reduce stress and invigorate your health. Walking, yoga, exercise, meditation—all of these possibilities are proven to help with stress management. It might seem that time and/or energy levels will not permit you to exercise, but exercising is worth it for your long-term health and wellbeing. A tired and cranky teacher is not the kind of teacher you want to be.

Taking time out to develop an action plan for your health can also be helpful. How are you going to sustain your practice as well as unwind and manage stress? Sometimes the unwinding part of your day will take more effort than you realise. Make a plan for this (see Chapter 2 for more information about your health). If you find you cannot relax, you may need to develop some new skills. Like everything else, this set of skills can be learned and practised.

Prac can be a demanding experience, since it is a sudden departure from your established daily routines, and probably much more demanding, requiring high energy levels. It is important for pre-service teachers to be proactive about their health and wellbeing both prior to, and while they are engaged in, prac. Being prepared in advance works for most people. Pre-service teachers have told us that the following strategies have been helpful:

- the incorporation of physical exercise
- a healthy diet
- maintaining involvement in personal hobbies and interests
- time with friends
- practices such as mindfulness and yoga.

It is important to think through strategies ahead of time. Good health can help you to enjoy your prac and provide the energy and enthusiasm you will need to do well.

The following are suggestions made by pre-service teachers asked to advise others on health and wellbeing while on prac:

- Be organised—food, clothes, family responsibilities, child-minding and pick-up, commitments, finances.
- Eat healthy meals—prepare them in advance.
- Get out and exercise.
- Get plenty of restful sleep.
- Take time to unwind.
- Check that all your immunisations are up to date.

- Discuss any significant medical or health issues with your doctor and then university supervisor.
- Maintain good hygiene—especially hand-washing.
- Recognise and manage your stress.
- Be kind to yourself—treat yourself a little.
- Ask for help if you need it.
- Universities generally offer support services such as counselling if you need someone to talk to about managing challenges.

Teacher professional standards: Practice, knowledge, values

Teachers often use teacher standards, codes of conduct and codes of ethics to reflect on their own professional development. If you look at your prac requirements, and the reporting formats by which you will be assessed, you will probably find that particular teacher standards and/or codes have been embedded as part of the assessment criteria.

Good teachers weave their understandings of teacher standards, ethics, conduct and values together in a way that is meaningful for their learners, and the context and community in which they work. As a teacher, it is important to understand the particular teacher codes and standards that relate to your teaching context. Finding out what current standards and codes relate to your teaching context will involve researching at national, state and local levels:

- What teacher standards and codes are relevant to your next prac?
- How are you going to use the teacher standards and codes on your next prac?
- Do you have one in particular that you would like to work on for the duration of this prac?

Did you know?

For more information on standards and codes, see the *National Professional Standards for Teachers* (Education Services Australia, 2011b).

In conversation

During my first week of prac, my supervising teacher asked me to lead the school prayer during assembly. This was an awkward moment. If I had read the teachers' code of conduct for that particular school, I would have realised that this was an expectation of all teachers and I could have discussed it with my supervising teacher earlier. (Robert, student teacher, 2012)

From time to time, a tricky situation might arise while you are on prac. It is probably wise for you to defer to your supervising teacher in the first instance. However, given time, you may be able to discuss the situation further with the parties involved, and use the code of ethics or other similar frameworks to guide your reflections and decision-making.

Where to from here?

The practical ideas included in this chapter are designed to help you engage further with your prac—whether you are preparing for your first prac experience or the last before you graduate. They will also be helpful for your early experience as a graduate teacher. Each prac setting has its own ways of working. As you progress through your preparation to become a teacher, you will need to continually re-engage with the ideas outlined in this book to help you navigate your way to success. Return to this chapter and the suggested practical ideas at different points throughout your teacher education program. This work will help your engagement with the 'art of a successful practicum'.

MacNaughton and Williams (2008) describe a range of teaching techniques that educators use when interacting with young children. Some, such as the technique of positioning equipment and materials, collecting and scheduling, relate to how educators create stimulating and challenging environments that provoke children's curiosity and sustain meaningful learning. Others, such as demonstrating, describing, listening, modelling, co-constructing, problem-solving and philosophising, describe techniques that educators can use either with an individual child or when working with a group of children. The technique an educator selects depends very much on what that educator is trying to achieve with and for a child or group of children, the content and discipline knowledge involved, and any number of other factors.

Teacher as researcher

- Critique the teacher standards and codes that will be relevant for your next prac. Examine how they work and the messages they convey. Consider how they will impact your teaching decisions and the curriculum that you create with your learners.
- Draw on a variety of different perspectives to examine the curriculum documents that will be relevant for your next prac. Examine what key theoretical ideas underpin the documents. Explore what they say about different approaches to learning—for example, how are active learning,

technology and play positioned? What is the role of the teacher and learner in these documents? Also consider how these documents might be read from different perspectives—for example, from the perspective of a parent or a student who is new to Australia, and competently speaks and reads in Spanish and Portuguese, but not yet English.

- Consider what 'learning experiences', curriculum, planning and assessment will look like with babies and toddlers. Investigate ideas for documenting learning and creating curriculum with very young children. The document *Belonging, Being and Becoming: The Early Years Learning Framework for Australia* (DEEWR, 2009) is a helpful start. Explore a range of theoretical perspectives for thinking about babies and toddlers' learning. A review of current articles in journals such as the *Australasian Journal of Early Childhood* and *Contemporary Issues in Early Childhood* will help you with this task.

Activity 5.4

Current teacher education programs operate with a framework that involves both university-based content and experiences, and field-based or prac content and experiences. Discuss:
- what you have learned at university
- what you have learned during prac experiences
- the value of having both university-based and prac-based learning.

Develop a framework to help you to plan learning experiences while on prac. What will you include and why?

There are numerous learning experience or 'lesson plan templates' available on the internet and in textbooks, and you have probably been provided with pro formas through your university coursework. But the template that will work best for you will be the one you design and continue to develop yourself. Think beyond the 'boxes' for filling in ready-made lesson plans to developing a workable and useful tool to assist your teaching.

Have you used a learning experience plan before? Did it work? Why or why not? Consider whether your learning experience plan will help you to teach well and focus on learners, or is just a list of 'boxes' to fill in to look good on paper. Discuss your ideas with your peers.

Healthy critique

- What might be the benefits of 'ready-made' curriculum resource materials or lesson planning guides?
- How might they support your teaching?
- What might be the disadvantage of 'ready-made' curriculum resource materials or lesson planning guides?
- How might they inhibit your teaching?
- Write down some ideas for creating a curriculum for children which reflects your current thinking around concepts discussed in your program of study so far: images of children, images of teachers, relationships, learners and teachers, cultures and contexts.
- What elements do you think are important?
- How will you integrate these into the curriculum? What will it look like?

Portfolio task

- *Plan ahead.* Examine your portfolio before you undertake your next prac. Identify areas that need further evidence and develop an action plan for focusing on these areas. If your prac is in a setting that you haven't engaged with before, consider what the teacher standards will look like in this new setting and what artefacts might be relevant for your portfolio. Brainstorm a list of ideas that you can discuss with your supervising teacher.
- *Review your portfolio.* Consider your layout, content, presentation and arte-facts. Investigate current teacher standards to assess any modifications that you might need to make. Share your portfolio by exchanging it with one of your peers, and then prepare some thoughtful and constructive feedback and questions to ask each other.

Further reading

Bird Rose, D. (1995). Ned Kelly died for our sins. *Oceania*, 65(2): 175–86.
Claxton, G. (2008). *What's the Point of School? Rediscovering the heart of education*. London: Oneworld.
Department of Education and Training (DET) (2013). *Early Years Learning Framework: Information on the Early Years Learning Framework for educators*, <www.deewr.gov.au/EarlyChildhood/Policy_Agenda/Quality/Pages/Early YearsLearningFramework.aspx>. Accessed 20 November 2014.
Early Childhood Australia (2006). *Code of Ethics*, <www.earlychildhood australia.org.au/wp-content/uploads/2014/07/code_of_ethics_-brochure_ screenweb_2010.pdf>. Accessed 20 November 2014.
Eaton, J. & Shepherd, W. (1998). *Early Childhood Environments*. Canberra: Australian Early Childhood Association.

Education Services Australia (2011). *Accreditation of Initial Teacher Education Programs in Australia: Standards and procedures.* <www.aitsl.edu.au/verve/_resources/Accreditation_of_initial_teacher_education_file.pdf>.

Epstein, A. (2007). *The Intentional Teacher: Choosing the best strategies for young children's learning.* Washington, DC: National Association for the Education of Young Children.

Fullan, M.G. (1993). Why teachers must become change agents. *Educational Leadership*, 50(6): 12–17.

Giugni, M. (n.d.). *Rethinking Images of Inclusion: A picture book for children's services*, <www.cscentral.org.au/Resources/PSC-picture-book.pdf>. Accessed 20 November 2014.

Hattie, J. (2003). *Teachers Make a Difference: What is the research evidence?* Paper presented at the Australian Council for Educational Research Annual Conference, Melbourne, 19–21 October.

MacNaughton, G. & Williams, G. (2008). *Techniques for Teaching Young Children: Choices for theory and practice* (3rd edn). Sydney: Pearson Education.

Neidjie, B., Davis, S. & Fox, A. (1985). *Australian Kakadu Man.* Sydney: Mybrood.

Rodd, J. (2013). *Leadership in Early Childhood: The pathway to professionalism* (4th edn.). Sydney: Allen & Unwin.

Ryan, M.E. & Ryan, M. (2013). Theorising a model for teaching and assessing reflective learning in higher education. *Higher Education Research & Development*, 32(2): 244–57.

6

Stepping up, stepping out: Your employability

In this chapter you will find:

- information about employment possibilities after graduation
- suggestions for personal attributes that will make you employable
- ideas about developing your personal standpoint statement
- tips for preparing for a job interview
- a discussion about ongoing professional development.

Throughout the four years of her studies, Shari only ever wanted to be a teacher in a primary school. She had always remembered her own Year 3 teacher, and that's who she modelled herself on. She really wanted to make a difference to 'needy kids'. On her final prac, she was placed in a school with a large population of recently arrived refugee children from African countries, and she found it so rewarding to see them grow in confidence and quickly learn the English language. After graduation, Shari waited a long time for a job. At first she was offered contracts (three months, six months, twelve months). In each of the schools in which she taught, she was disappointed that there was not much of a play-based curriculum.

Now she has taken up a permanent posting, not far from home. Most of the children come from fairly affluent families, and she wonders whether they realise just how privileged they are. It is a large school (over 850 children), and Shari has to work with the other four Year 3 teachers, so does not have a lot of autonomy. The school also takes the standardised testing regimes very seriously, as it has an established reputation as a high-achieving school. A large part of the curriculum is focused on those tests. Shari is pleased because her work is close to home, and the children are mostly very well behaved. Life is good.

Cari really loved her child care prac. She was prepared do 'country service'—teach in a rural or remote setting. Immediately after graduation, she was appointed as the teacher at a child care centre in small country town. She left home with great excitement, mixed with some trepidation about the 'unknowns'. After the first two months, she almost threw it all in. Everything was so difficult. She was coming into what was an already established team. Everyone in the small town seemed to know all of her business. However, she decided to stick with it for a year. She called one of her university lecturers, and they began to talk regularly.

It is now six months on, and Cari is still finding it tough. She is homesick, but she is starting to get to know some people in the community and is starting to feel more welcome in the team. She is also trying to use a lot of what she learned at university. Some things work, some don't. She is really enjoying the children and the work.

A supervising teacher's thoughts

What advice would you give to someone going for an interview for a job at your workplace?

Well, that's not easy to say. Some people definitely interview well, and that makes a strong impression. So . . . some practice with interviews doesn't hurt. I usually study their CVs and letters of application that they have sent through, and that carries a lot of weight with me. I have to tell you, I do take notice of their grades at uni. I know that's not always an accurate indicator, and for some it's not always the full story. My own grades were not that crash hot, if I recall. But it does tell me a lot of things, like . . . they can meet deadlines, they have worked hard

" "

The future is not just a matter of training but a matter of being able to think, and to think creatively and broadly. (Nobel Laureate scientist Peter Doherty, 1997 Australian of the Year)

and probably they are reliable and organised—at least it tells me they are taking teaching seriously. You want them to have the knowledge and some basic skills and strategies, of course. But, just as important, you want them to be able to be adaptable, to go with whatever gets thrown their way; you want them to be prepared to admit they don't know everything, and that they will keep learning. It's those 'overall' things, like being a team player, getting on with others and as long as they are enthusiastic, and willing to keep learning . . .

—Joanne, Head of Curriculum, 2012

In one sense, graduation is the culmination of many hours of studies, and the successful completion of your course is certainly cause for celebration. At the same time, you are in the midst of yet another of the many transitions you will experience in your life and, like many transition periods, this one brings with it a degree of mixed emotions—joy, anxiety, hesitation and enthusiasm for new horizons and experiences. As you approach the final months of your studies, it is a good idea to use some strategies to synthesise your learning across the course.

Some universities will offer a 'capstone experience' designed to assist you with this transition. In short, a capstone will take the form of a 'crowning' or 'cementing' experience, such as an internship or a problem-based assessment task. Here you are required to bring together all that you have learned throughout your course of study, and take your final opportunity to bring creativity, resilience and other important professional and lifelong attributes to a situation you are likely to encounter in the workforce where you are employed after graduation.

In an important sense, if you begin synthesising your learning at this last point in your studies, it might well be a case of too little too late. This chapter is designed around similar principles to those that drive a capstone experience:

- looking back over your program of study, reflecting, and revisiting
- building coherence and synthesising the various domains of knowledge, and bringing them together in a holistic understanding of what you need to know and be able to do, in order to be the teacher you want to be

- having a future focus and looking forward to the next phase in your life, with some realistic expectations of what to expect in the workforce—both the high points and the inevitable disappointments and struggles.

Whether this is part of your course requirements or you are left to do this yourself, it is important to bring together the knowledge and experiences you have acquired through your pracs and coursework. This will give you a confidence that will equip and prepare you for the future challenges you face as you transition into the workforce.

Through systematic, intentional reflection across units and disciplines, you can work to articulate the personal and professional meaning of your educational experience. Consider how you might engage with some of the following strategies:

- *Stories.* Teachers share stories all the time—about children, relationships, dilemmas, delights. Often these stories act as a form of 'teacher as researcher', as they are accompanied by reflections and questions, and can work as a means to address professional questions that are raised in the sharing of a vignette. Share with other students stories, vignettes, dilemmas, problems or issues that you have experienced throughout your teaching preparation, and work together on solutions and strategies that you might try in the future. Try integrating and synthesising the knowledge, skills and experiences you have gained throughout your course.
- *Future focus.* Talk with experienced teachers about what to expect, and analyse their responses in order to help you anticipate your own pathways. Find other means that will assist you to look ahead to your future entry into the world of work, understand some of the experiences and emotions you may encounter, and build resilience for some of these predictable experiences.
- *Make connections.* Connect with people, and with different knowledges and experiences. During your pracs, talk with a wide range of personnel, build relationships, stay in touch—even volunteer to come back and help out from time to time if this is possible. Build coherence and relevance across the various components of your course experience through actively connecting the specific threads of your studies. Career preparation includes making links between theories and practices, psychology and sociology, curriculum and pedagogies, your immediate experiences and your reflections, developmental theories and critical theories.
- *Portfolio.* Through a well-planned portfolio, demonstrate who you are and the kind of teacher you want to be. Include evidence of your achievement of overall course aims and objectives, specific skills and institutional and professional expectations—such as professional teacher standards.

In conversation

When I was at university, I thought teaching was all about the lesson plans and the teaching strategies. When I got out into the school, I was surprised to realise it was the stuff we learned in those sociology-type subjects that I needed the most! You know, like understanding why children come to school without breakfast, and realising that kids' childhoods and home lives are not all like mine was. (Millie, early childhood teacher, 2010, five years after graduation)

What are the universities teaching these days?

Graduating as an early childhood educator means that you are qualified to become a member of a workforce that is unique and diverse. In addition, you have a unique set of skills and knowledge that is valued by many in different but related employment contexts. Early childhood graduates are valued employees in institutions such as art galleries and museums, as well as corporations and organisations that seemingly are removed from the context of a 'classroom teacher'. Your skills and qualifications will also be recognised in other countries.

Activity 6.1

Make a list of occupations other than classroom teacher where your skills would be highly valued.

When you are applying for a teaching position, it is wise to develop a teaching portfolio that is tailored specifically to that position and setting. Review the artefacts and evidence that you have collated while at university and make decisions about your latest, best and most relevant evidence to include. In order to fine-tune your application, it is important to research the relevant professional teacher standards, codes of conduct and codes of ethics, as well as the particular organisation that you are approaching.

The skills, knowledge and attributes required to manage groups of children, and educate and care for them while sustaining communication and relationships with their families and communities are all transferable, and highly valuable to others. It is not every person who can deal with a wide range of people on a daily basis, within the contexts of genuine and caring relationships rather than simply service.

Anyone who has recently attended an international cricket match might have witnessed the amazing capacities of teachers of young children played out in a stadium filled with over 50,000 people. When the champion players take a break for lunch, groups of young children play a version of cricket, in small organised groups, dotted around the central field. Their efforts keep the crowd entertained as lunch is taken. What goes virtually unnoticed by most are the teachers who quickly have the children organised, oversee their game, act as umpire and coach, and briskly gather the children and shepherd them off the field at the end of the lunch break. And all the children enjoy themselves. Not everyone has the skills and attributes necessary to achieve this!

Your specialised preparation means you have the capacities and specialist skills to care for and educate children aged from birth to 8 years. This qualification to work with very young children is not shared by other teachers (such as primary or secondary teachers), so it gives you an 'edge' when it comes to competing in the labour market. Ironically, many graduates with an early childhood degree aspire to work only in the lower primary setting. According to recent research (see Gibson, 2013a), the large majority of graduates at one large university in Australia did not seek employment in the area in which they had specialised expertise—long day care and child care.

Did you know?

Professional requirements can vary from country to country and, in Australia, from one state or territory to another. It is important that you are familiar with these differences when seeking employment.

Think about it

- What makes a good early childhood teacher working in a child care context?
- Would you consider a position in a child care centre?
- What do early childhood teachers need to know and be able to do in order to work in long day care contexts?

The transition from university to employment is not always straightforward. You may need to be prepared to take on part-time, contract or self-employment opportunities; your academic qualification is one asset, and it can be your starting point for demonstrating your other attributes. The world of employment is changing rapidly. Once a graduate was appointed to a teaching post and remained employed by that employer for the rest of their lives, making their way through a series of promotions, or choosing to stay in the same place for many years. There is increasing evidence to suggest that this has changed irrevocably. Labour markets in Western economies are changing and organisations are becoming 'leaner' in response to globalisation, technology and competitive pressures. There is therefore an increasing need for workers who are mobile, adaptable and able to productively integrate a patchwork of contract, part-time and self-employment opportunities as the labour market and their personal circumstances require.

What are your employment possibilities?

In conversation

I'll be honest with you. When I first came back from my ECEC centre prac with children aged from birth to 3 years, my first reaction was, 'I don't understand—why didn't I do the kindergarten or prep prac?' I just didn't get it!

It wasn't until we came back to university and we had tutorials and lectures after the event—which allows you to sit back, reflect, talk about each other's experiences and really unpack—that I understood. Literally, those two weeks after prac that I had back at university, my whole viewpoint changed. I went from just wanting to work in kindergarten to 'I've got it! I really understand what teaching with babies and toddlers is about now!' (Josie, pre-service teacher after completion of a prac with babies and toddlers in a long day care centre, 2012)

Josie recognises the value of the reflecting, 'unpacking' work that goes hand in hand with her actual prac experiences. Independent and critical thinking will produce original and informed views, and will potentially help her to distinguish herself from other applicants for work. In times when there is an apparent over-supply of graduates, employers can take their pick. In a study that canvassed the views of prospective employers, researchers found that particular emphasis was placed on trying to assess attributes and skills during the selection process when recruiting new employees (Fallows & Steven, 2000). It was clear that graduate certificates and other qualifications were by no means the sole basis for decisions. Creativity, enthusiasm and the capacity for independent and critical thinking were the three 'skills' considered most important.

While your undergraduate course undoubtedly has a significant role to play in the development of the understandings, skills and attributes that will help you to make a success of your career, the university classroom is not the only place where you are able to develop desirable capabilities. Some skills—like creativity—are also acquired and developed in the activities of everyday life. You are well advised to anticipate the opportunities for skills development outside your university context, and take responsibility for this. It is not entirely as a result of your university course and your prac experiences that you will attain the skills required to make you a good teacher: a significant part of that responsibility lies with you.

Along with the many opportunities you will have to test out theories, practise skills and strategies, and build on your knowledge of young children and learning, prac blocks also provide you with opportunities to gain accurate impressions of your future workplace(s). An important aspect of career development is adjusting any misconceptions about work roles. The actual time you spend in early childhood settings will vary from university to university: you may have an internship built into your study program; you may have opportunities to volunteer for extra time, in education settings or beyond. In any case, by graduation you should have an accurate and clear understanding of what your chosen occupation involves, starting with the fundamental tasks and responsibilities. Ideally, you will also have a sense of mission or commitment to the profession. You will have an idea of the proper relationships between teachers and their 'clients' (young children, their families and the community). And you should have an idea of the proper conditions for performing your work.

You should also be aware that the unexpected may still occur. In any profession, the transition from graduate to practitioner involves surprises. As we have emphasised in this book, prac is not the same as being a teacher. There is no way to prepare for some degree of 'reality shock'. Nevertheless, there are some steps you can take that will reduce the impact of this change. In psychological terms, the move from university to work is a significant life transition causing stress, anxiety, shock, fear, uncertainty, loss, loneliness, sometimes depression and low self-worth—feelings that are not generally anticipated by students. This may sound grim. However, we also want to stress that you will also experience feelings of excitement, achievement, pride, satisfaction, a sense of accomplishment and delight. You *can* make a difference!

66 99

If you were asked in an interview, 'What did you learn at university?' or 'What do you know about teaching?', how would you respond?
Think about how you might best account for yourself.
Practise your responses with another student.

I'm not ready! I haven't learned a thing at university!

Yes, you have! Your graduation means that you are now employable as a teacher, qualified to join one of the oldest professions. It might be a comfort for you to know that many graduates, in many professions, feel exactly the same misgivings as the time for them to leave university and seek employment approaches. There are deliberate steps you can take to build your confidence, based on sound knowledge of all you have achieved and learned as you have become 'qualified' to teach.

Employability is more than getting a job, though. Your set of achievements includes a wide range of attributes and complex learning that goes beyond a set of 'core' skills and competencies. Graduates can demonstrate that their achievements include skills *and* understandings *and* personal attributes. This makes them more likely to gain employment and be successful in their chosen occupation. While a record of your grades provides some measure of your performance as a pre-service teacher, and might predict your success in the profession, there are other aspects of what makes a good teacher that defy measurement.

According to Pool and Sewell (2007, pp. 279–80), there are four elements of employability:

- employability assets (knowledge, skills, attitude)
- deployment (career management, job search skills)
- presentation (CV writing, work experience, interview techniques)
- personal circumstances (family responsibilities, external factors—labour market, etc.).

Taking it further

For more on your employability see Pool & Sewell (2007, pp. 279–80)

Each of the four components contributes to your employability. If one of these elements is neglected or missing, then your employability as a graduate is reduced. There is some overlap between the components, and the issues are likely to be revisited many times in an individual's employment pathway.

Future factor

Employability is a lifelong issue, and nobody is perfectly employable. You will build your portfolio throughout your working life, and regularly refine it, selecting your latest and best evidence and discarding artefacts that are no longer relevant. There will always be room for improvement—you do not graduate as a teacher and maintain employability for life. A commitment to lifelong learning will provide you with adaptability to the demands of a changing world, and a better chance of occupational satisfaction and success.

> **Think about it**
>
> What will you do when you get the job?
> Foreground some of the dilemmas in which you might find
> yourself.
> Will you abandon all your university learning and fill the children's days
> with the dreaded 'worksheets'?
> You are going to need resilience, resistance, strategies. But you will also
> need to use finesse, be a contributing member of a team, and some-
> times this will mean compromise. What is your 'line in the sand'? What
> things will you refuse to compromise about? Make a note of these.

Consider that in four years' time, there may be another student positioned where you are, and they will be thinking of you. Perhaps they have
completed a prac under your mentorship. They will have the very latest
cutting-edge theories that have been taken up at the university in response
to the latest research findings. Will you be open to their new learning, or
will you tell them 'You don't need all that' . . . and insist on opinions that
have been shaped by your earlier training and more recent experiences?
That student might be thinking, 'They're really stuck in the past.'

Standpoint

The early childhood settings in a particular region in Italy, Reggio Emilia,
have become famous worldwide, earning acclaim from all quarters for
the quality of the care and education provided for young children. These
centres have a particular history and a particular philosophical underpinning, based on images of children as competent and active citizens of the
world. The success of these settings is, arguably, due to their solid connection with a strong cultural context of community.

Taking it further

For more on early
childhood settings
in Reggio Emilia,
see Edwards et al.
(2011).

Each school in Reggio Emilia is unique and has its own identity,
shaped by the children, families and teachers. Partnerships between
children, teachers, families and communities are actively fostered and
developed. Decision-making is largely carried out through collaboration,
and the rights of the child are well understood by all. Working together
and cooperation make the difference, and interdependence is an important consideration within education.

Interdependence and connectedness are also important to many Indigenous Australian peoples. If the success of educational settings is closely

Taking it further

For more on Indigenous learning, read: Martin (2008), Nakata (2007), Phillips (2012a, 2012b) and Smith (2012).

connected with the culture of the community and the country, then it is important for all teachers to build their knowledge and understandings of local and national culture and history. One of the important starting points for Australian Indigenous people is a standpoint statement. This is a way to begin any negotiations and relationships, where each party makes a statement about who they are and where they come from; this usually also points to their values, beliefs and ways of being.

Your portfolio could begin with a personal standpoint statement, in which you clarify your values, beliefs, ethics and approaches to pedagogies, relationships and young children. If you are living and working in Australia, you could also include your understandings and knowledge about Australian Indigenous people as a means of recognising and paying respect to the original custodians of the land on which we all live and learn. If you are in another country, you would need to find out as much as possible about the indigenous population in that country, and pay them the same respect.

First encounters: Prac and the workplace

Taking it further

For much of the materials in this chapter, we draw from our own university's career counselling services (see www.careers.qut.edu.au). We have tailored their materials to suit our needs more particularly.

Check for a similar service in your own learning institution.

Another idea that threads through this book is transitions. We know that students experience a range of emotions before prac, wondering what to expect and feeling uncertain about all kinds of things. Similarly, when graduates take up their first teaching appointments, they can go through a similar gamut of emotions, beginning again with feelings of uncertainty and concerns over the unknown aspects of what lies ahead.

Some ideas about transitions were raised in Chapters 3, 4 and 5. Here, we follow on with a framework that comes from career planning literature and research, and is a predictive pathway for what you might experience—both during your prac, and perhaps (although in a different way each time) in your early days of employment as a teacher. Frameworks like this are useful to keep in mind—if only to help you recognise and be aware of what you are experiencing. Each time, there may be a range of ways in which you might respond to the experiences.

Think about it

- How does your background and view of culture inform your relationships and your approaches to cultural inclusion and cultural competence?
- What gives you a sense of belonging collectively and individually? What is the relationship between the two?
- What gives you a sense of not belonging collectively and individually? What is the relationship between the two?

(Giugni, 2011; Phillips, 2012a)

Anticipation

It is reasonable that, in the lead-up to prac or your first graduate position, you should have a degree of concern about the workplace. But the more you know, the more prepared you will be. Make notes beside any of the points in Table 6.1 that connect with you. These may change with each prac, and again on graduation.

Table 6.1: Workplace concerns

Anticipations	Acknowledge and clarify your feelings
What do I need to know before I start?	
Where/how/when will I find out?	
Will I fit in and be accepted as part of the team?	
What are my concerns and anxieties?	
How do I prepare?	
How will I make a positive first impression?	
Will I develop the skills and attitudes to maintain a good impression?	
What are my rights and responsibilities?	

Disillusionment

Sometimes, partly due to the intensity of the build-up, you can feel a little shocked after your first encounter. Instead of letting that set you back too much, consider the points in Table 6.2, and take some actions.

In the work we do in education in this country, we begin by acknowledging the Australian Aboriginal and Torres Strait Islander people, who are the original custodians of this land. We pay our respects to the elders, past, present, and those who are to come in the future. The children have always been important to the culture, and Aboriginal families are an important part of the social structure and kinship systems. In acknowledging the history of our relationships since 1788, we hope to move forward together in peace and reconciliation, working for the rights and wellbeing, the care and education of all the young children living in this country.

—*Acknowledgement of Country*

Taking it further

Part of the work of being an early childhood teacher is also being able to articulate our work to others. We need to be able to identify, understand, demonstrate and communicate the richness and complexities of our work to others in the community. On prac, you can practise this with your supervising teacher, and others with whom you are working. You will be building the skills required for navigating context, culture and people. You will be learning to 'read' each of these aspects, and work to find your place in them.

Table 6.2: Negative reactions

What's going on?	Examine and critique your assumptions
The workplace is not what I expected	
Feelings of dissatisfaction and frustration	
My support system	

Confrontation

In the process of gaining confidence and competence in the workplace, you may be challenged by interpersonal relationships. Make notes beside each of the points in Table 6.3, with the understanding that relationships often take time, and things can go wrong. The diversities in our workforce mean that you will work with any number of different supervisory styles, and the giving and receiving of constructive feedback are both an art (see Chapters 2 and 5).

Table 6.3: Relationships

Relationships and confrontation	Listening and reflecting
Gaining confidence and independence	
Dealing with interpersonal issues	
How supervisory styles differ	
How to give and receive feedback	

Competence

Once you have begun to feel more familiar with the environment, and you have a better understanding of who you are working with, and how to manage and sustain the key relationships, the ongoing concern may become managing your workload. While you are on prac, the workload will probably represent a marked increase from your 'normal' daily routines. You will not be simply be working the contact hours that many people assume (e.g. 8.30 a.m. to 3.00 p.m., the hours the children are in class at school). Most evenings, you will have plans to write up and reflections to record. At the weekend, you will probably need time for preparation and planning. When you graduate and begin work as a qualified teacher, you will find that the workload does not decrease. Find out how others in your field manage their workloads. Make notes about strategies that you find effective. Developing your capacity to manage the workload while on prac will be important for your health and wellbeing, both immediately and in the future when you are qualified. See Table 6.4.

Table 6.4: Work and workload

What makes a good/healthy teacher?	Research and strategies
Becoming invested in the work	
How to manage your workload	

Culmination

Eventually, the end of your prac will come round. At this stage, many students are so settled that they are reluctant to return to university, and express the desire to stay on prac! At this point, it is important to consider how you will reflect and assimilate the prac experience into your broader picture of the teacher you want to become. See Table 6.5.

Table 6.5: Assimilating your prac experience

Assimilating the experience	Notes and action plan
Review and reflect: • What worked? • What I would do differently? • What should I discuss back at university? • What did I disagree with? • What are my questions now?	
Performance review • My prac report • My performance review	
Assessing what I have learned	

Getting a job

No matter what your chosen career path or employment option, the employing body will have a process for selecting its employees, and, in most cases, it is safe to assume that you will not be the sole applicant. Find out what the process is, particular to the employing body you are seeking employment with. Do not presume about this process. Any application process will need to be taken seriously. If there are selection criteria, be sure to address them in your application.

In conversation

My early childhood teaching degree has been a great passport for travelling across different teaching settings and countries. I have had teaching appointments in primary schools, long day care centres, preschools, kindergartens and high schools. I have also had teaching appointments in other countries, including England, Spain and Italy. Being open to new challenges, keeping abreast of research developments, and being willing to constantly learn have all helped to facilitate my teaching adventures. (Lyn, ECEC professional, 2014)

If you are asked to attend an interview, be well prepared. Your portfolio will contain many useful artefacts that you have gathered over the course of your preparation. You may or may not refer to this portfolio during the interview. Nevertheless, by reviewing the portfolio and using the selection criteria as an organiser for your entries, you will give yourself a coherent and robust view of your strengths, capacities and the contribution you can make to your employer and the team.

This is an ongoing process and, as you progress through your career, you will from time to time call upon this portfolio as a support for articulating your strengths and accomplishments. Be sure to keep it current, and regularly renew it with your latest and best evidence.

Checklist for interview
- *Know your portfolio.* Use your artefacts to support your verbal response to questions.
- *Know your audience.* Be knowledgeable about current 'hot' issues in education, and be able to articulate non-biased, research-based understandings.
- *Dress for success.* Dress the part.
- *Start off on the right foot.* Be on time and ready, make eye contact and introduce yourself.

Checklist for portfolio

- Ensure you include brief reflective comments with the artefacts you have selected to sit with each of the selection criteria.
- Check for bias throughout your portfolio.
- Ensure that your presentation of artefacts meets the highest ethical standards.
- Include an action plan—a plan to support your developing and improving pedagogy. Assess your own development and make a plan to improve any weaknesses. This will demonstrate your commitment to professional growth as a teacher. You should indicate where you have come from, and what you plan to do now.

Professional standards for teachers

Professional standards for teachers have been mentioned in a number of chapters in this book, and we return to them again here as a potential structure for your portfolio. Teachers are guided by professional standards and codes, just like other professions such as law and medicine. Teacher standards and codes are generally developed with input from the profession. They outline an agreed set of parameters for guiding professional practice, values, knowledge and conduct. Teachers are expected to know the standards and codes, and how each of them applies to them.

The particular standards that are appropriate for your circumstances are determined largely by where, and in which context, you work. For example, national standards apply to all teachers in Australia. At the same time, teachers may be bound to honour more local codes of ethics and codes of conduct, depending on the institution, corporation, organisation, state, territory, community, or sometimes local authority—or even individual ECEC centres and schools. Areas of specialised teaching—such as early childhood, inclusion support and English as an additional language or dialect—also have particular ways of working with children and families, and these are often outlined in codes published by professional organisations. See, for example, Early Childhood Australia (2006) and ACECQA (2014a).

Teacher standards are generally framed around what teachers should know and be able to do. Good teachers need to 'know their stuff', and the Australian *National Professional Standards for Teachers* include statements organised around:

- professional knowledge
- professional practice
- professional engagement.

You will find statements about learners, curriculum content, engaging parents, learning environments and assessment in the *National Professional*

Taking it further

For more information about the *National Professional Standards for Teachers*, see AITSL (2014).

Standards for Teachers, and they can also provide a useful guide for informing a teacher's practice. Standard 1 stipulates that teachers must be able to demonstrate their capacity to:

1. Know students and how they learn
   This, in turn, is elaborated through a number of additional statements:
   1.1 Physical, social and intellectual development and characteristics of students
   1.2 Understand how students learn
   1.3 Students with diverse linguistic, cultural, religious and socioeconomic backgrounds
   1.4 Strategies for teaching Aboriginal and Torres Strait Islander students
   1.5 Differentiate teaching to meet the specific learning needs of students across the full range of abilities
   1.6 Strategies to support full participation of students with disability.

When preparing your portfolio, you might include a separate artefact or a piece of evidence for each of these separate sub-points. Or there may be one piece of evidence that will serve the purpose of demonstrating all the points at once.

Within the standards, your career level is taken into account, and it is possible for you to determine how, at the point of graduation, you are expected to demonstrate each of the standards. Later, your portfolio will need to be continually upgraded, and expectations will change along with your years of experience in the profession. It should be apparent, though, that the time to locate and address these standards is long before graduation. Knowing the standards can provide you with a useful framework for setting your goals for each prac.

For your portfolio: Values

In Chapter 3, we discussed values and ethics, and how knowing and understanding your values is a fundamental part of career planning. Read each set of values and their associated descriptions in Table 6.6, and highlight those with which you strongly agree. Once you have done this, take a moment to see whether there is a particular area that has more highlights than others. For instance, you might notice that you value more things associated with relationships than those about self and work.

Table 6.6: Values checklist

Personal	<ul><li>*Creativity:* Creating new ideas, things, strategies that do not follow a format previously developed by others</li><li>*Prestige:* Becoming well known and respected</li><li>*Accomplishment:* Having the sense that I have done well</li><li>*Feedback:* Receiving frequent feedback from others about my work</li><li>*Moral:* Significantly contributing to a set of moral standards that I feel are important</li><li>*Aesthetics:* Caring about beauty and harmony</li><li>*Independence:* Being able to do things the way I want to do them</li><li>*Integrity:* Working in a way that is consistent with my values</li><li>*Learning:* Being given opportunities to learn new things</li><li>*Risk:* Doing things that involve some level of risk</li><li>*Honesty:* Respectfully telling the truth to others.</li><li>*Health:* Living a healthy and fit lifestyle</li></ul>
Relationships	<ul><li>*Altruism:* Helping people in a direct way, either individually or in groups</li><li>*Contact with people:* Having a lot of day-to-day contact with people</li><li>*Working alone:* Working by myself and having little contact with others</li><li>*Teamwork:* Having opportunities to work in a team</li><li>*Family:* Spending quality time with my family or partner</li><li>*Balance:* Feeling a balance between family, work and leisure aspects of life</li><li>*Friendships:* Developing close personal relationships with people as a result of my work activities</li><li>*Community:* Living where I can be involved in the community</li></ul>
Work	<ul><li>*Power:* Being in a position of influence</li><li>*Status:* Being regarded as an expert in my field</li><li>*Advancement:* The opportunity to work hard and enjoy rapid career advancement</li><li>*Routine:* Having a work routine and job duties/tasks that are similar each day</li></ul>

	• *Variety:* Having tasks and duties that are frequently changing
	• *Excitement:* Experiencing a high degree of excitement and energy in my work
	• *Fast pace:* Working in circumstances where there is a high pace of activity
	• *Economics:* Having the money to lead the lifestyle I choose
	• *Physical challenges:* Having a job that is physically demanding
	• *Flexibility:* Being able to set my own working schedule
	• *Pressure:* Working to or meeting deadlines

Source: QUT (2014); Rodd (2013); Waniganayake et al. (2012).

Of course, your values will change over the years, with added experiences and knowledge. It is important to learn as much as you can about the values of the organisation where you are seeking employment, and then it is a relatively simple matter to tailor your application letter, CV and professional portfolio to best demonstrate a match between your set of skills, values and attributes and the kind of employee they are seeking. Once you have identified the sought-after skills and values, and assessed the degree to which you possess them, remember to document and market them.

Most contemporary universities offer support for your developing employability. Locate these services and connect with career counsellors, whose expertise will assist you from the beginning of your studies. Don't leave this until your final semester. Begin documenting and designing your portfolio with your very first prac experience—or even before. Knowing where your strengths and gaps are can help you approach your prac with your own individual purpose and direction.

Support network

When you start work as a teacher, you might be surprised by differences in your expectations. Sometimes graduate teachers describe feelings of disappointment, dismay or frustration when things don't go according to plan. It is useful to have support networks in place so that you have someone to turn to for support and encouragement. In Table 6.7, fill in the names of people in your network who can support you while making the transition into the workplace.

Table 6.7: Support network

	Who can I call on?
Academics	
Mentors	
Family	
Roommates	
Friends	
Other	

Source: QUT (2014); Rodd (2013); Waniganayake et al. (2012).

Table 6.8 presents a list of ways in which you can be supported. Consider each person you noted when mapping your networks in Table 6.7 and record the type of support they might provide.

Table 6.8: Roles of support network

What can they do?	Who can I call?
Listen to your concerns	
Provide advice	
Praise your current efforts	
Create a diversion (an opportunity for fun!)	
Comfort you ('chicken soup people')	
Challenge you to look at things in a different light	
Affirm your experience (those who have travelled in your shoes)	

Source: QUT (2014); Rodd (2013); Waniganayake et al. (2012).

Many students find that the demands of prac mean they are juggling their time and commitments, and find their personal resources stretched to the limits. When they are able to call in 'favours', and draw on their friends and networks for support, this can mean the difference between a successful prac and the need to take extra time to complete.

Think about the importance of relationships in every aspect of the good teacher's work, and how this is threaded through this book. Reflect on facets such as active listening, reciprocity, trust and honesty. Much of our discussion is about your role of the *teacher*, and how your development

Taking it further

This section draws on the expertise and support offered by the careers counsellors at Queensland University of Technology (2014). Locate the employability support available to you in your own university or learning institution.

In your portfolio, how could you demonstrate to your potential employer that you have the necessary skills and attributes to develop and maintain healthy professional relationships in the workplace?

of these traits will benefit the children and others with whom you work. At times, you will also experience relationships as a support for *you*, and it will be important to reflect on relationships from this perspective as well.

Relationships: Working with others

The diversity of the workforce in the field of early childhood is something we have also threaded throughout this book. In particular, one of the unique things about our field is the interconnectedness: the multidisciplinary philosophy and history on which the field is built, the holistic approach to pedagogies. In Chapter 5, we highlighted the many different roles and responsibilities attached to each of the variously titled early childhood teachers—group leaders, educators, teachers, assistants, directors, principals. Added to this are the many other professionals and para-professionals with whom we endeavour to work closely—occupational therapists, health workers, social workers, inclusion support officers. And, of course, we necessarily develop relationships with young children, their families and their communities. While each has an important role to play, each is also working with a shared interest and aim—the wellbeing and development of all children in our care. For this reason, relationships cannot be left to chance, and are essential to the success of our work and the parts we all play in giving all children the best chance of success.

With relationships taking on so much importance, it is important that you reflect on your own capacities. When there is room for improvement in a relationship, it might be that you think that relationships are something that some people are just 'naturally' good at, and others are not. Nothing could be further from the truth. Understand that successful relationships involve skills that can be learned and practised—particularly in the professional context. The following exercise should work as a provocation for you to give further consideration to this important capacity building.

Teaching teams

Teaching in teams brings a number of advantages, both for the children and the teachers. Children benefit from being able to access the expertise, support and knowledge of more than one person. Children spend a large proportion of their time in the company of their teachers and, if there are opportunities for these close and sustained relationships to be developed with more than one teacher, then the chances are that the children learn

Activity 6.2

Consider how you have interacted with people before. Think of an example where you had to interact with others in order to complete a task.

- Was the task completed/the goal achieved?
- Did you have a positive experience, or was it a negative one?
- How did you get on with the other person/s? Were you friendly, bossy? Did you argue?
- Did you find it difficult to carry on social interactions with the other person/s? Why do you think you answered this question in this way?
- How did you get the job done? What strategies/skills did you use?
- How did the other person/s respond to you? Were they friendly, sociable, assertive, bossy, other?
- Were there any conflicts? If so, how were they handled?
- Did you make any new friends as a result of this work? If not, why not?
- What did you learn from this?
- What would you have done differently?

Now start again with this activity, and this time begin by describing a second example of a situation where you had to interact with others in order to complete a task. Answer the same set of questions about this second example.

Take another look at both the examples you have described. Are there any similarities and or differences in answers between the two interactions?

Consider how each of these experiences might help you in your progress towards your career.

to adapt and interact with more adults, recognise differences in adults and broaden their experiences and learning. For the teachers, the benefits are similar, and include a sharing of expertise and attributes, opportunities for professional collaboration and peer support, and even possibilities for working smart and sharing workloads.

The circumstances that see a teacher spending all their days in a classroom or setting with a group of children, isolated from other adult company, can be both enabling and constraining. Alone, you have sole responsibility daily for the children and their learning while they are with you in your own classroom or setting. With this comes a degree of autonomy and control over your environment and all that occurs within. On the other hand, teaching as part of a team increases the range of attributes and expertise, and can enable specialisation over the need for a more generalist approach to pedagogies—this can come at some cost to autonomy and self-direction. When working as a member of a team, you need to share planning and make time for meetings and sharing communication. Working alone, you are able to fine-tune and adjust your plans at a moment's notice. You are likely to find yourself in both situations at different times—either on prac or after graduation.

The ability to contribute as a positive and productive team member is an important attribute that will add to your employability. Consider ways in which you might demonstrate your capacities in this area.

Provide an example of a situation where you have effectively worked in a team to achieve a given goal. This might be on prac, at another workplace, as part of your volunteer activities or through community involvement.

- What skills did you use to get along with other team members?
- How could you provide evidence of this be valuable information to a potential employer?
- What was the task?
- What skills did you use to get along with the others?
- Why is this valuable information?
- Is there anything else you can add?

Sense of self: Knowing your personal attributes

Throughout this book, we have returned several times to ideas about identities (Chapter 4), standpoints (Chapter 1) and images of teachers (Chapter 3). Having an understanding of who you are and how you respond to different situations can be useful while on prac and in determining what path and type of work you will be able to deal with when you graduate.

What follows are a number of personal attributes provided by Graduate Careers Australia (2014). You might well be strong in some attributes, but you may never have considered others. If you are able to demonstrate these attributes, this can assist you with your development and success on prac, and also contribute to your overall employability. Consider what evidence you might generate in order to demonstrate your capacities when it comes to being a good teacher.

Loyalty

If you are loyal, you are strongly committed to your centre, setting, school or other place of employment. You believe in what other people and your place of employment are doing. You consider that the work has value and meaning.

Can you think of situations where you have been loyal to someone and explain why? If so, can you think of situations where you have not been loyal to someone and explain why? Reflect on how these situations might help or prevent you from becoming the teacher you want to be. How could you demonstrate loyalty while on prac, and to a potential employer?

Reliability/responsibility

If you are reliable, you can be trusted to do what you have been asked to do. You are punctual and you take responsibility for your own actions and performance. Responsibility can also involve being willing to help solve a problem identified, even if this is not strictly your problem.

Can you think of examples where you have taken responsibility/been reliable? Explain how you recognised what needed to be done, and how willing you were to do it. How does this help you to become the teacher you want to be? How would you demonstrate your reliability/responsibility, both while on prac and to a potential employer?

Self-confidence

Sometimes you can feel very confident and at other times you don't. Self-confidence is an admirable attribute. A person who is high in self-confidence is highly employable. It is important then that you believe in your potential to succeed. You can positively and confidently portray your skills, education, and abilities to others while on prac, and to potential employers.

Leadership

In Chapter 5, we made the point that leadership is part of every teacher's work. While there is much talk about 'natural-born leaders', this gives a false impression that only a few can lead. In fact, leadership is a quality that anyone can develop. Evidence of leadership skills might include being captain of a sporting team, a trainer or a team leader.

On prac, consider how you might demonstrate leadership qualities that you think you have already developed or are developing. These may

Activity 6.3

On a scale of 1 to 10 (1 = low self-confidence, 10 = high self-confidence), indicate how confident you are at:

Public speaking	/10
Working individually	/10
Working in a team	/10
Problem-solving	/10
Taking risks	/10
Generating new ideas	/10
Leading a group	/10
Achieving set goals	/10

How do these attributes help you to become the teacher you want to be?

How would you develop these skills if you rated yourself low? On your next prac, try to focus on developing the necessary skills.

How will you demonstrate your self-confidence while on prac and to a potential employer? (Rodd, 2013; Waniganayake et al., 2012)

involve sharing information and ideas, showing genuine concern, being willing to take risks or showing initiative. How can these qualities assist you to become the teacher you want to be?

On your next prac, try to focus on developing any of the skills you think particularly need practice. Consider how you might demonstrate leadership to a potential employer.

Think about it

Employers are often looking for potential leaders—they have respect, poise, confidence, maturity, a sense of vision, the ability to think, communicate and take on responsibility.

Adaptability/flexibility

Adaptability and flexibility refer to your ability to positively adapt and be open to changing circumstances, and new ideas and concepts. When working with young children, your ability to adapt and change, depart from a plan and a routine, and deal with the unexpected is an essential attribute for teaching, and you will be called upon to demonstrate your capacity to cope with change—probably on a daily basis.

Think about it

Do you tend to respond to changes negatively or positively? Think of an example where you have positively managed a change in specific circumstances or in a particular environment.

What approach did you use to evaluate/solve a problem and/or adapt? What were your thoughts and feelings through this process?

How are these qualities essential to your becoming the teacher you want to be?

Consider how you might demonstrate adaptability and flexibility to a potential employer.

Persistence

When the going gets tough, a persistent individual has the mental strength and resilience to hang in there. Being persistent is an important attribute, and enables you to hold on to a strong desire to reach a goal, regardless of whether or not the goal is difficult.

Think about it

Make a note of some examples where you have shown persistence in achieving or completing a goal/task.

- What strategies did you use to motivate you to complete the goal?
- How will this attribute help you to become the teacher you want to be?
- How might you demonstrate persistence and resilience while on prac?

Energy and health

In Chapter 2, we introduced the idea of your having a health plan for prac. In Chapter 5, we discussed the need to maintain health and resilience under all sorts of circumstances. When considering teaching as a profession, you need to think about whether your health is good, average or poor. Some work environments can be physically and psychologically demanding, and teaching may not be the best option for you if you are not fit enough to cope.

You need to look carefully at the demands teaching will make on you—especially if you have any health problems, as they may be made worse due to the work you are required to do. Since we work with some of the most vulnerable people in our community—young children—we also need to consider our own health, as it might also affect the health of the children with whom we work.

Your first prac will be a good point for you to measure your personal health in relation to the demands of the work and expectations. Start by listing any aspects of your health and fitness that could positively or negatively influence your work as a teacher.

Ongoing professional development and learning

While your graduation marks the end of a long program of study, in another sense you are positioned again as a learner who is right at the beginning. Now you will be a newly graduated teacher, and you are beginning a new phase of your learning and development. Early in this book, we examined identities, and what it means to be a professional educator. At every stage along the way, you will have good reason to revisit these ideas, and look again at your identity and how it is shaped.

Any set of professional standards that applies to you will most likely include an article like the following, from the *National Professional Standards for Teachers*:

> *Standard 6: Engage in professional learning*
> These standards make explicit the elements that are considered essential for high quality effective teaching, and there is an expectation that teachers continue their professional learning and development, and document evidence of this learning. (AITSL, 2014)

Your portfolio will provide an excellent foundation for this ongoing work.

Depending on your organisation and employer, you will be expected to show evidence of having engaged with a usually prescribed amount of professional learning. For example, the *Children's Services Award* (2010) links in-service training with career progression, but does not prescribe the amount of time required. The *Queensland Teachers Award* (QIRC, 2012) details specific requirements relating to professional development, including that teachers will spend five pupil-free days each year engaged in professional development activities. Be sure to be familiar with all the information around this. Such engagement might, for instance, involve conference attendance, workshop participation and online learning experiences. At the same time, becoming a good teacher requires that you continue with the work of teacher as researcher, which means you are responsible for your own ongoing quality practices, informed by the latest and best thinking in the field.

Many teachers keep a reflective journal, and map their research questions and their inquiries over time. This journal can grow into a rich resource for you and your ongoing development, enabling you to revisit your thinking, turn a critical lens on your own practice and, at times, share with others for their input and advice.

Figure 3.1 provides a useful framework for a reflective journal, and the cycle can be repeated with each new question you select for reflection and research. At the end of a period of time, the process of mapping your research questions will provide another useful reference point for your assessment of your own growth and development, as well as the beginnings of an action plan for the future.

Activity 6.4

Do you see yourself as a 'professional'?
What are your professional characteristics and qualities?

Activity 6.5

Discuss with a friend what your ideal work environment looks and feels like.
What can you do to contribute to a positive working environment?
Write a brief statement (250 words) in response to this question, and keep this in your portfolio. Revisit each year, and note any changes. Reflect on the changes.

Did you know?

Teacher standards and codes are useful for informing policy development, as well as navigating particular issues that might arise. A code of ethics document, for example, helped Madeleine, a newly graduated teacher, when a parent requested information about her child's playmate, another child in the group. Madeleine was able to call on the code of ethics and explain that she was bound by this code, which clearly advised against her sharing that information, in the best interests of the child. This response was then recorded for future reference. Later, in collaboration with other colleagues and community members, Madeleine formed a policy statement that she was able to share with all staff and families.

Activity 6.6

Discuss your response to the following conversation involving graduating early childhood teachers:

Rory: Even when people say to me, 'So what does this degree get you?' I'll say, 'I can be a teacher. I can do this—or I can be a director or child care worker.' And the first thing they always say is 'Why? Why would you do it? Not if you've got a degree, you don't even need to.' And that is everybody's impression of child care.

Margie: And the status of teachers as opposed to the status of a child care worker.

Rory: Exactly. If you're a teacher, you're a professional. If you're a child care worker, you're a babysitter.

How might your portfolio address some of the issues raised here? Advocacy and activism are also important to the profession. What are the current issues around quality, childcare, and early childhood? How might you respond to these current issues? What action could you take?

Activity 6.7

Loyalty, reliability, responsibility, self-confidence, leadership, adaptability, flexibility, persistence, intellectual quality, other . . .
How will you demonstrate your personal attributes in your portfolio? Will they be organised in a separate section, or will you integrate them throughout the portfolio?
For which attributes do you already have best evidence? Which attributes do you need to target in the future? How will you address this?

Further reading

Early Childhood Curriculum Committee (1978). *What Do You Believe?*. Adelaide: Education Department of South Australia.

Edwards, C., Gandini, S. & Forman, G. (2011). *The Hundred Languages of Children: The Reggio Emilia experience in transformation* (3rd edn). New York: Ablex.

Fleer, M., Edwards, S., Hammer, M., Kennedy, A., Ridgway, A. et al. (eds) (2006). *Early Childhood Learning Communities: Sociocultural research in practice*. Frenchs Forest: Pearson Prentice Hill.

Giugni, M. (2011). 'Becoming worldly with': An encounter with the Early Years Learning Framework. *Contemporary Issues in Early Childhood*, 12(1): 11–27.

Martin, K. (2008). *Please Knock Before You Enter: Aboriginal regulation of outsiders and the implications for researchers*. Brisbane: PostPressed.

Nakata, M. (2007). The cultural interface. *Australian Journal of Indigenous Education*, 36(5): 2–14.

Phillips, J. (2012) Indigenous education in Australia. In S. Carrington & J. Macarthur (eds), *Teaching in Inclusive School Communities*. Brisbane: Wiley, pp. 139–62.

Rodd, J. (2013). *Leadership in Early Childhood: Pathways to professionalism* (4th edn). Sydney: Allen & Unwin.

Smith, L.T. (2012). *Decolonising Methodologies: Research and Indigenous people*. (2nd edn). New York: Zed Books.

Vecchi, V., Cavallini, I., Filippini, T. & Trancossi, L. (2011). *The Wonder of Learning: The hundred languages of children*. Reggio Emilia: Reggio Emilia Children.

Waniganayake, M., Cheeseman, S., Fenech, M., Hadley, F. & Shepherd, W. (2012). *Leadership: Contexts and complexities in early childhood education*. South Melbourne: Oxford University Press.

7

Young children, different settings: Managing and connecting across contexts

In this chapter you will find:

- information about the demands of different prac settings
- details of the roles and responsibilities of the pre-service teacher, the supervising teacher and the university mentor
- advice about how to make the most of feedback
- suggestions for making a good impression.

Rhiannon has had two previous pracs—one in kindergarten and one in lower primary. This one—in child care—should be a breeze. How hard can it be? She anticipated that this prac would involve mucking around with babies and children all day, and hopefully be pretty cruisy—without the after-school staff meetings, standardised testing 'palaver', not to mention those 'older children'. Yet when Rhiannon had her first day on her child care prac (with babies—aaah!) she was shocked. She could not believe that this could be 'what she had signed up for in her university degree'. It seemed ridiculous that she should be studying at uni, yet still expected to sweep the kitchen in the afternoons. Apart from the age of the children, there were 22 staff, most of them with no degree. It was very challenging for Rhiannon to treat them as fellow teachers when they really didn't seem to know anything (or at least they certainly didn't seem to get most of what she knew, and she thought they should know).

Jess had also had two previous pracs: her first was in child care (which she loved), then lower primary and now preschool. Before each prac, Jess spent time thinking about the context into which she was going— knowing that each context in early childhood has distinct operational and structural features. With this, her preschool prac, she jumped online to learn about the organisation with which the centre was affiliated. So she commenced the prac with some understanding (and comfort) about the context, as well as knowledge of the organisation (its history, operation and function). Alongside all of this, Jess was ready, willing and waiting to learn, grow and be challenged through this, her third prac.

Most early childhood pre-service teachers will undertake their prac in at least three quite different settings, each with similarities and differences:

- *Birth to 2 years.* Generally this is in a long day care centre. Sometimes the children in this age group are referred to as 'babies and toddlers'. There are those who object to labels such as this.
- *The year before compulsory school commence.* Terminologies vary, and this might be called kindergarten or pre-prep, prep or preschool. It might be located in stand-alone facilities—for example, C&K, KU, Lady Gowrie, state school, independent school—or within a long day care centre.
- *Primary school.* The early years might be prep or Years 1–3. Generally, early childhood is considered to include children aged from birth to 8 years, but some settings differ, and consider the age group as birth to 5 years. Some schools include Year 3 in an early years curriculum approach, while others do not.

In other teacher preparation programs (e.g. for qualifying as a primary or secondary school teacher), prac experiences can be designed developmentally. That is, objectives and aims might develop incrementally, with each time in the classroom building on the previous experience, and gradual increases in expectations and responsibilities as your knowledge expands.

In early childhood programs, while graduates are qualified to work across a variety of contexts, with this advantage come some differences. Block time spent on prac is rarely developmental. In a short period, you are required to experience a range of contexts, each with differences in programming, governance and cultures.

The divide between care and education is a topic requiring much more time than is possible in this book; nevertheless, the evolution of the various settings is tied historically to this traditional divide. We have deliberately decided to avoid such divisions. In Chapter 1, we gave some very brief histories of these various contexts.

Developmental psychologists have provided a framework for understanding children's growth and development that is closely linked to established age and stage schema, and that works to organise knowledges and understandings. This framework has proven so useful and applicable, and is so prevalent, that it is used to organise much of the knowledge in the field of early childhood. The trouble with such an all-encompassing framework is the risks involved in 'universalising' images of children, constraining knowledge to particular cultural and social standpoints. Any framework will work to both enable *and* constrain, and a critical lens will help make these effects visible. In our rhizomatic approach to supporting your prac, we have not divided our thinking according to ages, stages and their accompanying settings; nevertheless, while we know that prac is such a rich and intense learning period, we also recognise the need for some quick reference points, for those times when you are after immediate and concise understandings and support.

In the final two chapters of this book, we provide short, sharp, no-frills information. You might think of these two chapters as your 'emergency survival kit', for quick reference and direction. This book is designed with your success on prac, or your first teaching job, in mind—more detailed and subtle nuances will be addressed elsewhere in your course. When you are preparing for prac or starting work, come back to these chapters and check off the reminders as you go.

It is important to again remind you that strategies and pedagogies you apply on prac may not always be the most appropriate when you are a fully qualified teacher, working with a group of young children with whom you have the time and opportunity to establish mutually respectful relationships, listen to their ideas and interact with their families. But sometimes these conditions are not entirely possible on prac. For you to experience success on prac, you sometimes need some 'never-fail' ideas, and some clear understandings about the 'rules of engagement': who does what, what is expected of you, and your roles and responsibilities.

In this short chapter, we focus on the roles and responsibilities of the key people involved, and the various dynamics that connect you with others during your prac. Here we pay some attention to how these might vary between settings.

It seems that each prac is different. You barely have time to feel comfortable with one approach before you finish up that prac and move on to a completely different context. But this can be a real advantage for you. No two teaching contexts are the same anywhere, and you actually get to experience the importance of being flexible, responsive and adaptable—while making connections and developing strategies, skills and knowledges that can be adapted and fine-tuned, depending on the space, the place, the time and the child.

There can be vast differences between two classrooms situated side by side in one school, but a more traditional approach to prac will see one student teacher, in one classroom, with one teacher, for the duration—without the opportunity to recognise and learn about differences in pedagogical approaches and behaviours. At times, when you move from, say, childcare to kindergarten prac, you might find that some strategies that worked a treat in one prac context do not work in the next. This might be related to age/stage theories. It might also be due to other factors that come into play, such as traditions, folklore or 'the way it's always been done'. How will you know? And what will you learn?

For one thing, it is you who will make the connections. Just as the central person in Figure 7.1 is doing, you are carrying learnings and understandings from your previous prac to the next, and adapting and adjusting to fit the new. Elsewhere in this book, we make the point that prac is not the same as being a fully qualified teacher. One of the key differences is relationships. On prac, you will not have an opportunity to establish the same relationships with the children and their families that you will when you are their teacher. In addition, you will be managing a relationship with your supervising teacher, and other staff, that will be different again when you are a member of staff. Be aware of this. Do your best to establish appropriate and mutually respectful relationships in your position as a pre-service teacher. Think about what this relationship entails. Consider trust, respect, reciprocity, contributions, interactions, listening. The relationships of which you will be a part while on prac—and indeed elsewhere, including when you begin work—are all influenced, to varying degrees, by culture, ethics, politics and social dynamics.

Figure 7.1: You can make rhizomatic connections across the different prac settings

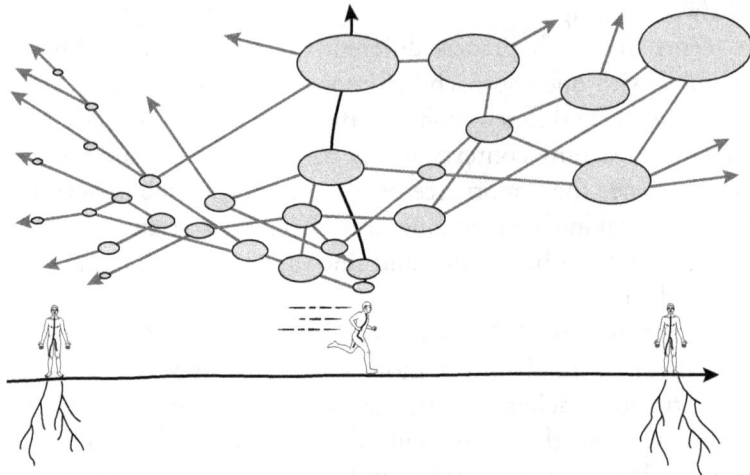

Source: Ngui (n.d.).

In conversation

My teacher on prac gave the kids stickers all the time—and they loved them. All the teacher needed to do was say that this was worth a sticker, and they would all sit up straight, and some kids would nearly burst trying so hard! I know you always tell us here at uni that stickers are not the way to go, but to be honest . . . they really work. I used them when I was on prac. It was the only way I could get everyone to listen to me. I don't really see what's so wrong, when something works like that! (Hassan, pre-service teacher, 2012)

Discuss:

• your response to the 'sticker' debate
• who would be the best person with whom Hassan could discuss this issue.

In Chapter 1, we painted a broad picture of what to expect on prac. Here, we expand in some detail, and take into account the ways in which some of the roles and expectations might vary between settings.

First, it is important to understand the degree of leverage and flexibility that might or might not be available to individuals and institutions.

Some of the conditions of prac are dictated by particular governance arrangements, authorising bodies, professional associations and government mandates—needless to say, for you on prac and as an individual beginning work in the field, these are non-negotiable. In the case of early childhood degrees, sometimes more than one set of mandated requirements and quality controls will apply:

> The program's professional experience would be expected to include at least 80 days' professional experience for undergraduate courses with children aged [from] birth to two, two to five and over five years old. This must include a minimum of 10 days' professional experience with children aged [from] birth to two. (ACECQA, 2013)

> The professional experience component of each program must include no fewer than 80 days of well-structured, supervised and assessed teaching practice in schools in undergraduate and double-degree teacher education programs and no fewer than 60 days in graduate entry programs. (Education Services Australia, 2011b, p. 14)

The combination of these two requirements usually means that early childhood pre-service teachers will have a minimum of 90 days' prac.

What am I supposed to be doing?

In Chapter 1, we used a triangular diagram to show the support relationships available to you while on prac, and briefly explained how each person in the triad has a particular part to play. Here, we represent this diagram (Figure 7.2), because it is important for the each person's relationships to be clear. If you are to make prac your learning experience, and take ownership of its progress and your success, then it is essential that you understand the relationships between all the support people, and the different relationships you will be managing. Keep this triad in mind as you go through the details below. In an attempt to try to capture the specifics of what is expected of you, we have listed roles and responsibilities, described some behaviours, and foreshadowed what you can expect of others across the varying settings and contexts.

One of the most difficult transitions for many people is to begin to see themselves as the teacher and not as subject to the teacher. Memories of our own schooling are often partial or incomplete (Britzman, 1991), but they stay with us, and shape how we see ourselves. Now, on prac, is the time to step up and be accountable, act and think and work like a teacher, and start to become the teacher you want to be. There is a lot to think about!

Figure 7.2: Triad for prac

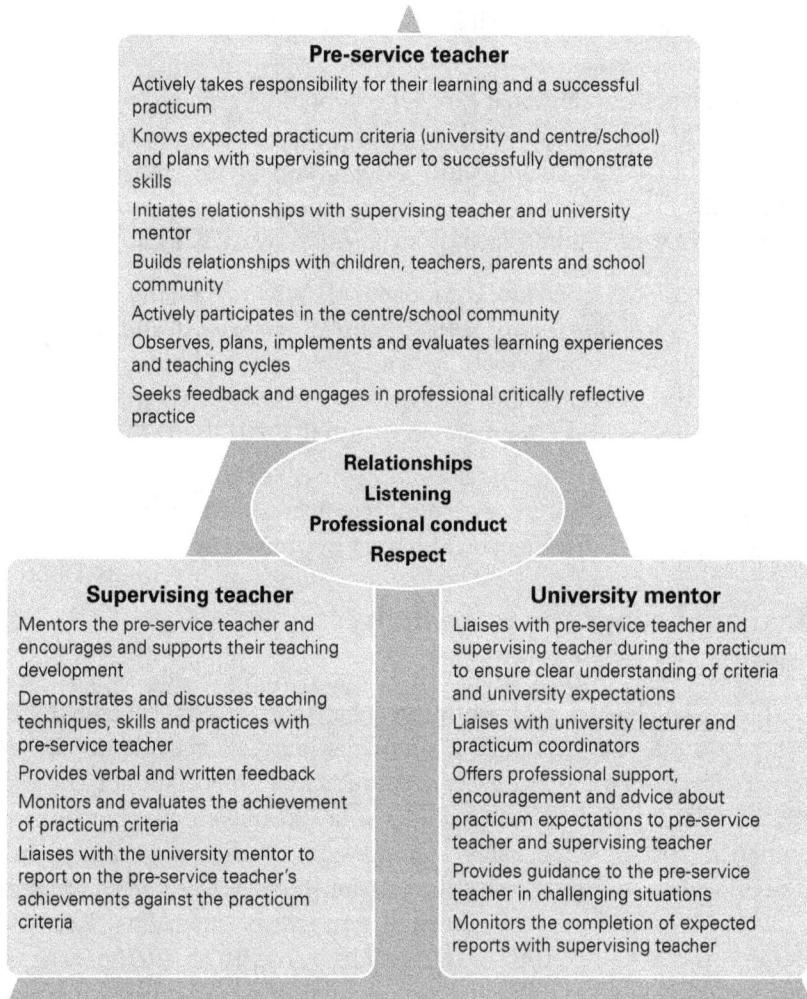

Pre-service teacher

Actively takes responsibility for their learning and a successful practicum

Knows expected practicum criteria (university and centre/school) and plans with supervising teacher to successfully demonstrate skills

Initiates relationships with supervising teacher and university mentor

Builds relationships with children, teachers, parents and school community

Actively participates in the centre/school community

Observes, plans, implements and evaluates learning experiences and teaching cycles

Seeks feedback and engages in professional critically reflective practice

Relationships
Listening
Professional conduct
Respect

Supervising teacher

Mentors the pre-service teacher and encourages and supports their teaching development

Demonstrates and discusses teaching techniques, skills and practices with pre-service teacher

Provides verbal and written feedback

Monitors and evaluates the achievement of practicum criteria

Liaises with the university mentor to report on the pre-service teacher's achievements against the practicum criteria

University mentor

Liaises with pre-service teacher and supervising teacher during the practicum to ensure clear understanding of criteria and university expectations

Liaises with university lecturer and practicum coordinators

Offers professional support, encouragement and advice about practicum expectations to pre-service teacher and supervising teacher

Provides guidance to the pre-service teacher in challenging situations

Monitors the completion of expected reports with supervising teacher

The pre-service teacher

Study each of the points below, and make notes for yourself on how you will enact each of them. Keep this list handy and refer to it regularly to track yourself and your performance.

Relationships

- Initiates and maintains relationships with supervising teacher and university mentor.
- Builds relationships with children, teachers, parents and school community.
- Actively participates in the centre/school community.

Responsibilities

- Actively takes responsibility for their own learning and a successful prac.
- Understands the graduate and professional standards, and knows how the prac criteria relate to these.
- Understands the expected assessment (university and centre/school) specific to the current prac, and plans with the supervising teacher to successfully demonstrate the required skills.
- Maintains confidentiality and engages in ethical and professional conduct at all times.
- Works with the supervising teacher to identify own teaching strengths and challenges.
- Seeks feedback and engages in professional critically reflective practice.
- Monitors own progress against the expected criteria, and engages in regular self-assessment and reflection.
- Provides regular written documentation to the supervising teacher. Supervising teachers usually like to see pre-service teachers' documentation on a daily basis, generally at the start of each day. You will need to be quite proactive in this regard, particularly if the supervising teacher is not in your room (this is the case for most students on baby/toddler pracs). It is *not* okay for no one to look at your folder.
- Communicates. Effective communication principles often require you to be proactive, and sometimes to draw on your resilience.
- Seeks out and understands the centre/school policies including practices and protocols for:
  - evacuation
  - suspected child protection issues
  - children's illness and communicable diseases
  - behaviour management
  - workplace health and safety
  - documenting children's learning
  - photographs of children.

Roles

- Pre-service teachers generally work under the direction of the supervising teacher to support children's learning and implement learning experiences.
- In a school setting, this might mean working directly alongside the supervising teacher in the same room.
- In prior-to-school settings (particularly long day care), this might mean working with other educators and in a different room from your supervising teacher.
- Observe, plan, implement and evaluate learning experiences and teaching cycles as appropriate.
- Be a teacher as researcher. Research how the supervising teacher teaches as well as engaging in research about your own teaching. How does your supervising teacher:
  - get children's attention
  - manage disruptive behaviour
  - start a learning experience/lesson
  - finish a learning experience/lesson
  - keep children on task
  - ask children questions
  - move from one activity to the next
  - check in with what children need
  - engage with parents
  - plan, assess and evaluate.
- What feedback will you ask for about your teaching?
- Depending on your university schedule, you might gradually work towards implementing more learning experiences as your prac progresses, to the point where you manage, plan, implement and evaluate most, or all, of the activities for the day.
- In school settings, this might mean being the 'teacher' for the day or for several days, managing all of the teaching and program requirements of the students.
- In prior-to-school settings, it might mean coordinating the shared planning and learning experiences of the day and collaboratively working alongside other staff to implement the daily program.
- Engage in all facets of teaching, including attendance at before- or after-school meetings and participate in bus duty, playground duty and other nominated duties.
- At times, pre-service teachers are asked to engage in roles outside the classroom. For example, you might be asked to join another class or group for an excursion; you might be asked to be a coordinator of events at a sports

day; you might be asked to join a staff team for a charity fun run; or you may be invited to help out with a stall on fete day.

Working with other teachers

Some relationships are easier to manage than others, and knowing yourself can help—especially when things are not going so smoothly. Whom do you work well with? Whom do you find challenging? What qualities do people bring to the relationship? You may need to recognise other people's strengths, value the ways in which they might be different from you, and move beyond your familiar ways of being. Sometimes this is not about you!

Think about how you might feel if someone that you didn't know came into your teaching space and starting reorganising the room and the children's program of learning.

- What might be the advantages?
- What might cause frustration?
- What could you do as a pre-service teacher to make this work successfully for teachers and children?

Working with other prac students

Often, there are a number of prac students at the one centre or school at the same time. During your prac, you might meet other pre-service teachers from different universities or different degrees. You might also meet students from the technical and further education (TAFE) sector or other organisations undertaking a prac, or high school students doing work experience. It is important that you conduct yourself professionally at all times and during all interactions with other pre-service teachers and prac students. While you are on prac, you are also representing your university. Sharing learning insights across different courses and experiences can be mutually beneficial, and can also provide great opportunities for working collaboratively with others.

Working in paired placements

Sometimes, pre-service teachers will be placed as a pair in a prac setting, and this calls for some application of the concepts underpinning teamwork and working in pairs, providing an attitudinal framework for collaboration.

It is hoped that, through this experience, the pre-service teachers will be well prepared to work in teams in their future teaching careers. Paired pracs have proven to be successful when the two students:

Taking it further

For more on paired placements see Walsh and Elmslie, Practicum pairs: An alternative for first field experience in early childhood teacher education (2005).

- share observations of children and ideas for follow-up experiences
- assist each other with the management of transitions, and the conduct of children's on-task learning experiences
- take turns in leading whole-class learning experiences with the children and playing a support role
- divide the whole group of children into two or more small groups for group activities
- take responsibility for different aspects of the program or groups of children
- engage in self and peer evaluation—evaluate, reflect upon and discuss their own work, and give constructive feedback about the work of their partner.

Activity 7.1

Try these questions, and then change the context and consider them again:

- What makes a good early childhood educator when working in the context where children are aged from birth to 3 years?
- What will this look like in practice?
- Will this involve different traits and skills from working in other contexts?
- What is your goal for this prac?

Activity 7.2

Try these questions, then change the context and reconsider them:

- How can you work on communication with children aged from birth to 3 years?
- What do you think will work?
- What will you plan to do?
- What new ideas will you try? How? When?

Document a plan, and add it to your portfolio.

Activity 7.3

Think of the different positions in early childhood. Build up a diagram, context by context, and include the positions within each (e.g. teacher aide, head of curriculum in primary school; teacher, director in child care). Now do some online research to find out the qualification requirements for each position. Look at Australia, and then other countries.

In conversation

I have had a bit of a slow start this field experience as I am still trying to get my head around this new way of thinking and documenting. But I am realising I need to just have a go and my work will evolve and improve as I go. (Randal, third-year pre-service teacher, 2010)

I think this field experience is going to be a great learning experience! I previously completed my Diploma of Children's Services, but the expectations of this field experience go far beyond what was expected when I completing my diploma, so I feel this prac will be a huge learning curve. (Maryann, third-year pre-service teacher, 2010)

So I have changed my way of thinking. Which I honestly thought wouldn't happen. This prac is not a waste of time. All my pracs have taught me valuable skills, and this prac has probably taught me the deepest, in terms of the essence of teaching. Having just written that, I remember the lecturer saying that to us back in week four or five. Reflecting can be so irritating at times, as it suddenly shows you things you've known all along, but didn't realise. (Xin, third-year pre-service teacher, 2010)

A checklist for your professional performance and relationships

According to Stonehouse and Duffie (2001), the essence of being a true professional is continually asking questions (like those suggested above), being confident and courageous enough to engage with what is difficult, challenging, frightening, worrying or unknown, and being wise enough to affirm and celebrate one's own success and achievements and those of others.

Supervising teacher

You might like to share this list with your supervising teacher. Check whether they would like you to make a copy. Often, supervising teachers mentor students from a number of different institutions, and it is easy for them to lose track of the information provided by each. If you can help distil this information for them, and make it easy for them to share your understanding of expectations, this is a good proactive strategy for improving communication and your relationship. You could copy this list and use it as the basis for your discussion at one of your 'On track on prac' sessions.

Relationships

- Works in partnership with the university and the centre/school to provide a supportive prac experience.
- Establishes a strong working relationship with the pre-service teacher.
- Liaises with the university generally via the liaison academic, or in some cases the prac coordinator.
- Liaises with the centre/school prac coordinator and other prac site-based staff, such as the educational leader and director (prior-to-school settings) and the principal and early years coordinator (school settings).

Responsibilities

- Establishes clear expectations for the pre-service teacher in accordance with the centre/school practices and the university criteria requirements.
- Negotiates times for meeting with the pre-service teacher to provide feedback on teaching practices as well as progress against the expected criteria.
- Monitors and evaluates the achievement of prac criteria according to stage of teacher education program.
- Provides regular ongoing verbal and written feedback to the pre-service teacher.
- Makes fair judgements about the pre-service teacher's performance. This is determined against the expected criteria and based on evidence.
- Advises the pre-service teacher if they are not meeting the expected requirements and discusses strategies with the pre-service teacher to improve performance.
- Liaises with the university mentor to report on the pre-service teacher's achievements against the prac criteria.

• Advises the university mentor immediately of any issues or concerns about the pre-service teacher's performance and progression against the criteria.

Roles

• Mentors the pre-service teacher and encourages and supports their teaching development.
• Models what the teaching standards look like in practice in own teaching.
• Demonstrates and discusses teaching techniques, skills and practices with the pre-service teacher.
• Discusses own professional engagement activities, experiences and the complexities of teaching.
• Discusses centre/school policy and protocols, and assists the pre-service teacher to access these documents and comply with expected practices.
• Provides ongoing constructive feedback to the pre-service teacher to encourage their teaching development. Uses examples, suggestions, reflections and strategies to support further improvement.

Other key relationships/personnel

Prior-to-school settings

Director

This person has the responsibility of overseeing the general operations of the early childhood centre. Pre-service teachers will liaise with the director in terms of centre orientation, policies, protocols and practices. They may or may not be the qualified early childhood teacher in the centre.

Educational leader

Early childhood centres are required to appoint an educational leader to 'guide other educators in their planning and reflection, and mentor colleagues in their implementation practices' (ACECQA, 2014b, p. 85). Pre-service teachers might liaise with the educational leader to discuss centre programming practices. This person may or may not be the director or qualified early childhood teacher in the centre.

Educators

Early childhood practitioners who work directly with children in early childhood settings (DEEWR, 2009, p. 5). Historically in many ECEC centres, educators have also been referred to as group leaders, room leaders and assistants.

School settings

Site or prac coordinator

Site coordinators have the role of coordinating the management of pre-service teachers during their prac. The site coordinator will often conduct an orientation to the school, its policies and practices with groups of pre-service teachers. Sometimes site coordinators engage in weekly group mentoring sessions with pre-service teachers.

Principal

Principals and assistant principals sometimes teach, but generally a large part of their role relates to the day-to-day management and leadership of the school. Sometimes principals engage in group mentoring sessions with pre-service teachers.

Early years coordinator

In larger schools, there may be one teacher who is the nominated early years coordinator. These coordinators organise meetings to plan curriculum across the early years classes, consider new policy and research developments, and collaboratively work with other early years teachers to organise early years networks and events. Sometimes early years coordinators engage in group mentoring sessions with pre-service teachers.

Prac resources

Supervising teachers can access modules that support them to be successful practicum mentors. These are available through the AITSL website (<www.aitsl.edu.au>). The modules align closely with the *National Professional Standards for Teachers* and focus on:

- building partnerships
- analysing teaching practice
- making fair judgements based on evidence
- understanding the graduate standards.

The modules are also accessible to pre-service teachers and are a useful resource. Your familiarity with these can help further your understanding of the role of the supervising teacher. You will also have a good idea of what might be expected of your performance as a pre-service teacher, particularly in primary school settings.

Resources such as videos, feedback templates and examples of pre-service teachers' work are also available on the site. Although these resources focus particularly on primary school settings, modifications and adaptations can be made to tailor them for prior-to-school settings.

Activity 7.4

Consider:
- what type of early childhood pre-service teacher you would like to have if you were the supervising teacher
- what would frustrate you
- what you would enjoy
- what would make the experience rewarding.

Discuss with other students. Discuss for each context.

Below are some extracts from students' emails to their university mentor (reproduced with permission). We have included them as indicators of how to document and make learning visible to others. They are also examples of good communication, reflection and learning.

In conversation

The staff at the centre are lovely and made me feel very welcome. The indoor and outdoor areas are very open and spacious. Throughout the day the children are able to make their own decisions regarding where they would like to play, and are not restricted to indoor or outdoor time. Our site coordinator shared with us some of their philosophies at the centre and brushed over a few theorists who have a huge influence on their beliefs and practices. (Abbie, 2013)

The experiences I have planned all stem from sensory perception. It started with a few observations which I then interpreted, made links to curriculum and theory, developed possibilities and then brainstormed follow up experiences. This concept has been growing ever since. The staff I am working with in the nursery room have really embraced this focus of mine. They have helped me to redesign the room and create wonderful displays. (Lauren, 2012)

When we were on our first prac, our host teacher told me I have to become okay with silence. At the time, I thought she was crazy. I'm a naturally loud person, but that doesn't mean I'm not okay with silence. This prac has made that comment make complete sense.

I'm not constantly talking or interacting with the children. At first I felt like I wasn't teaching and that this was a waste of my time. However, I now understand, after researching, reflecting, talking to others and the on-campus day.

Teaching isn't about telling the children what to do, or talking all the time. Sometimes it is about moving back and observing, listening, and using those rarely used (for me anyway) low-interaction strategies. Some may think this is a lazy way of teaching. I've come to believe that this, paired with mediating and explicit strategies, is what makes the great teachers. This is also what my first host teacher meant (I believe) about the silence. (Cat, 2013)

Activity 7.5

What expectations do you have of a supervising teacher? What could they do to help your teaching? What could you do to help them? Discuss with other students. Discuss for different contexts.

How will you build a relationship with your supervising teacher if they are not working beside you in the same room? What will be different? What might be the advantages of this arrangement? What might be the disadvantages? (*Note:* This situation will only arise in a long day care setting. In a school setting, you are not legally permitted to be alone, unsupervised with a group of children.) Why do you think this difference exists? Discuss.

University mentor

Relationships

- Liaises with pre-service teacher during the prac to ensure clear understanding of criteria and university expectations. Communication might include email and/or phone contact.
- Liaises with the supervising teacher and centre/school prac coordinator during the prac to ensure clear understanding of the criteria and university expectations.
- Liaises with university prac coordinator.

Responsibilities

- Monitors the completion of expected reports with the supervising teacher. This will include a final report and perhaps an interim report.
- Provides progress updates to the university prac coordinator and alerts them to any issues or concerns about the pre-service teacher's performance.
- May visit the pre-service teacher and the supervising teacher at the prac site, particularly if issues or concerns have been raised. This will be organised via the university prac coordinator.

Roles

- Offers professional support, encouragement and advice about prac expectations to the pre-service teacher and supervising teacher.
- Provides guidance to the pre-service teacher in challenging situations.
- Fosters professional partnerships between universities and centres/schools.

In conversation

At first I couldn't understand the purpose of having a university mentor during prac, especially someone I had never met face to face. I thought I could just email my lecturer if things weren't going right. Eventually I responded to my university mentor emails and found out that she was really very helpful. She was interested in what I was doing and gave me some good ideas to help deepen my reflections. (Matt, 2013)

The more feedback I get from others, the clearer the goals of my observations, plans and reflections are becoming—my two focuses for this prac are the environment and relationships. (Beck, 2012)

My planning is starting to make sense to me. Looking back on my previous reflections, I was so unfocused and my disappointment clouded my thinking. This is possibly because I felt, after my last prac, that I had a grasp on teaching, and this prac has just completely turned me on my head, and has been a huge challenge. It has definitely changed the way I view teaching. The way I plan is still similar; however, learning experiences for babies are so different to how I would plan lessons for Grade Ones! (Josie, 2012)

Other key university personnel

Unit coordinator

There is often one university lecturer who:
- liaises with other lecturers
- liaises with the course coordinator
- liaises with the head of school, department or faculty.

Field placement officer

- Generally responsible for finding prac placements and exchanging contractual agreements with supervising teachers.
- May ask students to nominate preferred geographical locations for undertaking prac.

Did you know?

A *placement officer or field experience officer* is the person at the university field experience sector who manages your preferences for placements, notifies you of your placement, and focuses on ensuring you have the information required in order to comply with key field experience requirements and adhering to policies and expectations.

Looking after yourself on prac

Consider:
- How will you relax?
- How will you let go?
- How will you keep on top of your workload?
- How will you debrief?
- How will you celebrate?

Giving and receiving feedback

In Chapter 3, we examined the importance of feedback, and you might like to revisit that chapter for more detail about this. It will be part of your ongoing professional life to both give feedback, as part of good teaching, and to receive feedback, as part of your professional development and growth.

Feedback is such an important component of prac that we are revisiting it here, with some very brief and concise points for you to review and remember. In particular, how you learn to receive feedback, and what you do in response to feedback, will be crucial to the kind of teacher you become. Receiving negative feedback is not easy for anybody, nor is giving negative feedback. Perhaps you won't always get it right, but use these experiences to practise and get better at it. Feedback is an essential component of effective teaching and learning.

Receiving feedback

As long as feedback is given in a non-judgemental and appropriate way, it provides valuable information for learning and for our continued development.

Dealing with constructive and positive feedback

Constructive feedback is critical for self-development and growth. Here are some points to bear in mind when you receive feedback:

- Constructive feedback is good and can be learned from. Welcome it!
- Accept feedback of any sort for what it is: information.
- Evaluate the feedback before responding.
- Make your own choice about what you intend to do with the information.

Dealing with negative feedback

Whether you are giving or receiving feedback, it is useful to bear the DAWA model (Table 7.1) in mind when it comes to people who receive negative feedback.

Taking it further

For more on giving and receiving feedback, see life coaching sites, such as <www.lifecoachingstudio.com/acom14.htm>.

Table 7.1: The DAWA Model

Denial	When people first receive feedback, they have a tendency to deny it. Please avoid immediate defensiveness—arguing, denying and justifying. This just gets in the way of your appreciation of the information you are being given.
Anger	After the denial stage comes anger. So you've been told that your work is not as good as it ought to be. You've said, 'It's as good as always', so you are denying it, then you become angry as it stews in your mind and body. The immediate reaction is to fume.
Withdrawal	After the anger has calmed down, the person has had time to reflect and ponder on the feedback. 'Well, I have been making more mistakes than normal.' This is when time is taken out to mull over the feedback and think about what it actually means.
Acceptance	The final part of this model is accepting the feedback, assessing its value and the consequences of ignoring it or using it: 'I *have* been making mistakes.'

Giving feedback

Providing feedback is always tough, but if it is constructive, you not only get the message across, but can also build a more cohesive and capable team as a result. In some prac situations, you will be working with other prac students, teaching assistants, teacher aides and administration staff. Being a good team member calls for open communication and honest feedback. Before providing feedback to others, be clear about your role and each person's responsibilities. It would be highly unlikely that you would be required to provide feedback to your supervising teacher, for instance. If it becomes necessary for you to provide feedback to your colleagues, there are a number of things to consider.

Choose correct timing for feedback

Praise is most effective when it is given as soon as possible after the behaviour has occurred, as it will help to reinforce a correct behaviour. When an incorrect behaviour is not corrected with feedback, your colleague may incorporate it into their interactions unknowingly. Provide feedback immediately or the next time the incorrect behaviour occurs.

Focus on specifics

When you focus on a specific correct or incorrect behaviour, you remove the feedback from the sphere of personality differences, and the other person will be more willing and able to change. For example, when providing corrective feedback:

- Do say: 'When you were talking to [child], I noticed that you forgot to use her name.'
- Don't say: 'You are not building rapport with the children.'

  When providing praise:

- Do say: 'When you spoke to X, I noticed that you used really good open and closed questioning techniques.'
- Don't say: 'You communicated well there.'

Limit feedback to a few important points

Restrict your feedback to one or two important points so that you do not overwhelm the other person with too much to consider. Just focus on the critical areas of improvement and help the other person address them one at a time.

Provide more praise than corrective feedback

When you give corrective feedback (which is often perceived as negative), remember to point out corrective behaviours first. This is as important as pointing out mistakes and areas that need improvement.

Positive reinforcement is one of the strongest factors in bringing about change, so always end the conversation on a positive note.

Some people refer to using the 'sandwich' technique here. When you have a 'negative' point to make, begin by referring to the strengths, and then sandwich the negative between the positives. End with a positive.

Give praise for expected performance

Praising anyone who meets established standards is as important as praising the exceptional performer.

Develop action plans

Work together to identify the desired performance or result and how/when it can be achieved.

Techniques for giving feedback

- *Use open-ended questions.* Start sentences with What? How? Who? Avoid closed questions starting with Tell me? Did you? Have you?
- *Reflect back.* Put what the other person has said into your own words and reflect it back.
- *Maintain silence.* Always give the other person time to think through their reply to a challenging answer.
- *Maintain eye contact and demonstrate an interest.*
- *Summarise.* The output of the meeting and action plan should be summarised to ensure that you have heard correctly and understood from the other person's perspective.
- *Conclude the discussion and focus on planning for the future.* Example: 'The three major issues you raised were . . .', ' To summarise then . . .'
- *Be sensitive.* Being sensitive to the needs of the person is important, as they may initially reject the feedback.
- *Initiate action and offer ideas.* Offer ideas without forcing your personal opinion.

Making a good impression

Finally, in this chapter of lists for quick reference, we also stress again the importance of first impressions, and the importance of your preparedness for the workplace. In Chapter 3, we discussed this in more detail, but here we provide a short, sharp reminder as you prepare to spend time in the workplace for your immediately, and are then very difficult to change.

It takes between thirty seconds and two minutes to form a first impression, so how you begin your first day at your workplace is important.

If you only do five things, when it comes to giving and receiving feedback:
1. Be well prepared.
2. Know what you want to say.
3. Practise your technique beforehand.
4. Check out your performance.
5. Be prepared to hear negative feedback.

First impressions

- Create a positive first impression and develop the attitude and skills to maintain it.
- First impressions are formed is very important.

The workplace is different

It is quite common to experience some form of disappointment with the workplace. The main reason for this is a difference between what you anticipated and what you really experience. This can result in a dip in morale. The workplace operates differently from university, so it is important to let go of the attitudes and expectations of university life when entering the workforce (see Chapter 3 for more on this).

Further reading

Hill, L.T., Stremmel, A.J. & Fu, V.R. (2005). *Teaching as Inquiry: Rethinking curriculum in early childhood education*. Boston, Pearson/Allyn & Bacon.

Nicol, D.J. & Macfarlane-Dick, D. (2006). Formative assessment and self-regulated learning: A model and seven principles of good feedback practice. *Studies in Higher Education*, 31(2): 199–218.

Sorin, R. (2006). Practice what you preach: Negotiated curriculum in early childhood teacher education. In *Proceedings of the 2006 Australian Teacher Education National Conference*, pp. 377–84. From Making Teaching Public: Reforms in teacher education, 5–8 July 2006, Fremantle.

Walsh, K. & Elmslie, L. (2005). Practicum pairs: An alternative for first field experience in early childhood teacher education. *Asia-Pacific Journal of Teacher Education*, 33(1): 5–21.

8

Your teaching toolkit: Never-fail strategies, tips and reminders

In this chapter you will find:

- a collection of 'never-fail' teaching strategies
- some essentials of behaviour management
- ways to document students' learning
- information on child protection: reporting suspected abuse and neglect
- a checklist for your portfolio.

Strategies and skills

A teacher can be an expert with discipline and curriculum knowledge, but unless they can first manage, engage, challenge, assess and encourage their students, they will not optimise the children's chances for learning and success. When pre-service teachers begin their early prac placements, it is not uncommon for them to struggle with enacting cutting-edge pedagogies if 'behaviour-management' issues, for example, get in the way.

Experienced teachers draw on a number of 'tricks of the trade' that have become so automatic that they hardly know how to articulate them.

If pre-service teachers are equipped with a toolkit of 'never-fail' strategies to draw on across a range of situations, they stand more chance of success with their earliest teaching experiences. The rhizomatic model favoured in this book places issues like management and leadership in a more complex context, while recognising that some 'tricks of the trade' work like a charm for teachers throughout their careers.

In this chapter, we have included some of our own 'tried and true' strategies for engaging children, and establishing an environment in which mutual relationships with the children can be begun. This way, you are able to use your prac time for testing theories and practising skills, techniques and pedagogies.

As you progress through your coursework, and through your series of pracs, we suggest that you add to this toolbox of skills and strategies. This will be a lifelong exercise, and the earlier you begin the better. You can 'collect' these tools by watching your supervising teacher, watching other teachers, reading, reflecting and documenting. Like any good set of tools, you will need to know them well, and you will need to be able to select the right tool for the right task.

Your toolkit might include jottings and examples of diverse strategies, such as planning ideas, use of voice, behaviour-management techniques and design ideas. In this chapter, we do not go into the theoretical underpinnings, but as you build your repertoire, it will be important that you critique, reflect and think carefully about the strategy and whether it fits with your principles of what makes a good teacher. For example, because a strategy 'works' at correcting children's behaviour, this might not be the only criterion for using it. Forty years ago, the use of the cane was considered a 'proper' strategy for managing children, and teachers who used the cane were considered 'good' teachers. Consider a framework for your selection of strategies, and test them against your beliefs about children, relationships and pedagogies:

- What worked for you on prac? What didn't work? Why? Why not?
- What does your teacher use? Is it effective? Will you do this? Why/why not? How are you evaluating?

Never-fail ideas, strategies and resources

Teaching doesn't always go to plan. Sometimes the most carefully prepared lessons and resources can't account for a loss of electricity, a reshuffling of classrooms and children, or the rescheduling of the day due to unexpected events. Good teachers can take this in their stride and always have ready-made back-up plans that they can enact at a moment's notice. The best ideas are open-ended and flexible so that they can be used across all teaching contexts and easily adapted to the ages, numbers and needs of a diverse range of children.

As a pre-service teacher, it is wise for you to start preparing a 'bag of tricks' for when you need it. The following list is a good starting point for you to prepare before you start prac and then build upon during your teaching years. Including at least one of each of the following ideas will help to get you started. To accompany these ideas, brainstorm a list of interesting learning activities that will engage the children with whom you are working.

- *Books and stories.* Carefully select five books that are written in different styles (e.g. poetry, picture book, novel), and that focus on different topics and different age levels. Keep recordings of a selection of short stories by great storytellers on your mobile phone or similar device. Books are engaging in themselves, but can also be a great stimulus for lots of extension activities such as children's own story-making, writing, drawing and performance.
- *A mystery box or bag.* Most children love a mystery. An interesting box or bag can instantly engage their interest. Have a selection of objects ready to put into your bag/box. Items such as a beautiful feather, shell or stone leave room for lots of ideas and activities. For example, discuss where it is from, write a letter to the owner, develop a story about the item, discuss it qualities and then draw or paint the item.
- *A deck of cards.* Cards can be used for anything from chance and data activities to grouping games.
- *A set of postcards.* Postcards collected from galleries, museums, cafés or holiday trips can be great discussion-starters that lead into engaging activities such as drawing, storytelling, dancing, painting, sorting, classifying and imagining.
- *An interesting or unusual item.* Antique shops, back sheds, gardens and kitchen drawers are great places to find interesting items. An eggbeater can become a character in a play, the source of a musical rhythm for a rap song or an item left behind by a mystery visitor.
- *Games.* Sometimes it's good to get outside and move with the children. Learn a set of simple games that don't need any equipment or only require a ball or a marker, and keep these in your bag of tricks.
- *Music and songs.* Young children in particular like rhymes and songs. Get to know a few simple songs and traditional nursery rhymes, as well as some songs in languages other than English, and from countries and

cultures other than Australia. Have some recordings of different music on your mobile phone or on a device. The music collection should include different rhythms, beats, sounds, eras, histories, cultures, voices and instruments. A great piece of music can be used as a movement activity for very young children or the basis of a rap song for older children to develop themselves.

- *Something of yourself.* Each of us has something (or many things) that make us unique, and if you share your skills, talents, interests and passions, children will become interested in you—they will see you as special. It may be that you are a great cook, an accomplished musician, a gymnast, love dogs or enjoy gardening. By sharing your passions, you will allow children to connect with you and get to know you.

In conversation

I was quite shy and dreading my final prac with prep (5-year-olds). While I had been able to 'bluff' my way through my other pracs, staying in the background as much as I could—observing and looking on—on this prac I was required to be in charge from pretty much day one—and for six weeks! Gradually I relaxed a little and allowed the children, parents and other teachers to get to know me. It wasn't until my last week of prac, after being at the school for over a month, that I brought my cello in and played for the children. Having completed my AMUS exams, I was an accomplished cellist. To my surprise, the children loved my music, and I subsequently created a project with the children about the cello and my music. The music was a powerful vehicle through which I was able to make connections with children and forge deeper relationships. I went from being shy and unsure to attaining a new sense of confidence—just through bringing a little of myself to the classroom. (Helena, pre-service teacher, 2011)

Collect good ideas when you are on prac

Relief/substitute teachers often have a mobile set of resources and ideas that they carry with them. Taking the time to exchange ideas with a relief teacher and watch them at work with a new group of children can be very insightful.

It is important to remember that resources are not neutral, and everything we do and say as a teacher has the potential to teach children—about themselves, others, their worlds, their possibilities. Maureen Ah Sam (in Phillips, 2007) developed a checklist for resources, with a particular focus on their appropriateness when it comes to Indigenous students and knowledges. We share a reduced version below. All the points are important for you to consider when choosing resources, such as story books, artefacts, dolls, puzzles and artworks. The list is not a yes/no exercise, but rather prompts thoughtful selection, based on your standpoint and your pedagogical beliefs and attitudes.

Participation

- Is the author an Aboriginal or Torres Strait Islander person?

Endorsement

- Has the resource been endorsed by local, regional and/or state/territory Aboriginal Education Consultative Groups (AECG)?

Authenticity

- Does the resource rectify historical distortions and omissions?
- Does the resource deal with factual information or historical events—are the details accurate?
- Is the setting of the story authentic? Is the story fact or fiction? When is it set: in the past or present?
- If the setting is contemporary, does the author accurately describe the situations of Indigenous people in Australia and elsewhere today?
- Is the resource material up to date?
- Are illustrations/photographs portraying Aboriginal people and Torres Strait Islander peoples positively? Are they authentic and non-stereotypical?
- Are Aboriginal and Torres Strait Islander people portrayed as unique individuals, with their own thoughts, emotions and philosophies, or are individuals positioned as representatives of particular racial or cultural groups?
- Does the material over-generalise?

Balanced nature of presentation

- Is there equal representation of genders in the material?
- Does the material trivialise female roles in Aboriginal society?
- Does the resource ignore females altogether?
- Are stereotyping and racist connotations present?

- Does the resource exclude some readers by assuming a 'European' background?
- Does the resource emphasise the 'exotic' to the exclusion of other cultural aspects?
- Does the material use derogatory terms to describe Indigenous people's actions, customs and lifestyles?
- Does the resource trivialise Aboriginal and Torres Strait Islander technology?
- Does the resource assume all Aboriginal people and Torres Strait Islander peoples live in the past?
- Is the resource biased and/or does it distort issues?

Sensitive issues that need clarification

- Does the resource accurately portray the customs and values of the diverse cultures of Aboriginal groups?

Exclusion of content of secret or sacred nature

- Does the material show and/or talk about secret or sacred items of knowledge?
- Does the resource use the name/s of deceased persons?
- Have the appropriate 'protocols' been followed if displaying or showing resource materials that include images of deceased persons?

The above list refers specifically to matters of concern for Aboriginal and Torres Strait Islander peoples. In order to take into account considerations for other groups of people, it is not simply a matter of transferring the points in this list. Start to record your own list of other considerations as you understand them, and help develop pedagogies that are authentically inclusive, and designed with success for all children in mind.

'Behaviour management'

When relationships are formed over time, based on mutual respect and with teachers who are active listeners, then 'behaviour-management' problems hardly arise. When children are seen as competent and capable, this gaze shapes their actions. And when curriculum is designed for children who are recognised as social beings, individuals and members of groups, with their own unique cultural knowledges and experiences, then 'behaviour management' is hardly an issue. But when a new pre-service teacher enters the established routines, and does not have the time to build those relationships, children's 'behaviour' can become problematic—for a number of reasons. You will learn more about these matters elsewhere in your studies.

If you are to have a successful prac, you will need to eliminate the behaviour 'problems' as quickly as possible, so that you can get on with the work of practising skills and techniques, and building on your knowledge about young children, their care and their education. The best way to do this is to engage the children's interest:

- *Be organised.* Have your plans clear in your mind and prepare your resources in advance.
- *Build relationships.* Find out what the children you are working with are interested in. Make connections between their learning and their interests.
- *Make your expectations clear.* Children work well when they know what is expected, and even better when they are involved in setting up the framework for expectations collaboratively with you.
- *Be consistent.* Children are aware of equity and fairness, and a degree of predictability helps children to feel secure. Routines also help to establish a rhythm in the day.
- *Be interesting.* Ensure that the learning experiences you have planned are engaging.

In Chapter 7, Hassan learned one important point about prac: even with the best of intentions, you might try to follow your own standpoint and pedagogical beliefs and resist the teachers' practices, but the children have soundly established behaviours. It is not always in the children's best interests to disrupt such patterns, and in any case you will often fail if you try. Your observations of the teacher's behaviour-management strategies should be most instructive, and could form the beginning of a very rich conversation (see the 'On prac on track' sections at the end of this chapter for some conversation starters).

As we have pointed out a number of times now, prac is not the same as when you have your own group of children, and you have the time to establish relationships and understandings. The following list includes some 'tried and true' tips for establishing a workable situation while on prac. Later, you will elaborate and/or refine these skills, and tailor them more appropriately as you come to know the children. They will be useful from the start of your prac.

- If noise levels rise, lower your voice and adjust the volume. If you are loud, the children will be louder.
- Move around a lot. Talk with the children. Listen to them. Sit at their level. Be with them.

Taking it further

Which of these strategies does your supervising teacher use: competition, praise, smooth transitions, quality of teaching and learning, environment, time out, responsible thinking room, naughty chair, non-verbal, ignore, rewards?

- Whenever possible, use the positive not the negative. Describe what you want to see, not what you don't want to see—for example, say 'I really think that's great to see you playing together and sharing' rather than 'Don't argue over the blocks. You're not sharing.'
- Do your planning. Be prepared. Don't try to 'wing it'. If children have to wait while you gather resources, or think of what to do next, you will lose their attention.
- Always say hello and goodbye to each child. Even if they are not making eye contact with you, let them know you are there, and that you want to build a relationship with them, rather than just sit on the sidelines.
- Ignore some things. If you stop to correct every 'misdemeanour', you will lose the thread and this will be at the expense of most of the children who are following along with you. Pretend you don't see some things if they are inconsequential.
- Scope. Always be checking to see what everyone in the space is doing. If you position yourself in a corner, or with your back to the space, you are neglecting your responsibility. When you want to have one-on-one conversations with individual children, position yourself so you can still keep an eye on the entire space.

Time management

Interruptions are normal in early childhood care and education, and a good teacher is always flexible and adaptable, and able to make changes to their schedule at a moment's notice. At the same time, when you are on prac, you are likely to be given staged tasks, learning experiences or even 'lessons', and you and your teacher will agree on the timing. Often this will change too, but it is important, as you are learning to teach, that you get an idea of how long processes and experiences can take. In addition, the teacher's existing schedule is important for many reasons. Refer to the indicators on which you will be assessed for your prac, and it is highly likely that 'time management' features somewhere. There are a number of strategies and habits that prove useful for efficient and effective time management. These include:

- Be organised—prepare everything ahead of time, rehearse if you are doing something for the first time.
- Wear a watch and take note of key time markers, such as when your learning experience should begin and then end, the conclusion of a session, when the transition to lunch begins, when children need to move to another area.

- Have ideas planned for fast finishers or children who have a slower pace than others.

Documenting children's learning

Researching alongside children to find out more about their interests and what is important to them helps teachers to understand their learning preferences, and so better target their planning. Learning experiences will be more authentic and engaging if teachers have taken time to plan ideas around what they know about their learners. Taking time to observe and interact with children is an important part of the planning process.

There are many different facets of learning that can be observed with children of all ages, including babies and toddlers. Brainstorming lists of observation ideas before prac will make it easier to think about what to do when you get there. Observations can take various forms—from jottings and sketches to annotations and journalling. Experimentation will help you to work out the pros and cons of each type.

Ideas for understanding children's learning

- How do the children interact with each other?
- What strategies do the children use to engage each other and adults?
- How do the children communicate? Use language (verbal/non-verbal)?
- How are the children using their bodies?
- What are the children wondering about?
- What theories are the children constructing and testing? How are they challenging these?
- Where do the children spend their time? Why? How?
- How do the children manage conflict?
- What problem-solving/discovery strategies do you see?
- What kinds of feedback are the children seeking?
- How are the children making meaning?
- What relationships and connections are the children making?
- Should you review your documentation?

There are many different ways to document children's learning—from the more traditional anecdotal records and activity samples to the more contemporary forms of journalling, photographing, videoing and compiling portfolios. Teachers experiment with different ways of recording children's learning according to the purpose of the documentation and its audience. When making decisions about different documentation techniques, teachers are helped to review their practices by critiquing the documentation content, format and layout. This helps them to assess whether the forms of documentation are meeting the required purposes.

Questions for reviewing/critiquing documentation

- Is the documentation useful? How am I using this documentation?
- What theories am I using to interpret this documentation?
- Are there other theories that would be helpful for thinking about this documentation?
- What images of children are emerging from the documentation?
- Does the documentation frame children as deficit or competent? Would a different format offer a different lens?
- Is there a better way that I could document this aspect of learning?
- Whose ideas and actions have been documented?
- Whose ideas and actions are missing?
- Whose voices are heard?
- Whose voices are silenced?
- What are the main ideas that are emerging?
- What further questions do I have about children's thinking?
- What questions are being prompted by the documentation?

Assessment

Assessment is an integral component of teaching, and is much more than simply giving children tests. Integrating assessment strategies throughout your planned learning experiences will help you to understand children's knowledge and learning strategies. This helps you to develop and improve your teaching.

Consider integrating the following assessment strategies and then add your own:

- Ask questions.
- Brainstorm ideas on the board.
- Draw or construct ideas.
- Use photographs (with ethical clearance and consent).

Documenting your own learning

There will be a lot to take note of when you are on prac. Developing good documentation systems will help to keep you organised and save time in the long run. The following essentials will get you started:

- a diary for recording prac tasks and events

- a journal for professional reflections—some of these you will share with your supervising teacher and others you might keep private or share with your university mentor
- a 'prac folder' for organising and collating documentation of:
  - children's learning (observations, records, artefacts, ideas)
  - curriculum decisions such as the learning experience plans and evaluations that you develop
  - a teaching and learning portfolio for demonstrating that you are meeting your university criteria and requirements.

In 2012, pre-service teachers at one university were assessed on the teaching and learning portfolios they compiled while completing their pracs in primary schools. Below is a list compiled to include choices made by the students. They included:

- observations, including photos of classroom activity
- lesson plans, which showed understandings of curriculum, pedagogies, assessment, effective learning, learning through experience, young children and their behaviours and capacities, and assessment
- newsletters to which the pre-service teachers had contributed
- parental involvement: activities designed to build partnerships between children, their families, and the learning environment/institution; communication examples; back-to-school night—a night/afternoon when parents come to school to visit their children's classrooms and hear about the curriculum
- peer critique: feedback from peers during field experience
- evidence of teamwork
- a summary of how feedback from interim reports was used and actively and thoughtfully responded to
- bulletin board displays: creative displays showcasing children's work
- a case study: a series of observations focusing on one or two children that creates a holistic perspective of their experience in the classroom
- a child study: a series of reading and writing assessments about a child that, after analysis, provides information for planned daily instruction
- a classroom management plan: a plan designed by the supervising teacher and the pre-service teacher to support student learning
- community involvement: events and communications (e.g. volunteering at the school fete)
- conferencing with families: parent–teacher interviews
- curriculum plans: knowing the curriculum; connecting national, state and local standards to children's learning

- cycle of learning: two or three successive plans demonstrating ongoing links and development of learning
- field trip plans: making learning real and experiential for children
- integrating technology plans
- journal entries: reflective practice showing knowledge of content, child development, sociology, critical thinking and ability to reflect
- letters from students and parents
- reflections: using references to the literature, theorists, curriculum frameworks
- samples of student work: documenting the pre-service teacher's ability to link student learning to prior knowledge, to meet students' needs, to encourage critical thinking, problem-solving and active learning
- pre-service teacher demonstrating their ability to critique, analyse and reflect
- examples of recognising and catering for diversity
- self-evaluation: reflective practice describing and documenting own development during a particular timeframe
- teaching evaluations from mentors or supervisors
- classroom organisation strategies/floor plans
- anecdotal record: notes taken during classroom observations or while teaching that may pertain to children's learning and development
- assessments: any artefacts that measure children's performances would be considered assessment. Pre-service teacher explained whether they have assessed children's performance, diagnosed progress or used the assessment to modify instruction.
- attendance at 'management committee' (e.g. P&C, school council or board) meetings or other school or centre functions: professional development is important
- action plan: addressing how field experiences link together. What have you learned? Where to now?

Recommended resource list

More and more resources are available on the market, with claims of improving young children's learning, building capacities, linking with brain research, amusing and entertaining active minds and bodies, and helping to improve the future chances of all children. The task for the good teacher is not so much locating resources as learning how to select and discriminate between the large number of materials available. In addition, the good teacher will learn how to be economical and 'scrounge', recycle and reuse resources that are simple, accessible and, above all, aids to quality learning experiences.

Earlier in this chapter, we shared a list compiled by a colleague who focused specifically on resources that were connected with Indigenous knowledges. As you build on your own experiences, as well as continue to develop your philosophy, your pedagogical repertoires and your standpoint, you will use other criteria for choosing resources. Prac is a valuable time for you to observe resources that are in use in your setting, how the children use them and how the teacher has selected them, and to make informed judgements about their appropriateness and value. Begin your own list of resources, and add to it with every opportunity.

Resources can also include the proliferation of 'ready-made' curriculum resource materials or lesson planning guides that are equally available, either online, or in books.

Think about it

What might be the benefits of 'ready-made' curriculum kits, never-fail lesson plans and pre-prepared worksheets?
How might they support your teaching?
What might be the disadvantage of 'ready-made' curriculum resource materials or lesson planning guides?
How might they inhibit your teaching?

In conversation

You can feel very safe in a syllabus document and someone's framework of how to do teaching; you actually don't have to expose much about yourself at all. This prac exposes you more. You can't hide behind a syllabus document and it's in that exposure that perhaps some students don't like child care. (Ellen, pre-service teacher, after completion of a prac in a long day care centre)

Recommended professional library

Ask your supervising teachers which books they use to help support their teaching. Teachers accumulate a number of books, beginning with their initial teacher preparation studies, and over the years as they continue their professional development and build on their own experiences as teachers. A professional library is something that you will develop, and it will be populated with the books to which you return again and again, as well as new books that appear and appeal to your own particular interests and/or needs. You can begin to build your professional library as a pre-service teacher, and discriminate between the textbooks that are useful for you now, and those that will probably remain part of your frame of reference well into your career as a teacher.

Here is an example of one teacher's professional library (an eclectic mix that covers leadership, sustainability, curriculum, pedagogy, planning and play):

Arthur, L., Beecher, B., Death, E., Dockett, S. & Farmer, S. (2012). *Programming and Planning in Early Childhood Settings* (5th edn). Melbourne: Thomson.

Cologon, K. (ed.) (2014). *Inclusive Education in the Early Years: Right from the start*. Melbourne: Oxford University Press.

Davis, J.M. (ed.) (2014). *Young Children and the Environment: Early education for sustainability* (2nd edn). Melbourne: Cambridge University Press.

Fleer, M., Edwards, S., Hammer, M., Kennedy, A., Ridgway, A. et al. (eds) (2006). *Early Childhood Learning Communities: Sociocultural research in practice*. Sydney: Pearson Prentice Hall.

Grieshaber, S. & McArdle, F. (2010). *The Trouble with Play*. Maidenhead: Open University Press.

Hassed, C. (2008). *The Essence of Health: The seven pillars of wellbeing*. Sydney: Ebury Press.

Rinaldi, C. (2006). *In Dialogue with Reggio Emilia: Listening, researching and learning*. Abingdon: Routledge Falmer.

Tobin, J., Hsueh, Y. & Karasawa, M. (2009). *Preschool in Three Cultures Revisited: China, Japan and the United States*. Chicago: University of Chicago Press.

Waniganayake, M., Cheeseman, S., Fenech, M., Hadley, F. & Shepherd, W. (2012). *Leadership: Contexts and complexities in early childhood education*. Melbourne: Oxford University Press.

Child protection: Recognising and reporting suspected child abuse and neglect

Maltreatment affects children's learning, and teachers have a responsibility to recognise and report suspected child abuse and neglect. Drawing on the extensive research and work of Walsh and Mathews (2010a, 2010b), we stress that this is a key professional area, and training is not a one-off.

You will need to ensure engagement with continual training in order to keep abreast with key policy and legislative changes.

Recognising child abuse and neglect is complicated because the manifestations can be indistinguishable from other childhood maladies. Teachers must be able to process multiple sources of information about the abuse, the child and the child's family. They need to be able to interpret and assess indicators and warning signs. During your program of study, you will learn about child abuse and neglect, your role and responsibilities, and the necessary knowledge and understandings in this area.

As a student on prac, you may observe incidents that unsettle you—where you wonder whether what you see constitutes child abuse and neglect. If this occurs, it is important to know who to talk to, and where to go for support. Reporting child abuse and neglect can be an emotive issue for many reasons.

Practical support is available to pre-service teachers from:

- university mentors,
- the field experience unit coordinator
- your head of school.
- the university's counselling services.

The following points are made here as reminders for you before you begin prac. They draw on the work of Walsh and Mathews (2010a) and other researchers in this field.

Recognising

Knowledge or reasonable suspicion is needed to make a report. Reasonable suspicion can be based on:

- first-hand observations of harmful treatment of a child (more likely for friends, neighbours, family members)
- the child's condition
- what the child says
- what the parent/caregiver says (actual disclosure/gives accounts of injuries that are highly questionable)
- prior reports.

Observe and make written notes as soon as you start to have concerns (be as factual as possible).

Reporting

Teachers are among the most common sources of reports—more than any other professionals apart from police. Teachers have a duty to report, legally, professionally and ethically. The teacher's job is not to investigate, but to report knowledge and reasonable suspicions of significant harm. If their suspicion turns out not to have any foundation, they cannot be held liable for a report made in good faith.

Resources

The following resources may be helpful to pre-service teachers, university mentors and unit coordinators.

What is child abuse?

- Queensland Government, 'What is Child Abuse?', <www.communities.qld.gov.au/childsafety/protecting-children/what-is-child-abuse>.

Mandatory reporting of child abuse and neglect

- Requirements about who is mandated to report and what must be reported vary across the different states and territories of Australia. See <www3.aifs.gov.au/cfca/publications/mandatory-reporting-child-abuse-and-neglect>.

Australian Child Protection legislation

- *Child Protection Act 1999* (Qld), <www3.aifs.gov.au/cfca/publications/australian-child-protection-legislation>.

Information

- Reporting suspected child abuse (in Queensland): <www.communities.qld.gov.au/childsafety/protecting-children/reporting-child-abuse>.
- Reporting in other Australian states and territories: <www.aifs.gov.au/cfca/pubs/factsheets/a141787>.

Child protection services in Australia

- Australian Capital Territory—Office for Children, Youth and Family Support: <www.communityservices.act.gov.au/ocyfs/services/care_and_protection>.
- New South Wales—Family and Community Services: <www.community.nsw.gov.au/docs_menu/for_agencies_that_work_with_us/child_protection_services.html>.
- Northern Territory—Department of Children and Families: <http://childrenandfamilies.nt.gov.au/Child_Protection/index.aspx>.
- Queensland—Department of Communities, Child Safety and Disability Services: <www.communities.qld.gov.au/childsafety/protecting-children/reporting-child-abuse>.
- South Australia—Department for Education and Child Development: <www.families.sa.gov.au/default.asp?navgrp=366>.

- Tasmania—Department of Health and Human Services: <www.dhhs.tas.gov.au>.
- Victoria—Department of Human Services: <www.dhs.vic.gov.au/for-individuals/children,-families-and-young-people/child-protection>.
- Western Australia—Department for Child Protection and Family Support: <www.dcp.wa.gov.au/ChildProtection/Pages/ChildProtection.aspx>.

Resources for professionals

- National Child Protection Clearinghouse: <www.apo.org.au/national-child-protection-clearinghouse>.
- National Association for Prevention of Child Abuse and Neglect: <http://napcan.org.au/>.
- Act for Kids (formerly Abused Child Trust): <www.actforkids.com.au>.
- Childwise: <www.childwise.net>.
- Department of Communities, Child Safety Services (Qld): <www.childsafety.qld.gov.au>.
- Department of Education and Training (Qld): <http://education.qld.gov.au>.

Taking photographs while on prac

Using photographs and digital recordings to document children's learning

During prac, you are required to observe children and build understandings of their learning and development. In recent years, the use of digital cameras and videos has grown to provide a means of making learning visible. The inclusion of carefully considered images of children in context can be used as a tool to assist teachers to reflect on children's learning as well as their own pedagogy. The use of visual images in the documentation of children's learning may also assist teachers to review and communicate learning processes with children and families. Thus, formative and summative assessment techniques may incorporate photographs, digital, audio or video recordings. What is important here is who knows about these photographs, who has access to the photographs and the purposes for which they are intended.

Privacy and personal information

It is strongly encouraged that particular care is given to handling images and other personal information about children. It is important that the images only be used for the purpose for which they were taken or for a

Taking it further

For more on issues of child abuse and neglect, see Walsh and Mathews (2010a).

Pre-service teachers should discuss the use of visual images in the documentation of children's learning with the supervising teacher.

directly related purpose, and must not be disclosed to other third parties unless you have been given express permission. Under no circumstances should the photographs be posted on a public space such as the internet.

Parental/guardian consent

Before photographing children, you must obtain the informed and voluntary consent of the parent or guardian of the child. Digital images and recordings created during prac should only be used for the express purpose of assessing and reporting, for which consent has been obtained. The images cannot be shared or displayed in environments that are external to teaching contexts unless further parental or guardian consent has been obtained.

Extra care should be taken to ensure that the material is appropriate, managed professionally and ethically, and respectful of the rights of children and compliant with the laws governing the photographing and use of material involving children.

A consent letter should be used to obtain permission from a parent or guardian of a child to photograph them for the required purposes. Your letter can use a basic form like the sample in Figure 8.1.

Figure 8.1: Consent letter for photographing children

[University letterhead here]

I am a pre-service teacher completing the Bachelor of Education (Early Childhood) at XXX University. As a requirement of this course, I will be completing my field experience in the infant and toddler room/prep class/preschool/kindergarten/school on the following dates:

Teaching dates: (insert dates) _____

I am really looking forward to working with your child, the staff and families who are connected with this setting. During my time here I will be observing and working with the children to further develop my understanding of how children think, play and learn. As part of my teaching responsibilities, I will be taking photographs, recording observations and perhaps video- or audio-taping a variety of experiences in which the children are involved. I would also like to obtain some of the children's work samples—with the permission of the child and the classroom teacher.

This documentation will be used to plan meaningful and engaging follow-up learning experiences for the children, in consultation with the teacher. As part of my teacher education program requirements, I am expected to develop a professional teaching portfolio. I would like to be able to include a selection of these photographs and written documentation in my portfolio and I would appreciate your permission to use items that may include images of your child in them.

These photographs and observations are for the purpose of 'bringing to life' the documents I present in my portfolio. They would be used only for educational purposes associated with my teacher education program (e.g. for assessment) and for sharing my portfolio during employment interviews. Potential employers will not be permitted to make copies.

Please tick one of the two statements below, sign and return this document to me by _____. If you have any questions at all, please let me know.

☐ I have read and understood this letter, and give consent for my child to participate in written observation and/or to be photographed or video or audio recorded in this educational setting for the purposes outlined in this letter.

☐ I do not give consent for my child to participate in written observation and/or to be photographed or video or audio recorded in this educational setting for the purposes outlined in this letter.

Child's name: _____

Child's signature (if appropriate) _____

Parent/guardian's name: _____

Parent/guardian's signature: _____

Date: _____

With best wishes,

_____

What goes in my reflections?

Throughout your studies you will learn about the importance of being a reflective practitioner. Good teachers constantly reflect on what they do. Your reflections will depend on what you know, circumstances, situations, the children, expectations, your aims and goals, your beliefs, your curiosities, your creativity, your questions.

Below, we provide a framework that is built on the earlier work by Bain et.al. (1999) and more recent work by Ryan and Ryan (2013). We list a set of questions that might be applicable across a number of settings. They are designed to prompt reflection on your work. Another layer of reflection would result if you were to answer these questions in a number of different settings, and then you put your responses side by side. What are the similarities? What are the points of difference? Why do you think this might be so?

Consider a focus for your purposeful reflections. For instance, your focus could be:

- The classroom and broader environment (centre/school)
- The organisational structure (centre/school)
- How the different staff members work together
- How the parents and the wider community are connected
- How the different groupings (classes/age groups) are connected (in the centre/school)
- How learning is supported, extended and scaffolded for individual children, groups of children, all children.

When you are on prac, you might plan to deliberately focus on one of the following matters:

- What do you currently do to create a learning environment that enhances children's learning?
- Do you note some play areas are more appealing to children than others? What could you do to attract children to the areas that are currently under-utilised?
- Does the structure of your day enable children to engage in long periods on uninterrupted play? If not, what could you do to ensure that children have time to engage deeply with what they are learning?
- Do the materials and resources provided for children encourage them to be imaginative and creative?
- What strategies are you using to support and extend children's thinking? What other approaches could you use?
- Do you know what theories children are currently constructing and how they are testing them?

Table 8.1: A framework for reflection

Levels of reflection	1	**Describing**	• What happened? • What is the issue? • What did you observe? • What are your feelings and responses? • What is your opinion? • What questions do you have?
	2	**Connecting**	• What connections can you make? • Have you seen this before? • What else have you observed? • Who else is relevant here? • What professional knowledge is relevant here? • What professional skills are relevant here?
	3	**Explaining**	• How would you explain the situation? • What are the contributing factors? • What experiences do you bring to this situation? • What does the literature say about this? • What theories might help you understand this?
	4	**Reframing**	• How can you think more deeply about this situation? • What further questions do you have and how will you answer these? • What multiple conclusions might you draw? • How will you further develop your understandings and professional practice? • How will you reframe your future practice? • What action plan will you develop for future practice?

A prac dialogue

Finally, we share some excerpts from an email exchange between one of our pre-service teachers and one of our favourite supervising teachers. Anne is a highly accomplished teacher who has been working at a community-based preschool in a suburb of Brisbane for more than fifteen years. She is always keen to host pre-service teachers, and sees this work as part of her professional responsibility (although she did take a break from hosting student teachers not so long ago, just to renew aspects of her own practice). We leave the last words to Anne, as we think they speak for themselves, demonstrating the extraordinary possibilities when an enthusiastic and committed pre-service teacher is paired with a talented and committed professional teacher, and together they share their thinking and observations, and collaborate on meaning-making—about the children, the community and their shared profession. Thank you Anne for your amazing teaching, and your willingness to build and sustain our long-standing relationships.

Pre-service teacher Cici (not her real name) sent this email to Anne after her first day observing at the centre:

So here are my observations (this is new to me!)

G stood watching from the lockers for a while as I was interacting with the children on the playdough table. She eventually came over to join us, after sitting quietly for a while she decided to share with me her creation. Speaking up and asking me to look. After about 5 minutes of play I got up to move inside. Grace came with me and I asked what she would like to do next, she pointed to the wooden blocks so I sat on a chair and watched as she began her creation.

(I took photos of all this with the silver camera.) Very carefully she put two tall blocks vertically, making sure they would balance before putting a shorter block across the top. She continued adding to her building, looking very proud when it would stay standing. Each time she came back to the carpet with more blocks she would look to me. She gradually became more talkative, explaining what the creation was. 'A castle, with a house and a tiny TV'. She then placed 5 blocks on the floor and said that it was 'A star' and was a road for the cars. She added a smaller building that was a bed and a roof, and then a bridge that was over the water. The blue carpet being the water. By the end of this small session of play she was chatting away to me.

. . .

T was sitting on the puzzle mat attempting to do the aeroplane puzzle that has 3 different possible pictures. He didn't seem to grasp how the puzzle was meant to work, instead was very excited when each piece fit over the holes, even if the pieces were hanging off the edge of the puzzle. I tried to guide him to look at the pictures on the pieces, how some of them had sky in the background which meant that the plane was flying, and others had white ground which meant that the plane was on the ground. He soon started to look for the sky or the ground, but still couldn't quite grasp the concept of them forming a picture. W (teacher) soon came and joined us and was keen to help me finish the puzzle as T had lost interest. We started talking about flying, and who had been on a plane. A plane flew overhead while we were doing this so that was exciting.

In the afternoon when everyone was outside working with the construction blocks (I'm not sure what they are called?) T came up to me with a 'long shooter', I asked him how many blocks did he think were in it. 'LOTS!' was his answer. I encouraged him to count them, and he counted while touching the blocks, but counted faster than the number of blocks he touched. (I know there is a specific term for this! But cannot think of it.) I asked if we could count them together. But he was adamant he had already counted them. I reassured him that yes he had. He relented grudgingly and said we could count them together. After counting them with me he then took some off, and showed me, we counted them again. There were less! He did this over and over until there were zero. He seemed very pleased.

Ok! That was a lot!

I would love some feedback about observations as I am going to have to do a lot of them! I will be showing you, Anne, every day my observations and reflections.

Thanks so much!

Anne replied to Cici's email, Both emails are much longer than the excerpts we have selected here. They include some exchanges on another three children, all equally detailed.

Welcome aboard and Good Morning Cici,

Great to see you leaping in where sometimes angels fear to tread!

It sounds like you have enjoyed playing alongside the children as well as really embraced the teaching opportunities inherent in the close interactions you have commenced. WELL DONE!

The first prac is a pivotal one . . . it can either make or break your enthusiasm and we are very keen to make sure it enhances yours.

Observations of a formal nature may indeed be new to you but as a mother of two and a mature aged student, might I suggest you are off to a strong start. I can see by your comments this far that you look and see the children's hearts and souls . . . and this is a strong starting place.

You could observe G's caution . . . she has only been enrolled for a brief while and so is still building her confidence and identify in the peer group.

You acknowledged her needs here, gave her the time and your willing interest to walk at her pace and she trusted and delivered her acceptance over time . . . Win/Win.

Your observations of her reflect my own over recent weeks so G is showing us her strengths and interests and her interest in showing us what she is very capable of doing. G is the third child in her family and her siblings, C, aged 8 and H, aged 6, have provided G with increased developmental capacity that is built upon already strong genetic capacity, to thrive . . . and thrive she will with two years of Kindy experience.

. . .

T . . . ah, the unique and delectable T!

What a wonderful reflection you have written here! It is both complex and interesting . . . we have a mixed age group here and within the age stage mixture we also have mixed capacities, interests and perspectives as you have already identified in your obs of G and T . . .

Do you think T was struggling with the puzzle? He may have been . . . but he may have also been learning far, far more through his efforts to work it out than any frustration experienced at not being able to complete the puzzle. Showing an interest in his effort and exploration and investigating his feelings and perspectives may have revealed his position . . .

Some questions to consider as you reflect . . .

Do you think T was interested in a unique puzzle?

Might T have been on a different journey than the one you thought him to be on?

How might we work with a child such as T to find out what he is doing?

The doing of the puzzle is one goal, the exploration of the possibilities of the puzzle another, the problem identification yet another, the purpose yet another . . . for every child this might be a different experience. How do we know?

Should puzzles be the same challenge for every child?

Great to see you stepping forward to investigate . . . when pausing a moment to observe and inquire as to that which the child is intrigued by, one might see a different pathway of imagination and inquiry . . . or one may be told, 'I can't do it.' . . . and one can then ask . . . 'Shall I work with you?'

I think your last obs of T, i.e. the construction and counting one in the pm . . . is very telling about who T is and how complex his style of thinking is . . . a wonderful obs . . . T is a quiet and deep thinker, worker and achiever. Staff are wondering if T needs more support to socialise or whether T is happy to be in his own thoughts and experiences . . . this is a tricky assessment to make . . . suffice to say he is a deep thinker and loves to have moments 1 on 1 with adults and peers . . . he's not yet ready for, or comfortable with being the centre of large group experiences . . . a gentle and deep soul.

For day one, Cici, you have done a wonderful job. Exciting to read, wonderful obs for us to add to the children's profiles . . . and a great start to your prac!

Can't wait to begin this journey alongside you . . . have a wonderful holiday and [I] look forward to catching up in the new term.

Warm regards,

Anne

On track on prac

We conclude this chapter with a number of sections titled 'On track on prac'. Your relationship with your supervising teacher is important, and sometimes it might be easier if you have a starting point for initiating some extended conversations. These are designed to 'break the ice' and help build a relationship of mutual trust and respect between you and your supervising teacher.

If you think it is appropriate, photocopy one of the 'On track on prac' pages, and make a set time for you and your supervising teacher to sit—maybe over a coffee—and 'interview each other' in order to share your views on the prompt questions.

You might use these more than once, or you might use one for each different context. You could also document the conversations as a teacher/researcher, and keep them for your journal reflections—even add them to your portfolio.

Remember that these are designed as a way to start the conversation. It will be your judgement that guides you on how best to use them.

On track on prac 1

This is your time to talk with your supervising teacher about keeping your prac on track. Find a time and space that works for you both, and give some attention to some of the unique operational features of this particular context. If possible, both of you should give some thought to these prompt questions. They are designed to help exchanges of information, thinking, ideas and advice.

Consider:

* What are the key factors that are important to understand about this context (whether it be child care, kindergarten, preschool, lower primary)?

* How will the specifics of this context shape this prac experience?

* How do you sustain your engagement during this prac?

* What arrangements do you need to make to ensure you are able to fulfil the university requirements and your supervising teacher's/ student teacher's expectations, and at the same time look after yourself?

* What is your health plan so you remain strong and healthy and are able to keep on track?

On track on prac 2

Setting aside time for professional conversations with supervising teachers can help you to develop deeper understandings about teaching and the profession. Preparing your questions and ideas in advance, and organising time for these meetings, will help to optimise the opportunities they provide.

Discuss and share:

• Why did you choose to join the teaching profession? What prompted you? Have you worked in other professions? Why do you teach?

• Who has inspired you as a teacher? Was it another teacher or somebody else? How? From where do you continue to draw your inspiration? What inspiration do you hope to gain from this prac experience?

• What do you think about how teachers are prepared? What have you used from your teacher preparation program? What would you have liked to know about before you started teaching? What other courses have you completed since your initial teaching qualification?

• How do you build relationships with children? What strategies do you use for challenging relationships? What relationships do you build with families?

• What philosophies and standpoints do you draw on for your work? How would you describe your philosophy in relation to children, parents, teaching and education?

track**On track on prac 3**

aside time for professional conversations with supervising teachers can help you to develop deeper understandings about teaching and the profession. Consider the following ideas for formulating your own professional conversations with your supervising teacher. Preparing your questions and ideas in advance and organising time for these meetings will help to optimise the opportunities they provide.

Discuss and share:

- What do you think are the most important issues/debates currently occurring in the field of education?

- How would you describe your position when it comes to these issues/debates?

- Who do you go to when you want advice about your work?

- Who do you give advice to when it comes to education?

- Do you regularly attend conferences or professional learning experiences? Which ones? How frequently? Why?

On track on prac 4

Setting aside time for professional conversations with supervising teachers can help you to develop deeper under-
standings about teaching and the profession. Consider the following ideas for formulating your own professional conversations with your supervising teacher. Preparing your questions and ideas in advance and organising time for these meetings will help to optimise the opportunities that they provide.

- Who are some good mentors you have had during your (teaching) career? During this conversation, you can also discuss each other's expectations for mentoring during your prac.

- What are your key ideas for creating curriculum? How do you actually do it? What components are involved? What do you prioritise? How did you start creating curriculum as a beginning teacher?

- What does leadership mean to you in this workplace? What are the attributes of good leaders with whom you have worked? What leadership activities do you engage in? What role do you have in leadership?

On track on prac 5

Setting aside time for professional conversations with supervising teachers can help you to develop deeper under-standings about teaching and the profession. Consider the following ideas for formulating your own professional conversations with your supervising teacher. Preparing your questions and ideas in advance, and organising time for these meetings, will help to optimise the opportunities they provide.

Discuss with each other your involvement in the profession:

- Do you subscribe to newsletters or journals?

- Are you an active member of a network group?

- Are you a member of a union?

- Are you a member of a professional association?

- Where do you look to for information and ideas?

- Which conferences or professional development opportunities have you found most useful?

- Which leadership activities are you involved in?

Further reading

Bain, J.D., Ballantyne, R., Packer, J. & Mills, C. (1999). Using journal writing to enhance student teachers' reflectivity during field experience placements. *Teachers & Teaching*, 5(1), pp. 51–73.

Phillips, J. (2007). EDB007 Culture studies: Indigenous education. Tutorial guide. Brisbane, QUT.

Ryan, M.E. & Ryan, M. (2013). Theorising a model for teaching and assessing reflective learning in higher education. *Higher Education Research & Development*, 32(2), pp. 244–57.

Walsh, K. & Mathews, B. (2010). Maltreated children in the early years: International perspectives on the teacher's role. In V. Green & S. Cherrington (eds), *Delving into Diversity: An international exploration of diversity issues in education*. Hauppage, NY: Nova Science, pp. 195–207.

References

Ailwood, J., Black, A.L., Ewing, B.F., Heirdsfield, A.M., Meehan, C.J. et al. (2006). Supporting transitions from student to professional: A mentoring case study from early childhood education. In G. Rienstra & A. Gonczi (eds), *Entry to the Teaching Profession: Preparation, practice, pressure and professionalism.* Canberra: Australian College of Educators, pp. 48–55.

Angelou, M. (1994). *The Complete Collected Poems of Maya Angelou.* New York: Random House.

Australian Bureau of Statistics (ABS) (2011a). *50 Years of Labour Force Statistics: Now and then*, <www.abs.gov.au/AUSSTATS/abs@.nsf/Lookup/4102.0Main+Features30Dec+2011#changing>. Accessed 20 November 2014.

—— (2011b). *Childhood Education and Care, Australia, June 2011*, <www.abs.gov.au/ausstats/abs@.nsf/Latestproducts/4402.0Main%20Features3June%202011?opendocument&tabname=Summary&prodno=4402.0&issue=June%202011&num=&view>. Accessed 20 November 2014.

—— (2012). *As a Matter of Fact*, <http://agencysearch.australia.gov.au/s/search.html?query=working+week&collection=agencies&form=simple&profile=abs>. Accessed 20 November 2014.

Australian Children's Education & Care Quality Authority (ACECQA) (2013). *Guidelines for Approval of Early Childhood Education and Care Qualifications*, <http://files.acecqa.gov.au/files/Quals/2Guidelines%20Approval%20of%20ECEC%20qualifications_v040313.pdf>. Accessed 20 November 2014.

—— (2014a). *National Quality Framework*, <www.acecqa.gov.au/national-quality-framework>. Accessed 20 November 2014.

—— (2014b). *Guide to the Education and Care Services National Law and the Education and Care Services National Regulations 2011*, <http://files.acecqa.

gov.au/files/National-Quality-Framework-Resources-Kit/2014/NQF02%20 Guide%20to%20ECS%20Law%20and%20Regs_web.pdf>. Accessed 20 November 2014.

Australian Institute for Teaching and School Leadership (AITSL) (2014). *National Professional Standards for Teachers*, <www.aitsl.edu.au/australian-professional-standards-for-teachers/standards/list>. Accessed 20 November 2014.

Ayers, W. (2004). *Teaching the Personal and the Political: Essays on hope and justice*. New York: Teachers College Press.

Biddulph, S. (2006). *Raising Babies: Should under 3s go to nursery?* London: Harper Thorsons.

—— (2008). *Raising Boys: Why boys are different—and how to help them become happy and well-balanced men* (2nd edn). Berkeley, CA: Celestial Arts.

Bird Rose, D. (1995). Ned Kelly died for our sins. *Oceania*, 65(2): 175–86.

—— (2000). *Dingo Makes Us Human: Life and land in an Australian Aboriginal culture*. Cambridge: Cambridge University Press.

Boomer, G.A. (1981). *Negotiating the Curriculum*. Washington, DC: Falmer Press.

Bredeson, P.V. (2003). *Designs for Learning: A new architecture for professional development in schools*. Thousand Oaks, CA: Corwin Press.

Britzman, D. (1991). *Practice Makes Practice: A critical study of learning to teach*. Albany, NY: State University of New York Press.

Butler, J. (2011). *Your Behaviour Creates Your Gender*, <http://bigthink.com/videos/your-behavior-creates-your-gender>. Accessed 20 November 2014.

Caldwell, R. (2007). Agency and change: Re-evaluating Foucault's legacy. *Organization*, 14(6): 769–92.

Children's Services Award (2010). <www.airc.gov.au/awardmod/awards/MA000120.pdf>. Accessed 20 November 2014.

Claxton, G. (2008). *What's the Point of School? Rediscovering the heart of education*. London: Oneworld.

Council of Australian Governments (COAG) (2008). *A National Quality Framework for Early Childhood Education and Care: A discussion paper*. Canberra: COAG.

—— (2009). *Investing in the Early Years: A national early childhood development strategy*. Canberra: COAG.

Dahlberg, G. & Moss, P. (2005). *Ethics and Politics in Early Childhood Education*. London: Routledge.

Darling-Hammond, L. & Bransford, J. (eds) (2005). *Preparing Teachers for a Changing World: What teachers should learn and be able to do*. San Francisco, CA: John Wiley & Sons.

de Botton, A. (2009). *The Pleasures and Sorrows of Work*. Harmondsworth: Penguin.

Department of Education (2013). *National Early Childhood Education and Care Workforce Census,* <https://education.gov.au/national-early-childhood-education-and-care-workforce-census>. Accessed 20 November 2014.

Department of Education Employment and Workplace Relations (DEEWR) (2009). *Belonging, Being and Becoming: The early years learning framework for Australia*, <www.deewr.gov.au/EarlyChildhood/Policy_Agenda/Quality/Pages/EarlyYearsLearningFramework.aspx>. Accessed 20 November 2014.

—— (2012). *Child Care Service Handbook: 2012–13*, <www.communities.wa.gov.au/education-and-care/nqfgb/Documents/child_care_service_handbook_2012_13.pdf>. Accessed 20 November 2014.

Dewey, J. (2010). To those who aspire to the profession of teaching (APT). In D.J. Simpson & S.F. Stack (eds), *Teachers, Leaders and Schools: Essays by John Dewey*. Carbonale, IL: Southern Illinois University Press, pp. 33–6.

Duncum, P. (1999). What elementary generalist teachers need to know to teach art well. *Art Education*, 52(6): 33–7.

Early Childhood Australia (ECA) (2006). *Code of Ethics*, <www.earlychildhoodaustralia.org.au/wp-content/uploads/2014/07/code_of_ethics_-brochure_screenweb_2010.pdf>. Accessed 20 November 2014.

Eaton, J. & Shepherd, W. (1998). *Early Childhood Environments*. Canberra: Australian Early Childhood Association.

Education Services Australia (2011a). *Accreditation of Initial Teacher Education Programs in Australia: Standards and procedures*, <www.aitsl.edu.au/verve/_resources/Accreditation_of_initial_teacher_education_file.pdf>. Accessed 20 November 2014.

——(2011b). *National Professional Standards for Teachers*, <www.aitsl.edu.au/docs/default-source/default-document-library/national_professional_standards_for_teachers.pdf?sfvrsn=4>. Accessed 25 March 2015.

Edwards, C., Gandini, S. & Forman, G. (2011). *The Hundred Languages of Children: The Reggio Emilia experience in transformation* (3rd edn). New York: Ablex.

Epstein, A. (2007). *The Intentional Teacher: Choosing the best strategies for young children's learning*. Washington, DC: National Association for the Education of Young Children.

Fallows, S. & Steven, C. (2000). Concluding observations and plans for institutional implementation. In S. Fallows & C. Steven (eds), *Integrating Key Skills in Higher Education: Employability, transferable skills and learning for life*. New York: Routledge, pp. 217–30.

Feiman-Nemsar, S. (2003). What new teachers need to learn. *Educational Leadership*, 60(8): 25–9.

Fleer, M., Edwards, S., Hammer, M., Kennedy, A., Ridgway, A., Robbins, J. & Surman, L. (2006). *Early Childhood Learning Communities: Sociocultural research in practice*: Sydney: Pearson Education.

Fullan, M.G. (1993). Why teachers must become change agents. *Educational Leadership*, 50(6): 12–17.

Gibson, M. (2013a). 'I want to educate school age children': Producing early childhood teacher professional identities. *Contemporary Issues in Early Childhood*, 14(2): 127–37.

—— (2013b). Producing and Maintaining Professional Identities in Early Childhood, unpublished PhD thesis, Queensland University of Technology.

Giugni, M. (2011). 'Becoming worldly with': An encounter with the early years learning framework. *Contemporary Issues in Early Childhood*, 12(1): 11–27.

—— n.d. *Exploring Multiculturalism, Anti-bias and Social Justice in Children's Services (NSW PSC)*, <www.cscentral.org.au/Resources/Exploring_Multiculturalism.pdf>.

—— (n.d.). *Rethinking Images of Inclusion: A picture book for children's services*. Canberra: ACT Professional Support Coordinator, <www.cscentral.org.au/Resources/PSC-picture-book.pdf>. Accessed 20 November 2014.

Grace, R. & Trudgett, M. (2012). It's not rocket science: The perspectives of Indigenous early childhood workers on supporting the engagement of Indigenous families in early childhood settings. *Australasian Journal of Early Childhood*, 37(2): 10.

Graduate Careers Australia (2014). Website, <www.graduatecareers.com.au>.

Hargreaves, D. (1997). Student learning and assessment are inextricably linked. *European Journal of Engineering Education*, 22(4): 401–9.

Hattie, J. (2003). *Teachers Make a Difference: What is the research evidence?* Paper presented at the Australian Council for Educational Research Annual Conference, Melbourne, 19–21 October.

Hettler, B. (1976). *Six Dimensions of Wellness Model*, <www.nationalwellness.org/?page=Six_Dimensions>. Accessed 20 November 2014.

Hill, L.T., Stremmel, A.J. & Fu, V.R. (2005). *Teaching as Inquiry: Rethinking curriculum in early childhood education*. Boston: Pearson Education.

James, A., Jenks, C. & Prout, A. (1998). *Theorizing Childhood*. Cambridge: Polity Press.

James, R. & McInnis, C. (2001). *Strategically Re-positioning Student Assessment: Discussion paper for the AUTC project 'Assessing Student Learning'*, <www.cshe.unimelb.edu.au>. Accessed 20 November 2014.

James, R., McInnis, C. & Devlin, M. (2002). Assessing learning in Australian universities: Ideas, strategies and resources for quality in student assessment, <www.cshe.unimelb.edu.au/assessinglearning/docs/AssessingLearning.pdf>.

Kincheloe, J.L. (ed.) (2005). *Classroom Teaching: An introduction*. New York: Peter Lang.

Latham, G., Blaise, M., Dole, S., Faulkner, J. & Malone, K. (2006). *Learning to Teach: New times, new practices*. New York: Oxford University Press.

Luke, A., Cazden, C., Coopes, R., Klenowski, V., Ladwig, J. et al. (2013). *A Summative Evaluation of the Stronger Smarter Learning Communities Project: Vol. 1 and Vol. 2*. Brisbane: Queensland University of Technology.

Luke, A., Woods, A. & Weir, K. (2013). Curriculum design, equity and the technical form of the curriculum. In A. Luke, A. Woods & K. Weir (eds), *Curriculum, Syllabus Design and Equity: A primer and model*. New York: Routledge, pp. 6–39.

McArdle, F. (2010). Preparing quality teachers: Making learning visible. *Australian Journal of Teacher Education*, 35(8): 60–78.

—— & Wong, K.-M.B. (2010). What young children say about art: A comparative study. *International Art in Early Childhood Research Journal*, 2(1), <http://artinearlychildhood.org/artec/images/article/ARTEC_2010_Research_Journal_1_Article_4.pdf>. Accessed 20 November 2014.

McLaughlin, J., Whatman, S.L. & Nielson, C. (2013). *Supporting Future Curriculum Leaders in Embedding Indigenous Knowledge on Teaching Practicum.* Brisbane: Queensland University of Technology.

MacNaughton, G. & Williams, G. (2008). *Techniques for Teaching Young Children: Choices for theory and practice* (3rd edn). Sydney: Pearson Education.

Malaguzzi, L. (1993). For an education based on relationships. *Young Children*, 49(1): 9–12.

—— (1994). Your image of the child: Where teaching begins. *Child Care Information Exchange*, 96: 52–61.

Manne, A. (2005). *Motherhood: How should we care for our children?* Sydney: Allen & Unwin.

Martin, K. (2008). *Please Knock Before You Enter: Aboriginal regulation of outsiders and the implications for researchers.* Brisbane: PostPressed.

Ministerial Council for Education Early Childhood Development and Youth Affairs (MCEECDYA) (2008). *Melbourne Declaration on Educational Goals for Young Australians*, <www.curriculum.edu.au/verve/_resources/National_Declaration_on_the_Educational_Goals_for_Young_Australians.pdf>.

Ministry of Education (NZ) (1996). *Te Whāriki.* Wellington: Learning Media.

Nakata, M. (2002). Indigenous knowledge and the cultural interface: Underlying issues at the intersection of knowledge and information systems. *International Federation of Library Associations and Institutions* (IFLA), 28(5): 281–91.

—— (2007). The cultural interface. *Australian Journal of Indigenous Education*, 36(5), 2–14.

Ngui, M. (n.d.). *Thousand Plateaus*, Bumblenut. <www.bumblenut.com/drawing/art/plateaus/index.shtml>.

Organization for Economic Co-operation and Development (OECD) (2006). *Starting Strong II: Early childhood education and care policy.* Paris: OECD.

Osgood, J. (2006). Deconstructing professionalism in early childhood education: Resisting the regulatory gaze. *Contemporary Issues in Early Childhood*, 7(1): 5–14.

Penn, H. (2011). *Quality in Early Childhood Services: An international perspective.* Maidenhead: McGraw-Hill.

Phillips, J. (2007). *EDB007 Culture studies: Indigenous education. Tutorial guide.* Brisbane: Queensland University of Technology.

—— (2011). Resisting Contradictions: Non-Indigenous pre-service teacher responses to critical Indigenous studies. PhD thesis, Queensland University of Technology.

—— (2012a). Indigenous education in Australia. In S. Carrington & J. Macarthur (eds), *Teaching in Inclusive School Communities.* Brisbane: Wiley, pp. 139–62.

—— (2012b). Indigenous Knowledge Perspectives: Making space in the Australian centre. In J. Phillips & J. Lampert, *Introductory Indigenous Studies in Education: Reflection and the importance of knowing*. Sydney: Pearson Education, pp. 9–25.

Pool, L.D. & Sewell, P. (2007). The key to employability: Developing a practical model of graduate employability. *Education & Training*, 49(4): 277–89.

Productivity Commission (2014). *Childcare and Early Learning Draft Report, July 2014*. Canberra: Commonwealth of Australia.

Queensland Industrial Relations Commission (QIRC) (2012). *Teachers Award—State 2012*, <www.qirc.qld.gov.au/resources/pdf/awards/t/t0110_ar10.pdf>. Accessed 3 March 2015.

Queensland University of Technology (QUT) (2014). *Career Modules*, <www.careers.qut.edu.au/>.

Raths, L., Harmon, M. & Simon, S. (1966). *Values and Teaching*. Columbus, OH: Charles E. Merril.

Rigney, L.-I. (2010). Indigenous Education: The challenge of change. *Every Child*, 16(4): 10–11.

Robinson, K. & Davies, C. (2008). Docile bodies and heteronormative moral subjects: Constructing the child and sexual knowledge in schooling. *Sexuality & Culture*, 12: 221–39.

Rodd, J. (2013). *Leadership in Early Childhood: The pathway to professionalism* (4th edn). Sydney: Allen & Unwin.

Ryan, M.E. & Ryan, M. (2013). Theorising a model for teaching and assessing reflective learning in higher education. *Higher Education Research & Development*, 32(2): 244–57.

Schein, E.H. (2010). *Organizational Culture and Leadership* (4 edn). San Francisco, CA: John Wiley & Sons.

Smith, L.T. (2012). *Decolonising Methodologies: Research and Indigenous people* (2nd edn). New York: Zed Books.

Stonehouse, A. & Duffie, J. (2001). *NSW Curriculum Framework for Children's Services: The practice of relationships—Essential provisions for children's services*, <www.community.nsw.gov.au/docswr/_assets/main/documents/childcare_framework.pdf>. Accessed 20 December 2014.

Sumsion, J. (2005). Putting postmodern theories into practice in early childhood teacher education. In S. Ryan & S. Grieshaber (eds), *Practical Transformations and Transformational Practices: Globalization, postmodernism, and early childhood education. Advances in early education and day care*. Amsterdam: Elsevier JAI, vol. 14, pp. 193–216.

Tayler, C. (2011). Changing policy, changing culture: Steps toward early learning quality improvement in Australia. *International Journal of Early Childhood*, 43(3): 211–25.

Timperley, H. & Alton-Lee, A. (2008). Reframing teacher professional learning: An alternative policy approach to strengthening valued outcomes for diverse learners. *Review of Research in Education*, 32(1): 328–69.

Walsh, K. & Elmslie, L. (2005). Practicum pairs: An alternative for first field experience in early childhood teacher education. *Asia-Pacific Journal of Teacher Education*, 33(1): 5–21.

Walsh, K. & Mathews, B. (2010a). Maltreated children in the early years: International perspectives on the teacher's role. In V. Green & S. Cherrington (eds), *Delving into Diversity: An international exploration of diversity issues in education*, Hauppage, NY: Nova Science, pp. 195–207.

—— (2010b). Child protection. Queensland College of Teachers annual lecture, 3 December. Brisbane: Queensland University of Technology.

Whitton, D., Sinclair, C., Barker, K., Nunlohy, P. & Nosworthy, M. (2006). *Learning for Teaching: Teaching for learning*. Melbourne: Cengage.

Wollons, R.L. (ed.) (2000). *Kindergartens and Cultures: The global diffusion of an idea*. New Haven, CT: Yale University Press.

Woodrow, C. (1999). Revisiting images of the child in early childhood education: Reflections and considerations. *Australian Journal of Early Childhood*, 24(4): 7–12.

Zeichner, K. (2006). Reflections of a university-based teacher educator on the future of college and university-based teacher education. *Journal of Teacher Education*, 57(3): 326–40.

—— (2009). Teacher education and the struggle for social justice. New York: Routledge.

Index

For Product Safety Concerns and Information please contact our EU
representative GPSR@taylorandfrancis.com
Taylor & Francis Verlag GmbH, Kaufingerstraße 24, 80331 München, Germany